TAXES IN AMERICA

WHAT EVERYONE NEEDS TO KNOW

TAXES IN AMERICA

WHAT EVERYONE NEEDS TO KNOW

LEONARD E. BURMAN
and
JOEL SLEMROD

OXFORD
UNIVERSITY PRESS

OXFORD
UNIVERSITY PRESS

Oxford University Press is a department of the University of Oxford.
It furthers the University's objective of excellence in research, scholarship,
and education by publishing worldwide.

Oxford   New York
Auckland   Cape Town   Dar es Salaam   Hong Kong   Karachi
Kuala Lumpur   Madrid   Melbourne   Mexico City   Nairobi
New Delhi   Shanghai   Taipei   Toronto

With offices in
Argentina   Austria   Brazil   Chile   Czech Republic   France   Greece
Guatemala   Hungary   Italy   Japan   Poland   Portugal   Singapore
South Korea   Switzerland   Thailand   Turkey   Ukraine   Vietnam

Oxford is a registered trademark of Oxford University Press
in the UK and certain other countries.

Published in the United States of America by
Oxford University Press
198 Madison Avenue, New York, NY 10016

Library of Congress Cataloging-in-Publication Data
Burman, Leonard.
Taxes in America : what everyone needs to know / Leonard E. Burman,
Joel Slemrod.
p. cm.
Includes bibliographical references and index.
ISBN 978-0-19-989026-2 (pbk. : alk. paper)—
ISBN 978-0-19-989027-9 (hbk. : alk. paper)
1. Taxation—United States.   I. Slemrod, Joel.   II. Title.
HJ2381.B79 2013
336.200973—dc23
2012026106

978-0-19-989026-2 (pbk.)—978-0-19-989027-9 (cloth)

1 3 5 7 9 8 6 4 2
Printed in the United States of America
on acid-free paper

*To our wives, our most valued friends
and trusted advisors*

CONTENTS

PART II THE COSTS AND BENEFITS OF TAXATION

6 Taxes and the Economy   133

7 The Hidden Welfare State   150

8 The Burden of Taxation   163

9 Tax Administration and Enforcement   171

PART III A TOUR OF THE SAUSAGE FACTORY

10 Misperceptions and Reality in the Policy Process

PREFACE

Who are we?

Leonard E. Burman is the Daniel Patrick Moynihan Professor of Public Affairs at the Maxwell School of Syracuse University and holds appointments in the departments of public administration and economics, as well as the law school. Prior to coming to Syracuse, he co-founded and directed the Tax Policy Center (TPC), a nonpartisan joint venture of the Urban Institute and Brookings Institution. TPC is widely respected in Washington policy circles for the quality, objectivity, and clarity of its analysis of complex subjects. Burman previously served as Deputy Assistant Secretary for Tax Analysis at the Treasury Department and senior economist at the Congressional Budget Office. He was president of the National Tax Association (NTA), the leading American organization of experts in the theory and practice of taxation, from 2010 to 2011. He often testifies before Congress on tax and budget policy issues and his commentaries have been published in top newspapers and aired on public radio. He is the author of a book, *The Labyrinth of Capital Gains Tax Policy: A Guide for the Perplexed*.

Joel Slemrod is the Paul W. McCracken Collegiate Professor of Business Economics and Public Policy at the Stephen M. Ross School of Business, and Professor and Chair in the Department of Economics, at the University of Michigan. He also serves as Director of the Office of

Tax Policy Research, an interdisciplinary research center housed at the Ross School of Business. He has served as the senior economist for tax policy at the President's Council of Economic Advisers, has been a member of the Congressional Budget Office Panel of Economic Advisers, and has testified before Congress on domestic and international taxation issues. From 1992 to 1998 Slemrod was editor of the *National Tax Journal* and from 2006 to 2010 and from 2008 to 2010 was a co-editor of the *Journal of Public Economics*. In 2005 to 2006, he was president of the NTA. He is co-author with Jon Bakija of *Taxing Ourselves: A Citizen's Guide to the Debate over Taxes*, whose fourth edition was published in 2008 and whose fifth edition will be published any day now.

Why did we team up to write this book?

Mostly because we're old friends and like working together. We go way back. Indeed, Len was Joel's first Ph.D. student when we both were at the University of Minnesota. Since then we have kept in close touch through the ups and downs of tax policy and have shared a commitment to educating the public about sometimes opaque tax issues, even while acknowledging that we don't have all the answers and sometimes even have differing views. Once before we took a shot at something like this, co-authoring in 2003 an article for *The Milken Institute Review* entitled "My Weekend with Nick and Adam: Tax Policy and Other Willful Misunderstandings." Some traces of that article, available at http://www.urban.org/UploadedPDF/1000554.pdf, survive in this book. Slemrod has co-authored a book (*Taxing Ourselves*) with another former Ph.D. student, Jon Bakija, who is Professor of Economics at Williams College. That book is used in many undergraduate and master's level classes on public finance and taxation (and is highly recommended to people who decide they want to delve more deeply into tax policy).

After talking for years about doing this, now we've done it.

What's the book about?

Taxes have always been an incendiary topic in the United States. A tax revolt launched the nation and the modern day Tea Party invokes the mantle of the early revolutionaries to support their call for low taxes and limited government.

And yet, despite the passion and the fury, most Americans are remarkably clueless about how our tax system works. Surveys indicate that they have no idea about how they are taxed, much less about the overall contours of federal and state tax systems. For instance, in a recent poll a majority of Americans either think that Social Security tax and Medicare tax are part of the federal income tax system or don't know whether it is or not, and more than six out of ten think that low-income or middle-income people pay the highest percentage of their income in federal taxes. Neither is correct.

Thus, there is a desperate need for a clear, concise explanation of how our tax system works, how it affects people and businesses, and how it might be made better. The timing could not be better for an engaging and illuminating book on tax policy. The president and Republican leaders have all embraced the idea of major tax reform (although their respective visions differ considerably). The dangerous explosion in the public debt has, most experts believe, also created an urgent need for more revenues, ideally generated in a way that would boost economic growth and make the tax system simpler and fairer. Finally, the debate about taxes has become a proxy war in the battle about the size and scope of government.

The book focuses on U.S. tax policy, but includes information about other countries where it is enlightening. For example, we talk about U.S. tax burdens compared with the rest of the world and discuss the value-added tax (VAT), which is not currently part of the U.S. tax arsenal, but is ubiquitous elsewhere and is often on the drawing board for would-be reformers in this country. We offer an overview of state and local taxation in the United States, but our main focus is on federal taxes.

The book has three main sections. Part I discusses how we are taxed in the United States. It starts with a broad overview and then more detailed discussion of personal and business taxes, taxes on spending (such as the VAT), and other taxes (such as the estate tax). Part II discusses the costs and benefits of taxation. We begin by discussing how taxes affect the economy, the trillion plus dollars of spending that are channeled through the tax system (sometimes called the Hidden Welfare State), the burden of taxation and notions of fairness, and how the Internal Revenue Service (IRS) runs the U.S. tax system. Part III ("A Tour of the Sausage Factory") covers tax politics and tax reform.

Although taxes can be a mind-numbing topic, we hope to key our discussion to issues that are or are likely to be on the mind of the average taxpayer and be in the news, as well as supply interesting information that many readers might not know about (such as how the IRS decides whom to audit). We have tried to employ a light touch, interjecting tax humor and political cartoons where appropriate and illustrating key data with very simple graphics.

Who provided invaluable assistance on this project?

Joe Jackson and Terry Vaughn at Oxford University Press first pitched the project to us and have provided encouragement and granted deadline extensions with a generosity that the IRS does not typically offer taxpayers.

At Syracuse University, Burman's Tax Policy and Politics class beta-tested parts of the book and provided useful feedback. Heather Ruby provided invaluable research assistance and found many of the cartoons.

At the University of Michigan, Ph.D. student Sutirtha Bagchi read carefully and researched the chapters that Slemrod drafted initially and Katie Lim helped with compiling many tables. Several people in addition to Sutirtha read and offered valuable comments on a first draft of the book—Mary

Ceccanese, Maureen Downes, Bob Mull, and Allison Paciorka. Mary Ceccanese, who will celebrate her 25th anniversary as Coordinator of the Office of Tax Policy Research in 2013, spearheaded the arduous process of turning a draft into a polished final product, and did so in her usual meticulous, efficient, and good-natured way.

Finally, we are grateful to Bob Williams of the Tax Policy Center for allowing us to adapt its excellent glossary for this volume.

PART I

HOW ARE WE TAXED?

1

THE VIEW FROM 30,000 FEET

Why is everyone always so worked up about taxation?

Taxes in America amount to about 30 percent of national income or roughly $12,000 per man, woman, and child. Now, that's a lot of money that could otherwise be spent on privately provided goods and services that people value and enjoy, so it's no surprise that Americans pay very close attention to whether we are getting our money's worth and whether our own tax bill is too high.

Legendary Supreme Court Justice Oliver Wendell Holmes, Jr. once said that "Taxes are the price we pay for a civilized society." This is true in the sense that tax dollars fund the basic architecture of a free society: a court system, fire and police departments, national defense. But governments in 2012 do much more than that. They support large social insurance programs that provide income and medical care to the elderly and low-income non-elderly, as well as schools, highways, bridges, dams, national parks, public housing, and so on.

Although Justice Holmes called taxes a price, taxes differ from prices in some essential dimensions. With most goods and services, paying more entitles you to more stuff or better-quality stuff, or both. But, with one exception, that is not true of what you "get" from government. You can't bring your 1040 to Yosemite and demand VIP treatment because your tax bill is higher than most other Americans. (You could try, but we doubt you'd get very far with the Park Ranger.) Also, unlike other goods and services, you don't get to choose what you spend your tax liability on. This is decided through a political process, and probably no one ends up completely happy with how much, and on what, the government spends the money. Some want a bigger military and less aid to education, while others would prefer more spending on education, and less on foreign aid, and so on. And, unlike deciding whether to buy a Starbucks latte or rent a fancy condominium, you do not have a choice—evasion aside—about whether to remit taxes.

The income tax is the most common point of contact between people and the government. The filing deadline of April 15 is as well-known a date as April Fools' Day, and not many events bring on more stress than a tax audit. It's really no surprise that, according to public opinion polls, the Internal Revenue Service (IRS) ranks near the bottom of American government institutions in popularity,[1] while the Social Security Administration (SSA) tops the list: for most Americans the IRS cashes your checks, while the SSA sends checks out. This image persists even though in recent years the IRS has dispersed hundreds of millions of payments related to, for example, the Earned Income Tax Credit and stimulus programs. Not only that, but the process of calculating what is owed is for many a complex, time-consuming, intrusive, expensive, and ultimately mysterious process, where the right answer is elusive. As the noted humorist Will Rogers said decades ago, "The income tax has made more liars out of the American people than golf has. Even when you make a tax form out on the level, you don't know when it's through if you are a crook or a martyr."[2] Many taxpayers suspect that they are suckers—when others find loopholes to escape their tax liability, they're left holding the bag.

Taxes can impose a substantial cost on people over and above the purchasing power they redirect to public purposes because they can blunt the incentives to work, save, and invest and can also attract resources into tax-favored but socially wasteful activities such as tax-sheltered orange orchards or construction of "see-through" office buildings (which could be profitable in the early 1980s because of tax benefits despite a dearth of tenants).

Tax policy affects the rewards or costs of nearly everything you can think of. It increases the price of cigarettes and alcohol, lowers the cost of giving to charity, reduces the reward to working, increases the cost of owning property or transferring wealth to your children, lowers the cost of homeownership, and subsidizes research and development. For this reason, tax policy is really about everything, or at least everything with an economic or financial angle. Some want to extend the reach of tax policy even further, supporting proposals for a tax on fattening or sugary foods (the fat tax, not to be confused with the flat tax). Proposals in Denmark and Ireland, as part of initiatives designed to combat global warning, would tax cattle owners on cow flatulence (over $100 per cow per year in Denmark), a key source of methane (Note: the fart tax should not be confused with either a fat tax or a flat tax).

What is a tax?

A tax is a compulsory transfer of resources from the private sector to government that generally does not entitle the taxed person or entity to a quid pro quo in return (that's why it has to be compulsory). Tax liability—what is owed to the government—may be triggered by a wide variety of things, such as receiving income, purchasing certain goods or services, or owning property.

Although once triggered the tax liability is not voluntary, the amount of any given tax that is due generally depends on voluntary choices made by people or corporations. Thus, in principle, one can legally avoid income tax by not earning any income (or have income below a threshold amount), avoid retail sales tax by not buying anything, and avoid property tax by not owning any residential or commercial property. Of course, earning no income at all is not advisable even though it lowers tax liability; our point is that the *amount* of tax due depends on what you do and how you arrange your financial affairs. What's more, taxes are often borne by people other than those who write the check—so you may bear the burden of a tax even if you never file a return. (See page 22, "Who really bears the burden of tax?")

What are the major kinds of taxes?

Taxes can be classified on a number of dimensions. One important distinction is between impersonal and personal taxes. With the impersonal kind, how much tax is triggered is the same regardless of *who* undertakes whatever action triggers the tax. The usual retail sales tax is an impersonal tax, because any consumer (not a business—more on that later) buying a $20 hammer in a state with a 5 percent sales tax triggers a $1 tax liability regardless of who sold it or who bought it. If Warren Buffett buys it, $1 in tax is due and if either of us buys it, it is still $1. The impersonality certainly simplifies the tax collection process, as the retail business need not verify anything about the buyer such as his or her income, wealth, age, marital status, and so on. On the other hand, as we'll discuss later, this aspect of a sales tax limits the extent to which tax liability can be linked to people's income and wealth, which bothers many who are concerned with the fairness of the distribution of tax burdens.

A graduated income tax is a personal tax because the tax due per dollar of income earned depends on characteristics of the household. In particular it depends on their level of income—where higher-income households are usually subject to higher tax liabilities and higher tax liabilities per dollar of income—but also on other characteristics such as marital status, their charitable contributions, medical expenses, and so on.

How are taxes like ducks?

What is, and isn't, called a tax sometimes becomes a high-stakes political game. Because of the heightened political resistance to anything called a tax, sometimes governments desiring revenue do their best to call taxes something else. The Reagan administration euphemistically referred to "revenue enhancement" when it proposed to raise taxes in the early 1980s.

At the 1988 Republican national convention, George H. W. Bush famously promised, "Read my lips—no new taxes." Once elected, Bush's designated budget director, Richard G. Darman, backed the president-elect's pledge not to raise taxes, saying he would recommend that President Bush reject any measure that the public might perceive as a tax increase. At his confirmation hearings before the Senate Governmental Affairs Committee, Darman indicated that he would not hide behind semantic niceties. Rather, he would apply the "duck test" to determine if a proposal could be perceived as a tax increase: "If it looks like a duck, walks like a duck and quacks like a duck, then it is a duck."

The distinction between a tax increase and a spending cut is not at all clear because our income tax code includes many items that may be better characterized as spending programs that just happen to be delivered through the tax

" First, there will be NO NEW TAXES . . or I'm not six feet tall. "

Figure 1.1 www.CartoonStock.com

system. Indeed, one of the largest antipoverty programs in the United States, the Earned Income Tax Credit, is delivered through the tax code (more on this later). Is cutting back on subsidies a duck? Prominent conservatives disagree on that question. In early 2011, antitax crusader Grover Norquist accused conservative Republican Senator Tom Coburn (R-OK) of breaking his no-tax-increase pledge by proposing an amendment to end a tax credit for ethanol. Norquist objected to the elimination of the credit because he views it as a tax increase, while Senator Coburn considered it to be a spending cut.[3]

Are there "hidden" taxes?

Some taxes are more visible, or salient, than others. Hidden taxes, like hidden fees, operate under the radar of at least some of those affected. Most retail stores (at least the ones we shop at) don't remind us of the sales tax until we arrive at the cash register. On many e-tailing sites, the sales tax is added only at the very end of the transaction. Some conservatives are upset by this because they fear that it makes consumers, who are often also voters, underestimate the cost of government and therefore soften their vigilance regarding big government. Of course, the retailers are aware of the tax because they have to remit the amount owed regardless of how visible the tax is to the consumer.

This discussion helps sort out what it means when a retail store—for some reason usually furniture stores—advertise that "we pay your sales tax!" as part of a sales promotion. The truth is that the store *always* has to remit "your" sales

Figure 1.2 www.CartoonStock.com

tax. And that certainly means that their prices are higher than otherwise. The sales-tax claim is just another—apparently appealing—way to claim that they are offering a special low price. As always, a purchase subject to a 6-percent-off sale, or any price discount, is only as attractive as the price before the discount.

Hidden tax burdens are a bigger issue. The tax law specifies which person or business entity is legally obligated to remit taxes. But who must remit the tax does not pin down who ends up bearing the burden—the burden may be shifted. That burdens can be shifted is well-known. Any parent knows that the burden of a school science project that is nominally the child's responsibility ends up costing the parent long hours. High parking meter charges not only increase shoppers' costs, but end up burdening local business owners through decreased sales.

"Could you make it a dollar and four cents, sir? — The Government says I have to collect sales tax."

Figure 1.3 www.CartoonStock.com

Shifting of tax burdens is common, and it is almost never the case that the individual or business that remits the tax is the only one who is made worse off. At first glance, taxes on the income of a corporation appear to decrease the income of its owners, the shareholders. However, ultimately, these taxes may also lead to higher prices of what the business sells, burdening consumers; they may also reduce wages, thereby burdening workers as well.

Are there ways to raise revenue other than taxes?

Yes, but these days, non-tax revenue sources play a relatively small role in the U.S. tax system.

Some non-tax revenue-raising schemes probably should be called taxes. Think about state-owned liquor stores that charge more than what would cover costs; from the consumer's point of view, this is not much different from allowing private retailers to sell liquor subject to an excise tax.

There are more important ways for governments to get control over resources that don't involve raising money directly. Take the military draft. Until 1973 the United States required (and nearly 100 countries still do require) that many citizens of a certain age serve in the military.[4] A military draft has many of the features of a tax—it is compulsory and there is no quid pro quo, aside from a usually minimal salary. Just like a tax, many draftees would prefer not to bear the burden of service. Centuries ago it was common for governments to require compulsory labor service for other purposes. In Egypt, the use of forced labor on public works projects was used from the time of the pyramids until the mid-1800s. Forced labor was common in medieval Europe when peasants were required to work for feudal lords, and it even occurred in the U.S. colonies.

The federal government could get resources by printing money and buying things with it, an option that is not available to state or municipal governments. Compared to, say, a personal income tax, this practice (called "seigniorage") really obscures who bears the burden, but there is a burden nevertheless. Printing money causes inflation, which erodes the value of dollar-denominated assets such as government bonds or cash. Thus, the government gets resources at the expense of those who hold these assets. People understand this, and so when future inflation looks likely, people will not voluntarily lend to the government unless they are compensated with higher interest rates. Sometimes governments require financial institutions to hold public bonds at below-market interest rates—a practice called "financial repression"—which is another way to effectively obtain wealth from the private sector.

The United States does not typically print money to fund a nontrivial fraction of its operations. But in the past century several countries in desperate fiscal situations have resorted to the printing press, causing hyperinflation and disastrous consequences for the economy. During the single year of 1923, the Weimar Republic of Germany saw its price level increase by the mind-boggling factor of 481.5 billion.[5] The printing presses ran all night and issued notes of larger and larger denomination, while workers immediately purchased goods with their paychecks as the currency depreciated by the minute. In the spring of 2006, the *New York Times* reported that in hyperinflating Zimbabwe, toilet paper cost 417 Zimbabwean dollars—not per roll but per single two-ply sheet—a roll cost $145,750, and Zimbabwe printed $100,000,000,000,000 (100 trillion dollar) bank notes!![6]

Why not just borrow the money instead of raising taxes?

The federal government can borrow money to fund its operations, and in recent years has been doing this to an unprecedented degree. But borrowing is fundamentally different from raising money through tax, or taxlike, means. For one thing no one coerces anyone to lend to the government. They do so voluntarily because they find the interest rate attractive given the minimal default risk. Thus, government borrowing does not eliminate, or even reduce, the burden of government spending; but rather just postpones the reckoning of this burden, which will be felt through some combination of higher taxes in the future and cutbacks in future government spending or the inflation tax just discussed. (See page 146, "Why not run deficits forever?")

How can taxes be like regulations?

In most cases taxes are designed to raise revenue, and the changes in behavior they induce are unintended, undesirable byproducts. No policymaker intends to deter an automaker from building a plant in Michigan, but the corporate income tax may do that. Likewise, no politician wants to discourage spouses from entering or staying in the workforce, but the individual income tax can do that.

Some taxes, though, are intended to change behavior. One reason for taxing gasoline is to induce people to use less energy. Carbon taxes are designed to reduce emission of greenhouse gases that most scientists believe exacerbate the gradual warming of the climate. Instead of using tax policy to achieve these aims, one can imagine regulations that restrict, limit, or proscribe the activities. For example, a cap-and-trade system can have similar effects to a carbon tax. Under this system the government sets a limit on total emissions, and then allocates or auctions a number of permits equal to that amount. The permits can then be bought and sold, which establishes a market price. This market price has the same effect as a tax would—making the polluting activity more costly. If the explicit tax, or the implicit tax due to the market price of the permits, is equal to the social cost of the polluting activity, then decision-makers are induced to take heed of the social cost of their actions. (See page 97, "What is a Pigouvian tax?")

How have taxes changed over time?

Beginning about a century ago, the role of government began to expand all over the world, and the United States was no exception. A century ago taxes levied by all levels of government comprised less than 3 percent of national income. Now they are almost 30 percent. So, as a share of the economy, taxes are ten times as big as they were in 1912. But nearly all of that phenomenal growth occurred from 1912 to 1962. Since that time, federal taxes as a percentage of national income have gone up and down quite a lot, but have not trended upward or downward, while state and local taxes have drifted upward.

How do state and local taxes vary?

The Tax Foundation has calculated, for each state, taxes paid (including fees) to state and local governments as a percent of income. The ratio varies from a maximum of 12.2 percent in New Jersey to a low of 6.3 percent in Alaska. More than three-quarters of states are between 8.0 and 10.3 percent.[7]

How does the composition of tax vary across federal, state, and local governments?

The federal government's revenue comes predominantly from individual income taxes (43.5 percent in 2009) and social insurance and retirement receipts (42.3 percent), while only 6.6 percent comes from corporate income taxes and about 3 percent from excise taxes.[8] In contrast, state and local governments get about two-thirds of their revenue from sources hardly used at all by the federal government: 32.7 percent from sales taxes and 33 percent from property taxes, while only 22.3 percent of their revenue derives from the individual income tax and 3.8 percent from corporate income taxes (figure 1.4).[9]

How do tax burdens vary around the world?

Quite a bit. As figure 1.5 shows, among the developed countries the ratio of taxes to national output in 2008 varied from 48.2 percent in Denmark to 26.1 percent in the United States.[10]

It may come as a shock that in 2008 the United States had the rock-bottom lowest tax-to-income ratio among developed countries. But it's true.

Closer examination reveals that the United States raises about the average share of GDP from income taxes. What sets us apart from other developed economies is how little we collect from consumption taxes such as retail sales taxes or excise taxes, where the total tax is determined by the amount of spending, not income or wealth. The typical European country raises about the same share of income as the United States does from income taxes, but about as much revenue from a type of consumption tax called a value-added tax, which the United States—alone among developed countries—does not have.

In those countries with higher taxes, governments provide services we have to pay for out of our own pockets here. Completely free health care is the developed-world norm, heavily subsidized child care is common, generous child-

State

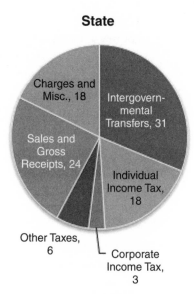

Local

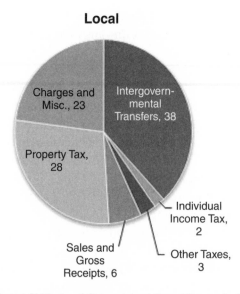

Figure 1.4 Percent Distribution of State and Local General Revenue by Source, 2008. *Source*: Tax Policy Center, State and Local Government Finance Data Query System. http://www.taxpolicycenter.org/taxfacts/displayafact.cfm?Docid=527, http://www.taxpolicycenter.org/taxfacts/displayafact.cfm?Docid=529

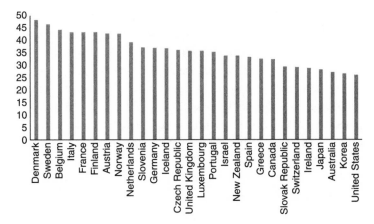

Figure 1.5 Tax burdens around the developed world: Tax as a percent of GDP in 2008.
Source: http://stats.oecd.org/Index.aspx?DataSetCode=REV

bearing and child-raising benefits are usually provided, and unemployment benefits are high and long-lasting.

Federal taxes in the United States have been at about 18 percent of GDP for 50 years. Does that mean that this is the natural rate of taxation?

Not in any meaningful economic sense. Economies can thrive with much different levels of tax. But 18 percent may represent a sort of political equilibrium that reflects the level of private consumption Americans have been willing to give up for what the federal government provides. When revenues have risen significantly above the historical norm, policy makers have chosen to cut taxes.

Why is the long-term fiscal outlook so dire?

Looking forward, there is a huge mismatch between the promises we have made regarding Social Security, Medicare, and Medicaid and the taxes we have in place to fund them.

The so-called entitlement programs are projected to grow much faster than the economy (and tax revenues), because (1) Americans are living longer, so that the ratio of benefit recipients to working, taxpaying Americans is rising, and (2) health care costs continue to grow faster than other prices. Medicare pays for acute care for the elderly and Medicaid pays for about half of nursing home care. By one reputable calculation, the gap between promised benefits and taxes in place amounts to over $50 trillion (yes, trillion!) over the next 75 years.[11] Given this mismatch, benefits will need to be cut, taxes increased, or both.

Can taxes be discussed without getting into government spending?

In the rest of this book, we will try our best to focus on the tax side of government budgets. But inevitably at several points along the way, we will have to talk about spending.

One reason is that sometimes the distinction between taxing less and spending more, or between taxing more and spending less, is arbitrary, reflecting semantic distinctions that are inconsequential from an economics perspective. Sometimes these inconsequential distinctions are reflected in official government accounting, so that of two programs that are effectively the same, one looks to be a tax cut and the other a spending increase. Later we will address the notion of *tax expenditures*, which are really just spending programs embedded within the income tax system. (See page 151, "What exactly is a tax expenditure?")

The appropriate level of taxes should reflect a comparison of the benefits of what government spending provides—be it national security, social insurance, fire departments, or national parks—with the cost of taxes. When comparing the benefits to the costs, we need to bear in mind that the cost of taxes should also incorporate the disincentives and misallocations that taxes inevitably cause. For this reason a bridge that costs $500 million to build should promise benefits quite a bit higher than that. (See page 134, "Why do economists think that raising funds costs much more than the tax sticker price?")

The link between what government provides and what it collects shows up repeatedly in public opinion polls. About one-half of Americans say that the amount of tax they pay is too high, according to a 2011 Gallup poll, and only 4 percent say it is too low.[12] But when asked whether taxes should be reduced if that means cutbacks in Social Security, Medicare, education, or defense spending, the antitax fervor dims: more than six in ten oppose cuts in these programs. This pattern of answers does not dispose of the issues, because one should inquire into how much such programs would have to cut back, and how. But pairing the tax question and the spending question is definitely the right way to think about fiscal issues. Spending without taxing does not provide free services. But the underlying benefit-cost analysis gets blurred because the federal government can borrow. When it does, the immediate, visible signal of the cost of government—taxes due—understates the true cost of government spending. *The cost of government is measured much more accurately by what it spends than by what it collects in taxes.*

Thus, a claim that taxes are too high is either a statement that (1) the government should just borrow more or, (2) the government spends too much. The first is just bad economics or wishful thinking, because borrowing does not lower the cost of government and in most cases increases it by directing private saving into government bonds rather than productive capital. As to the second, we should always inquire exactly what government programs should be axed or slimmed down.

Many Americans care little about the abstract question of whether overall taxes are too high, too low, or just about right. They care much more about *their* taxes, and their own tax liability. That's a whole different matter, because whether my tax burden is $25,000 a year or $50,000 a year has absolutely no effect on the strength of our national defense, the viability of the Medicare system, or whether the local park system is well manicured. At the macro level, determining the right allocation of tax burdens depends on resolving what is fair—always a contentious issue—and how alternative tax systems that assig n tax burdens differently affect economic growth. We will do our best to answer these—and other—questions in the rest of this book.

2

PERSONAL INCOME TAXES

What's the difference between personal taxes and business taxes?

Some taxes are levied on people and some are levied on businesses. This distinction is less important than you might think. The fact is the person or business entity that writes the check doesn't necessarily bear the burden of the tax. Consider the corporate income tax. Many people like the corporate income tax because they think businesses should pay taxes, not people. But the fact that the business writes the check doesn't really tell you whose bottom line is affected by it. It could be the company's shareholders. It could be the workers. The tax could be passed through to consumers in the form of higher prices. Or it could be some combination of all of the above. The fact that the corporation "pays" the tax doesn't tell you much. In fact, in this book we will do our best to avoid using the term "pays tax" because it could mean one of two different things: who writes the check (i.e., *remits* the tax) or who bears the burden of a tax.

Most people know what the individual income tax is. It's the tax that has made April 15 as iconic as the Super Bowl, without the parties or the popcorn. It's probably the most salient tax for most people, even though these days most people owe more in payroll taxes than income taxes.

The federal payroll tax is earmarked to fund Social Security retirement, survivors, and disability insurance and

Medicare. Sometimes it's called the FICA tax after the legislation that enacted it (the Federal Insurance Contributions Act). For self-employed people, it's called the SECA tax (the Self-Employment Contributions Act). We have no idea why there are two names for basically the same tax, but it's a fun fact that will impress your friends at cocktail parties.

Sales taxes and property taxes are mostly collected by state and local governments. Indeed, those are two of the three most important taxes collected at that level. Most states also collect income taxes.

Taxes nominally leveled on businesses include federal and state corporate taxes, a portion of payroll taxes (including taxes administered by state governments to cover unemployment and disability insurance), and excise taxes. Businesses also remit the value-added tax (VAT), which is common throughout the world, but is not levied in the United States. The VAT is a kind of sales tax. (See page 98, "What is a VAT?")

Some taxes are remitted by other entities. For example, the estate tax is remitted by the fiduciary of the estate of somebody who has died (typically somebody fairly wealthy). Fiduciaries of trusts also remit taxes. Those are effectively personal taxes, but the entity that writes the check is the trust that manages the assets, not the person on whose behalf the trust is administered. And nonprofit organizations may have to remit tax if they engage in certain profit-making activities.

But, as a practical matter, these distinctions are not particularly important because, as noted, the entity that writes the check may have very little effect on who actually bears the burden of the tax.

Who really bears the burden of tax?

The answer is often more complicated than you might think. Let's get back to the example of the corporate income tax. As we've discussed, somebody bears the burden of the tax, but it's not obvious who. For a long time, the conventional wisdom

SIDEBAR 2.1 Taxing the "Rich" and Jobs

President Obama has proposed raising income tax rates on couples making over $250,000 per year (and singles making over $200,000). This is roughly the top 2 percent of households. The President argues that he's just asking the well-off to pay their fair share. Critics counter that such a tax would hurt workers because a lot of the top 2 percent are entrepreneurs who would cut jobs if their income tax went up. In other words, the critics are saying that a significant part of the incidence of the millionaires' tax would fall on labor—ordinary folk.

among economists was that owners of capital, and not just owners of corporate capital, bore the tax burden because it pushed business activity into noncorporate activities, driving down the rate of return. But more recent research suggests that workers bear at least part of the tax burden because their wages are lower than they would be if the corporate tax weren't imposed. This could have a big effect on people's assessment of the tax. If you think the tax translates into lower wages, you might be less enthusiastic about it than if relatively rich shareholders are worse off because of it. We'll talk more about this later.

Let's take another example: the payroll tax. Half of FICA taxes are levied on employers and half on employees. What does that mean? For almost all employees both halves are withheld and remitted by their employer to the government. Would it make much difference if we called it all an employer tax, or all an employee tax? No. Employers decide to hire workers based on what it costs to employ them. They don't really care whether the cost comes in the form of wages or payroll taxes or, for that matter, health insurance. All that matters is the total compensation cost, including taxes and fringe benefits. So if the employer's payroll taxes fell, they would be willing to pay higher wages. If payroll taxes increased, they'd cut cash wages. Probably not instantaneously, because workers think wage cuts are unfair and that can hurt morale, but wage increases would be slower than they would otherwise be until compensation was back in line with worker productivity.

Although it's conceivable that consumers or capital owners could bear part or all of the tax burden, statistical studies have almost uniformly concluded that workers bear the entire burden of both the employer and employee portions of the payroll tax.

The economic incidence of other taxes is less clear.[1] For example, it's commonly assumed that households bear the cost of the individual income tax, but there's little reason to think that this is so, especially when the individual income tax has all sorts of credits and deductions intended to subsidize particular activities. For example, one tax credit is designed to encourage purchase of fuel-efficient hybrid vehicles. The extra demand due to the subsidized price almost surely pushes up the price of such cars. This might be a good thing if the purpose is to encourage more car makers to produce green vehicles, but it means that part of the benefit of the tax credit goes to producers, not consumers. There are, however, no good empirical estimates of how much of the income tax is borne by households and how much by others.

The bottom line is this: The person who ends up bearing the tax may be very different from the person (or entity) that writes the check to the government or the person or business entity that the tax law proclaims that the tax is "on."

Are there cases in practice where it does matter who writes the check?

Yes. For one thing, who writes the check can matter when not everyone is scrupulously honest. For example, the IRS collects a much, much larger share of what is owed from withholding taxes remitted by employers than from income tax owed by self-employed people, even though the formula for calculating liability is exactly the same. If your employer is responsible for remitting the tax, it usually makes it to the IRS. If you have to self-report, on average you're much less likely to send in all of what you owe.

Another example is sales and use taxes. If you live in a state with a sales tax, you owe the tax whether you buy something at the corner store or order it over the Internet from an out-of-state merchant. The store owner remits the tax in the first case, whereas the purchaser has to remit a "use tax" in the second. Do you send in all the use tax you owe on your Internet purchases? If so, you're in very exclusive company. The entity that writes the check matters.[2]

We'll talk more about this in the chapter about compliance and enforcement.

Can taxes affect asset prices?

Yes. A tax on the return an asset provides generally reduces its value, while a subsidy increases its value. This effect, known as capitalization of the tax into the asset's value, is more likely to occur in cases where the total supply of the asset is not easily adjusted. The tax change can produce a penalty or a windfall for current asset owners, but it has little or no effect on the affordability for future buyers.

An important example of capitalization that troubles some economists (including us) is the mortgage interest deduction. Middle-class homeowners think of this as their big tax break—if they itemize their deductions, they get to deduct interest from taxable income—and it's one of the biggest tax breaks in the code. But suppose it makes people want to live on bigger properties? In places where land is scarce, that would just bid up land prices because you can't make more land. So some of the tax break is dissipated in higher property prices. This is a boon to property owners at the time the tax break is enacted, or expanded, but means that on average prospective homeowners may not benefit much. People in top brackets who get the biggest tax breaks probably come out ahead. People with lower incomes, who because they don't itemize or are in a low tax bracket might get little or no benefit from the deduction, might be worse off than they would be if mortgage interest wasn't deductible. And if it also pushes up the market price of rental housing, renters are unambiguously worse off.

What is the personal income tax?

Pretty simple: It's a tax on individual income collected by the federal government and most states.

The federal tax is progressive, which means the tax rate rises with income. (More on this later.) Defining income, however, is not as straightforward as you might think. The standard economist's definition of income is the sum of what you spend and what you save. Spending is pretty straightforward. But measuring saving is a little more complicated. It includes what we put in the bank, mutual funds, retirement accounts, and other kinds of investments. But increases in wealth that we don't spend also add to savings (and hence to income). In many cases this unfamiliar definition lines up with the more familiar meaning—what you are paid if you are employed plus what you make from owning a business and from investments—but, in some cases that we'll expand on later, it differs in important ways.

The income tax is much more than a tax on income. While some deductions account for the cost of earning income—for example, you can deduct the cost of uniforms that you have to wear to work—many deductions, exemptions, and tax credits are intended to provide subsidies of some sort or another. They often have little to do with the measurement of income.

Isn't the income tax a fraud?

Some tax protesters argue that the 16th Amendment to the Constitution, which authorized the personal income tax in 1913, was improperly ratified or otherwise invalid. You can find many of these people in jail. Courts have repeatedly concluded that the income tax is indeed constitutional and

---

BOX 2.1 **How Is Federal Income Tax Calculated in the United States?**

Adjusted Gross Income (AGI) =
  wages and salaries
  + self-employment income
  + capital income (taxable interest, rents, royalties, capital gains, dividends)
  + income from pensions and retirement accounts
  + a portion of Social Security benefits (for higher-income people)
  + random other stuff (like some alimony payments)
  − "above-the-line" deductions for things like contributions to retirement accounts, some educational expenses, and moving costs
Itemized Deductions =
  state and local taxes
  + mortgage interest
  + charitable contributions
  + casualty and theft losses
  + some employee expenses
  + some medical expenses
  + "miscellaneous deductions"
Taxable Income =
  AGI
  − personal exemptions
  − itemized deductions or the standard deduction (whichever is greater)
Income Tax =
  Tax from tax tables
  + alternative minimum tax (if applicable)
  − nonrefundable tax credits (can be no more than total tax liability before credits)
  − refundable tax credits

---

excoriated those who question its validity as frivolous, ridiculous, or worse.[3]

You may not like the income tax, but it is legal and valid.

What are exclusions, deductions, exemptions, and credits?

They all reduce tax liability, but in different ways.

An exclusion is a kind of income that doesn't count in the measurement of gross income. For example, if your employer provides you with health insurance, that's part of your compensation, but it's excluded from income for tax purposes.

A deduction is an expense that you subtract from gross income. Some deductions are available to all taxpayers who meet eligibility requirements, like contributions to Individual Retirement Accounts (IRAs). Others are only available to those who elect to itemize deductions rather than claim a standard deduction—an amount that doesn't require documentation to claim. In 2011, the standard deduction is $5,800 for single filers, $11,600 for married couples who file a joint return, and $8,500 for single parents who file as head of household. (About two-thirds of tax filers choose the standard deduction.)[4] And taxpayers are allowed to claim exemptions for themselves and their dependents.[5] This is just a fixed dollar amount that is subtracted in calculating income for tax purposes ($3,700 in 2011), so a couple with two kids could claim $14,800 in personal exemptions. Add to that the standard deduction for a married couple of $11,600, and no federal income taxes are owed until income exceeds $26,400.

All of these deductions reduce taxable income. They reduce tax liability too, but the amount depends on your tax bracket. For example, a $100 deduction reduces tax liability by $10 for someone in the 10 percent bracket, but it reduces tax liability by $35 for a high-income person in the 35 percent bracket.

Tax credits are different. A tax credit offsets tax liability dollar for dollar. For example, the tax code includes a $1,000 per Child Tax Credit. If you have two qualifying children, you get $2,000 off your taxes. There are tax credits to help pay for child care, encourage people to buy fuel-efficient vehicles, induce people to weatherproof their house, and do all sorts of other stuff. Sometimes, like the Child Tax Credit, the credit is a fixed dollar amount. Sometimes the credit is a percentage of what you spend on a qualifying activity. But the common characteristic is that credits are effectively vouchers that are run through the tax system. They're like cash payments except that, in most cases, the cash can only be used to reduce your taxes.

"THE INCREASED CHILD TAX CREDIT IS SUPPOSED TO STIMULATE THE ECONOMY... SO HOW ABOUT A RAISE IN MY ALLOWANCE?"

Figure 2.1 www.CartoonStock.com

An exception to the last statement is a special class of tax credits called refundable tax credits. Refundable tax credits can be claimed even if you have no tax liability. The most important refundable tax credit is the Earned Income Tax Credit, or EITC (table 2.1). Eligible filers can claim the credit and get its full value even if they don't have any income tax liability at all. The credit is substantial for families with children—worth up to $5,751 in 2011 to a family with three or more qualifying children.

The Child Tax Credit, which is currently set at $1,000 per child, is partially refundable. Currently, you may claim a refundable credit of up to 15 percent of earnings in excess of $3,000. (Technically, the refundable part is called the "additional child credit." That plus the regular nonrefundable child credit may not exceed $1,000 per child.) For example, someone with earnings of $13,000 and two or more children may claim a refundable Child Tax Credit of up to $1,500—15 percent of $10,000 (the amount of earnings above $3,000). This is less than

Table 2.1 Earned Income Tax Credit Parameters, 2011

Number of children	Credit rate (percent)	Minimum income for maximum credit	Maximum credit	Phase-out rate (percent)	Phase-out range Beginning income	Ending income
0	7.65	$6,070	$464	7.65	$7,590	$13,660
1	34.00	$9,100	$3,094	15.98	$16,690	$36,052
2	40.00	$12,780	$5,112	21.06	$16,690	$40,964
3 or more	45.00	$12,780	$5,751	21.06	$16,690	$43,998

Note: The beginning and end of the phase-out range is $5,080 higher for married couples filing joint returns.

Source: Tax Policy Center, http://www.taxpolicycenter.org/taxfacts/displayafact.cfm?Docid=36.

the $2,000 sticker value of two child credits, but much more than the value of a nonrefundable credit because this person would have no income tax liability before credits.

Why are there itemized deductions? Isn't it unfair that most people don't benefit from them?

Every income tax filer has the choice of totaling up their deductible expenses or taking a standard deduction that varies only by marital status. The option to claim a standard deduction is intended to be a simplification. Policymakers could eliminate the standard deduction and make everyone itemize deductions. Because their itemizable deductions add up to less than the standard deduction (that's why they've chosen the latter option, after all), this would increase taxes on most of the two-thirds of filers who do not itemize. They might feel better that they could take a charitable deduction like their richer neighbors, but the warm glow would wear off when they saw their taxes increase. Also those who do not itemize have no record-keeping requirement to verify their deductions. In a sense, the first $11,600 of deductions for a couple is a freebie. You get them even if you have no deductible expenses.

So it's not really unfair, but there's some evidence that taxpayers perceive it to be unfair: "Why can't I take a deduction for the contribution to my church?" This perception may help explain why several recent tax reform plans would eliminate the whole concept of itemized deductions. Some, like the deduction for state and local taxes, would simply disappear. Others, like the deduction for charitable contributions, would be allowed for everyone—not just for itemizers.

At what income level do people start owing income tax?

It depends on your marital status, whether you have children eligible for tax credits, and your age. In 2011, taxpayers with simple returns started owing income tax after credits at an income of $11,304 for a single filer with no children, but at an income of $37,887 for married filers with two children (table 2.2).

Although few senior citizens qualify for the EITC or Child Tax Credit because they don't have child dependents and often don't have earned income, most are exempt from income tax because there is an additional standard deduction for filers age 65 and over and most Social Security benefits are exempt from the income tax.

For people who really take advantage of tax breaks, the threshold can be much higher. For example, a filer can have millions of dollars of interest from tax-exempt municipal bonds and not owe any federal income tax if that is her only source of income.

Table 2.2 Income Tax Thresholds before and after Tax Credits, 2011

	Single		Married	
	No children	1 child	No children	2 children
Before Credits	$9,500	$15,900	$19,000	$26,400
After Credits	$11,304	$31,484	$19,000	$37,887

Note: Assumes filer is a wage-earner under age 65 with no other income who claims the standard deduction and EITC (if eligible); children qualify for the dependent exemption, EITC, and Child Tax Credit.

Source: Tax Policy Center, http://www.taxpolicycenter.org/taxfacts/Content/Excel/entry_thresholds_chart.xls and http://www.taxpolicycenter.org/taxfacts/Content/Excel/individual_rates.xls.

Is it true that half of households owe no income taxes?

The Tax Policy Center estimates that about 46 percent of tax units (for the most part, households) will not owe federal income tax in 2011. That sounds bad—like all the burden of government is being dumped on the other half of households. But that statistic is somewhat misleading for a couple of reasons.

The vast majority of working families are indeed subject to taxes. Most Americans owe more in payroll taxes than income taxes (and that is even before considering the employers' share, which many economists think workers ultimately bear). And state and local taxes take a much bigger chunk of lower-income families' incomes than federal income taxes (figure 2.2).

Less than 20 percent of households are subject to neither income tax nor payroll tax. Of these, more than half are elderly people who are exempted because they have little or no earnings and their Social Security benefits aren't taxed. (Higher-income households do owe income tax on up to 85 percent of their Social Security benefits.) Among the non-elderly, the vast majority of this untaxed group is not taxed because they're really poor (i.e., have incomes under $20,000). President Ronald

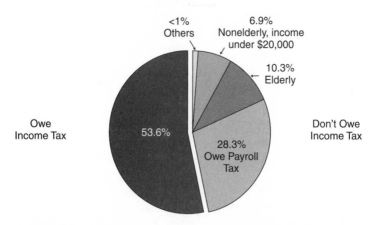

Figure 2.2 Characteristics of Households Who Do Not Owe Income Tax. *Source*: Tax Policy Center: http://www.taxpolicycenter.org/taxtopics/federal-taxes-households.cfm

Reagan made the decision that, as part of the 1986 tax reform, families living below the poverty level should be exempt from income tax, and that is still largely true.

In addition, the large fraction of Americans who escape federal income tax reflects in part the decision of policymakers to run big pieces of the social safety net through the income tax. For example, the refundable Child Tax Credit and Earned Income Tax Credit together are much bigger than any other cash assistance program for low-income working families. There are good reasons to run these programs through the tax system rather than through welfare offices, but the consequence is that it looks like a lot of people owe no income tax. Another perspective is that they get more in benefits than they owe in tax.

The Tax Policy Center calculated that if all of those tax subsidy programs were eliminated, or became explicit expenditures, only 20 percent of households—mostly those with very low incomes—would avoid owing income tax, compared to 46 percent now. Only 2 percent of households with incomes over $20,000 would owe no income tax.[6]

Is this bad for democracy?

It could be if a large portion of the population thought that government was "free," and therefore supported any spending program that benefited them to any extent. However, it's not clear if that is true, or what to do about it if it were. Do we really want to impose more tax liability on seniors or people with incomes below the poverty level?

One thing that might help clarify matters would be separating the revenue-raising function of the income tax from the subsidy-providing function. If subsidies were treated as spending, which they essentially are, the fact that many people get more in tax subsidies than they owe in tax might not seem so alarming. Lots of people benefit more from government programs than they owe in tax.

Taxes? They're a penalty for doing well.

Figure 2.3 www.CartoonStock.com

Do we tax capital income the same as labor income?

No. Labor income (wages, salaries, and self-employment income) is generally subject to both income taxes and payroll taxes whereas capital income (interest, dividends, capital gains, rent, and royalties) is generally only subject to income tax. (Starting in 2013, however, there will be a 3.8 percent tax levy on capital income earmarked for Medicare.) Capital gains and dividends are taxed at lower rates than other income; interest on municipal bonds is generally exempt from tax. Pensions, 401(k) plans, and IRAs are also ultimately tax-free, as we explain below. Economists sometimes say that we have a hybrid tax system—part consumption tax (in which the return to savings is tax-free) and part income tax (in which the return to savings is fully taxed). It represents a compromise between two competing objectives. On the one hand, we want to encourage people to save and, on the other, most Americans believe that the wealthy should bear proportionately higher tax burdens than those with more modest means. Partially, taxing capital income represents a compromise between those competing goals. (We'll talk about others later.)

What is economic income?

In some situations what most people think of as income doesn't provide a very good measure of a household's economic status. For example, suppose you're lucky enough to own a million shares of Apple corporation stock. As of this writing, your nest-egg would be worth about $600 million. Not only that, but your wealth has increased in value by over $250 million during the past year. If you didn't sell any shares, you wouldn't have any "income" as conventionally defined, and as defined by the income tax code, because Apple stock has never paid a dividend. Common sense suggests that you're a lot better off because your Apple shares have soared in value. Economic income would include the increase or decrease in value in your shares whether or not you sell them.

Economic income also includes other noncash sources, like the value of fringe benefits you receive from your employer. Health insurance is typically the biggest of these. It can be worth over $10,000 for a family, but it is not reflected in your paycheck or in taxable income.

Why do economists think my home earns me rent?

Funny story about that. One of us (Burman) used to work as Deputy Assistant Secretary for Tax Analysis at the U.S. Treasury. It's a great job for a public finance economist because every proposal for a new credit or deduction comes through that office for review. He got to meet the president. He got to hang out with Treasury Secretary Larry Summers before the movie *The Social Network* made him famous. All very cool.

But he'd also get crank calls at night from people who were outraged that the Treasury wanted to tax the rent on their home (box 2.2). "I'm a homeowner, not a renter! I don't pay rent. That's the whole point of being a homeowner. And I'm not a landlord. Nobody pays me rent. What are you crazy bureaucrats thinking?"

BOX 2.2   **Bill Archer Thinks "Economic Rent" Is Crazy Talk**

"Imputed rent? That's the rent a person would pay for his house if he didn't own it," Scholz said.

"This is incredible," responded Archer. "Americans will never accept all that as part of their annual income."

Source: Fred Barnes, "Every Man a King," *The Weekly Standard* 2, 44 (July 21, 1997), available at: http://www.weeklystandard.com/Content/Protected/Articles/000/000/008/511wdrpr.asp. (Relating the story of Treasury Deputy Assistant Secretary John Karl Scholz's exchange with House Ways and Means Committee Chairman, Bill Archer.)

Here's the backstory. Back in the Reagan Administration, in order to get a more accurate picture of how the tax burden varied across households of different levels of well-being, Treasury economists decided they'd calculate taxpayers' economic income. Economic income includes all those noncash forms of income mentioned above and "imputed rent." The economic notion is that your home is an investment and part of the return it provides is the rent you save. Imputed rent is basically the tax-free income your home generates.

A simpler way to put it is that a homeowner is clearly better off than a renter, all else equal, because the homeowner has a valuable asset. But Treasury never proposed to tax "imputed rent," in part because the concept is impossible to explain to real (i.e., noneconomist) humans. But the concept is perfectly valid.

Why don't we tax economic income?

Some economists think this is a terrific idea. If it could be measured properly, economic income would better measure taxpayers' ability to pay, and so be a more equitable basis for determining tax liability. But there are two practical problems (as well as a giant insuperable political one). One is that economic income can be difficult to measure accurately. For example, a good measure of imputed rent on owner-occupied housing would require a comprehensive annual survey of rents for comparable properties. For some kinds of properties that are rarely rented out, accurate estimates would be very hard to come by. And even for easier-to-evaluate properties, it would be very costly to estimate rental values every year. Imputed rent could be estimated based on property assessments made by local governments to collect property taxes, but those estimates would be very imprecise.

Unrealized capital gains would be easy to measure for shares of publicly traded companies, like Apple, but much harder to come by for privately held businesses. And even the value of employer-provided health insurance and pensions is difficult to estimate and allocate among employees. Further, consider the difficulty in valuing extremely rare art, intangible assets, or other items that are not commonly sold, and for which no up-to-date market price may exist. It's also problematic to assess tax when people don't necessarily have cash in hand to pay it. For example, if we counted as taxable income the $250 million of capital gains that the lucky

---

SIDEBAR 2.2 The Simplest Tax Shelter

- Borrow $10 million at 5 percent interest.
- Invest $10 million that will pay a 5 percent return, making the investment worth $10,500,000 after a year. The return comes in the form of a capital gain.
- Borrowing generates a $500,000 interest deduction. At a 35 percent tax rate, that reduces your federal income tax by $175,000. (There may also be state tax benefits.)
- The $500,000 capital gain is taxed at 15 percent. That adds $75,000 to your tax bill.
- On net, you save $100,000.
- Because of the tax savings, this deal would be worthwhile even if the investment paid less than $500,000 (even though, absent taxes, it would make no sense).

NB: this scheme is so obvious that it is not permitted. However, a whole industry is devoted to finding economically equivalent deals.

"... a tax shelter is a deal done by very smart people that, absent tax considerations, would be very stupid."—Michael J. Graetz, 100 Million Unnecessary Returns (New Haven: Yale University Press, 2010), 116.

Apple stock holder accrued, that would entail a very large tax bill. Some of that stock might have to be sold to meet the tax obligation, if it could not be used as collateral for a loan. That might not be considered a tragedy, but for a closely held business, forcing liquidation of the business to pay the tax could seem unfair and counterproductive. Economists have come up with approximations that would produce the same incentives and the same amount of average tax as taxing economic income, but they're politically impractical because they can sometimes require taxation on a theoretical gain even when the asset actually produced a loss.

So economic income is a helpful analytic tool for understanding the effects of tax policies, but not very practical as a tax base.

How do we tax capital gains and dividends?

Long-term capital gains (those on assets held at least one year) and qualifying dividends are taxed at a top rate of 15 percent. By comparison, the top tax rate on other income is 35 percent.

While long-term capital gains have been taxed at lower rates than other income for most of the history of the income tax, dividends have only been taxed at a lower rate since 2003. (This lower dividend tax rate is set to expire at the end of 2012, but don't hold your breath—it was also set to expire in 2008 and 2010, but was eventually extended). The argument for a lower dividend tax rate is that corporation income is already taxed at the company level, so taxing the dividends as well corresponds to double taxation. A similar argument is often made to justify lower capital gains tax rates. However, the lower rate is a very imperfect offset. While some corporations remit a lot of tax, some are able to use tax breaks to significantly reduce their effective corporate tax rate. And assets other than corporate stock have capital gains, so this double taxation argument does not apply to them.

The ideal adjustment for corporate double taxation—at least from the economist's perspective—would be to "integrate" the individual and corporate taxes. In other words, corporate income would be allocated to shareholders and taxed at individual rates, much as the tax system works for partnerships. For technical reasons, however, this is much easier said than done.

What are the arguments for and against lower capital gains tax rates?

While avoiding double taxation is a fairly convincing rationale for tax breaks on stock gains and dividends, the lower tax rate also applies to noncorporate capital gains. This is harder to justify. Proponents argue that capital gains tax breaks are desirable for various reasons: (1) a significant portion of capital gains simply represents inflation and we shouldn't tax that; (2) a lower tax rate on capital gains encourages risk-taking and entrepreneurship; (3) loss deductions are limited so it's unfair to tax gains in full; and (4) high capital gains tax rates create an inefficient "lock-in effect."

These arguments are less convincing than they appear at first blush. While it is true that when prices are rising a significant fraction of capital gains may represent inflation, that is also true of other forms of capital income. For example, at a 3 percent inflation rate, the first $3 of interest on a $100 savings account simply offsets inflation, but it is taxable nonetheless. For the same reason, interest expense is also understated due to inflation. Now, two wrongs (taxing illusory capital income and deducting illusory costs of borrowing) don't make a right, but if capital gains are taxed at lower rates, then either interest expense should be deductible at lower rates or else you create large incentives for tax sheltering.

It is probably true that a lower capital gains tax rate encourages risk-taking (although MIT economist James Poterba has found that much of the capital that finances new investments is not subject to capital gains taxes and, thus, is unaffected by capital gains tax breaks). The question is whether such encouragement is warranted. Investments of "sweat equity" are already treated very favorably by the income tax. As an entrepreneur, you don't have to pay tax on the value of your labor until it produces income. This is a very valuable tax break.

A more persuasive argument is that, while positive capital gains are taxed (at a preferential rate), there is a strict limit on how much losses can be deducted against other income. Capital loss deductions must be limited to prevent wealthy taxpayers with large diversified portfolios from selectively realizing losses and indefinitely deferring gains. The losses could offset tax due on other income—such as wages—while tax liability on the assets with gains could be avoided entirely by holding them until death (see "Angel of Death" loophole below) or donating them to charity. However, the loss limit can put a real burden on someone who holds a single asset—such as a business—that suffers a loss. If the loss is quite large, it might take many years to fully deduct it. However, such situations are very rare. The vast majority of taxpayers with losses can fully utilize them within a few years.[7]

Finally, consider the lock-in effect, which means that people will be hesitant to sell their stocks in order to avoid triggering capital gains taxes. It is certainly true that a capital gains tax discourages people from selling assets, and therefore acts as a barrier to achieving one's desired portfolio. You can postpone the tax indefinitely simply by holding the appreciated asset. However, our research and the research of most other scholars generally conclude that the "lock-in effect" is relatively modest, at least in the range of tax rates we've recently had.

The argument against providing capital gains tax breaks is twofold: first, lower capital gains tax rates encourage tax shelters, and those are generally inefficient. Second, the vast majority of capital gains are realized by people with very high incomes. Tax breaks on capital gains disproportionately benefit the rich and undermine the progressivity of the tax system.

What is the "Angel of Death" loophole?

One way to avoid capital gains tax is to die. Yes, it's an extreme measure, but it happens to all of us eventually. Columnist Michael Kinsley dubbed this the "Angel of Death" loophole.

When you die, the tax "basis" for your appreciated assets becomes the value at time of death. Thus, for your heirs it's as if they bought the Apple stock at its price when they inherited it; your heirs never have to pay tax on the gains that accrued during your life due to your clever stock-picking.

This is surely an important factor in the lock-in effect discussed above. Postponing a tax is good, but avoiding it altogether is the ultimate tax shelter.

Note that there is another way to avoid paying capital gains tax—donate appreciated assets to charity. Although there are limits, donors can generally deduct the full value of contributions of property without owing any tax on the accrued gains. This makes contributions of highly appreciated property much more attractive than contributions of cash—and explains why nonprofit organizations with wealthy donors spend a lot of time selling things that donors have given them.

If we want to favor capital gains and dividends, does it make sense to do it via lower rates?

Not really. The alternate rate schedule for capital gains is really complicated. Look at the 37-line worksheet in the instructions for Schedule D (where capital gains are reported) to see how mind-numbing the calculation really is.

There is an alternative. A portion of capital gains and dividends could be excluded from taxable income. For example, if 60 percent of long-term capital gains were excluded, the effective tax rate on capital gains for people in the top bracket would be 14 percent (40 percent of 35 percent). And the calculation would be pretty straightforward: 40 percent of capital gains would be included in income and the other 60 percent would be disregarded. This is the way capital gains were taxed before 1987.

You might wonder why Congress decided to cap the tax rate on long-term capital gains in 1987. The Tax Reform Act of 1986 lowered ordinary income tax rates and fully taxed capital gains as part of a grand compromise. However, conservatives were concerned that income tax rates would creep up from the 28 percent rate that applied to high-income people and they did not want the tax on capital gains to rise as well. So the rate on capital gains was capped at the then-extant maximum rate of 28 percent. Of course, income tax rates did increase, first in 1990 (when President Bush fatefully broke his "no new taxes" pledge) and again in 1993, but the tax rate on capital gains remained capped at 28 percent. Legislation in 1997 cut the top rate to 20 percent and the rate was cut further to 15 percent in 2003.

What is the AMT?

AMT stands for alternative minimum tax. It is an addition to regular income tax that was designed to ensure that, in spite of the proliferation of what might be called loopholes in the tax law, millionaires paid at least some tax. Unfortunately, it is poorly designed, inordinately complex, and is today more likely to hit upper-middle income families than millionaires.[8]

Here's how it works. First you calculate your regular taxable income and income tax liability. Then you start over, and add back a bunch of tax breaks to taxable income, deduct a flat AMT exemption amount ($74,450 for couples and $48,450 for singles in 2011) and calculate the tax at rates of 26 or 28 percent. If the tax under this alternative calculation is more than tax owed under the regular income tax rules, you must add the difference to your tax bill; this is equivalent to owing the higher of the two tax liability calculations. Hence, the logic behind the name "alternative minimum" tax.

Ironically, the bulk of the AMT's taxable income adjustments have nothing to do with anybody's notion of a loophole. The largest is the deduction for state and local income and property taxes, which accounted for 68 percent of all AMT adjustments in 2008. Personal exemptions—the $3,700 deduction (in 2011) for each family member and dependent—account for another 19 percent of AMT add-backs, and so-called miscellaneous itemized deductions, such as employee business expenses, make up 12 percent of the total.

Not surprisingly, given the preponderance of middle-class preference items among the add-backs, the people most likely to be hit by the AMT are big families living in high-tax states. Although originally targeted at well-heeled tax avoiders, the AMT's reach is expanding deep into the middle class. The Brady Bunch—six kids, professional dad, stay-at-home mom living in Southern California—would be hit big time by the AMT, because dependent exemptions are not allowed against the AMT. It also can make long-term financial planning extremely complicated.

Where the heck did this turkey come from and why is it so hard to get rid of?

In 1969, Treasury Secretary Joseph Barr testified to Congress that 155 high-income tax filers had paid no income tax in 1967. This provoked a firestorm of protest. According to law professor Michael Graetz, in 1969 Congress got more letters about this tax issue than about the Vietnam War—and the war was certainly agitating people that year. People thought it was really unfair that folks earning over $200,000 (the equivalent of over $1 million in today's dollars) could totally avoid income tax.

In response to the outcry, Congress might have reformed the tax code to close loopholes or it could have tried to convince the public that the tax breaks were warranted, but it didn't like either option. Tax reform would have angered the people who were exploiting the juicy tax shelters (who also were often rich donors) and it would have been hard to make the case for many of them, so lawmakers chose to put a Band-Aid on the income tax.

Originally, the minimum tax was an additional tax paid by those with very high incomes who took advantage of certain tax shelters. But as time went on, it morphed into its current form.

Today almost nobody defends the AMT and most major tax reform proposals would eliminate it; but, like a vampire, it's very hard to kill. The main reason is that it raises a lot of revenue. The Tax Policy Center estimates that repealing it would cost at least $1.4 trillion over the next decade under current law. If the Bush tax cuts are extended past their scheduled expiration in 2012, the cost would grow to $2.5 trillion. So the AMT appears to be a prodigious revenue generator.

But that does not account for the "AMT patch."

What is the AMT patch?

Ever since 2001, Congress has raised the AMT exemption amount every year or two to avoid a flood of new AMT taxpayers. These temporary fixes have been dubbed "the patch." They basically amount to ad hoc indexation of the AMT for inflation. This is needed because, unlike the regular income tax, the AMT exemption amount does not automatically adjust to reflect inflation. The consequence is that, without the patch, more people would be thrown onto the AMT every year because their AMT tax liability grows relative to liability under the regular income tax.

As of this writing, the patch runs through 2011. If Congress does nothing, in 2012, the AMT exemption will return to its pre-Bush level, $45,000 for a couple and $33,750 for a single filer. As a result, almost 27 million more households will owe AMT—31 million households (19 percent of tax filers) will owe AMT—compared to 4.3 million (2.6 percent) in 2011. Because Congress doesn't want to field 27 million angry letters, they will do something. Most likely, they'll increase the temporary exemption level to reflect inflation for the next year or two and we'll repeat this silly exercise again.

What is the "Buffett Rule"?

President Obama invented the "Buffett Rule." It is the principle that millionaires should pay at least as high an average tax rate as middle-income people. Warren Buffett, the billionaire investor and chairman of Berkshire-Hathaway, inspired the eponymous rule when he pointed out that he owed less income tax than his assistant. Most of Mr. Buffett's income comes from capital gains and dividends, which are taxed at a top income tax rate of 15 percent and not subject to payroll taxes. Mr. Buffett's assistant probably owes at least a 15 percent income tax rate on her Berkshire-Hathaway salary and another 15.3 percent in payroll taxes. Assuming that is most of her income, she probably faces a combined income and payroll tax rate of 30 percent or more. There are no details on how much this person actually earns or owes in taxes, or even which of Mr. Buffett's several assistants he had in mind, but her boss and the president have made Warren Buffett's "secretary" the poster child for tax inequity.[9]

The president has said that the Buffett Rule is not a particular proposal, but a principle for tax reform. Senator Sheldon Whitehouse (D-RI) proposed legislation inspired by the Buffett Rule that would require millionaires to owe income and payroll taxes equal to at least 30 percent of income. (The tax phases in between $1 and $2 million of income, so the rule does not apply with full force until incomes are at least $2 million.)

Critics (including one of us) have pointed out that the proposal would be tantamount to a second AMT, adding new complexity and inequity to the tax code.[10] A better approach would be to deal with the underlying aspects of the tax code that allow millionaires to avoid income tax. For example, several recent tax reform proposals would tax capital gains and dividends the same as other income, eliminating the source of inequity in the Buffett anecdote. (See page 225, "Are there some sensible tax reform ideas?")

Senator Whitehouse's bill does include a "sense of the Senate" resolution calling for tax reform and saying that the new minimum tax is an interim step. But using an act of tax code sabotage as a way to motivate tax reform sounds like a legislative strategy inspired by Machiavelli's *Prince*.

What are hidden tax brackets?

Whenever a tax break phases out with income—which is very common—it increases the tax triggered by earning an additional dollar. For example, the $1,000 per Child Tax Credit phases out at a rate of $5 per $100 of income over $110,000 for a couple. So, if your income increases from $110,000 to $111,000, you lose $50 of Child Tax Credits; your tax bill goes up by 5 percent of your additional income. It is just like a 5 percent "surtax" (a tax on top of another tax) added to your regular income tax.

The AMT features a very large surtax of this kind. The AMT exemption phases out at a rate of 25 percent of income over $150,000 for couples. If income increases from $150,000 to $160,000, the AMT exemption falls by $2,500. Because AMT taxable income is the difference between income as defined under the AMT rules and the exemption, taxable income increases by $12,500, so AMT taxpayers pay 25 percent more tax on the additional income than they would without the phantom tax. Those in the 26 percent AMT bracket see their *effective* rate increase to 32.5 percent (125 percent of 26 percent); in the 28 percent bracket, the effective rate becomes 35 percent.

Does Uncle Sam really want you to live in sin?

Probably not, but the tax code does treat married couples differently than single people. When you marry, even if your incomes don't change, your total taxes may go up, down, or stay the same. Marriage can affect your tax bill because we have a progressive income tax and tax families rather than individuals. If your taxes go up, you face a "marriage penalty"; if they fall, you get a "marriage bonus."[11] The Bush tax cuts eliminated marriage penalties for most middle-income families, so you're more likely to pay less tax than more when you tie the knot, but penalties have not been eliminated.

BOX 2.3 Vivien Kellem's Tea Party Revolt and the
Origins of the Marriage Penalty

Until 1948, married taxpayers in the United States filed as separate
individuals (as they still do in most of the world). High-income couples attempted to game this system by allocating capital income to
the lower-earning spouse who was subject to lower tax rates, but that
couldn't be done in community property states such as California.
In those states, capital income had to be allocated equally to the two
spouses, resulting in a higher total tax bill. In response to complaints
about the resulting inequities depending on one's state of residence, the
United States instituted joint filing in 1948. At first couples owed twice
the tax that a single person would with half the couple's income. This
scheme eliminated marriage penalties altogether, but it also maximized
marriage bonuses—single penalties.

The presence of single penalties was not lost on Vivien Kellems, a
successful and outspoken single business woman. It galled her that she
owed much more tax than a man with similar income and a stay-at-home
spouse would. She organized a group called War Widows of America
complaining that the tax system was unfair to women who, through no
fault of their own, lost their spouses and the valuable tax savings that
would accompany them. The fact that Kellems and many others in her
group had never been married was not mentioned. She campaigned tire-
lessly through the 1960s to eliminate tax penalties on singles.

In 1969, her campaign was partially successful. Congress cut taxes on
single filers while leaving taxes on joint filers unchanged, creating the
first marriage penalties while cutting the extent of single penalties. (With
a graduated tax schedule, there's no way to eliminate one without creating the other.) Ironically, those marriage penalties became a rallying
cry for later generations of tax protesters as married women entered the
work force in droves, creating many more penalized couples.

Source: Michael Graetz, *The Decline (and Fall?) of the Income Tax* (New York:
W. W. Norton & Company, 1997).

The easiest way to see why marriage penalties and bonuses
arise is to imagine a simple (and therefore hypothetical!)
flat-rate income tax where the first $10,000 of income is untaxed
and income above that threshold is taxed at a 25 percent rate.
This tax scheme is slightly progressive because the tax rate as
a share of income rises with income; for example, it's zero for
people earning $10,000 or less and 20 percent for a taxpayer

Figure 2.4 www.CartoonStock.com

earning $50,000. Now suppose the same schedule applied to couples and singles. A couple with each earning $10,000 would be tax-free if single, but the couple would owe $2,500 in tax on their $20,000 in household income if they married. That $2,500 in extra tax is the marriage penalty.

To eliminate this marriage penalty, the exemption threshold could be doubled for couples to $20,000. But that creates the possibility of marriage bonuses, or looked at differently, single penalties. If someone earning $20,000 married someone who doesn't work, her tax bill would fall by the same $2,500—a hefty marriage bonus. The government could split the difference—say, setting the exempt threshold at $15,000 for couples. In this case the first couple would still pay a penalty and the second receive a bonus, but penalties and bonuses would be cut in half.

Our tax system is way more complicated than this simple example, and the Bush tax cuts made it resemble the very marriage-friendly second example above for all but very high- and low-income couples. But it's still true that couples

Figure 2.5 www.CartoonStock.com

where each spouse has similar income are more likely to pay penalties than couples with very unequal incomes.

A lot of provisions can create marriage penalties, and they're not just in the income tax. In 2004, the U.S. General Accounting Office counted 1,049 laws "in which benefits, rights, and privileges are contingent on marital status" (although not all convey penalties or bonuses).[12] For example, Social Security provides benefits for spouses even if they have paid little or no payroll taxes, a substantial marriage bonus. The estate tax has an unlimited exemption for bequests made to a surviving spouse—a potentially huge marriage bonus that is not available to unmarried partners. The AMT can create big penalties and bonuses depending on circumstances. The EITC—like traditional welfare programs—can also create marriage penalties (because a spouse's earnings can raise the couple's earnings into the range where the EITC is reduced or eliminated).

How does inflation affect the income tax?

Part of your income simply reflects inflation. For example, if you earned $50,000 in 2008 and $51,900 in 2009, your income, as measured by purchasing power, didn't really change because prices went up by the same 3.8 percent between the two years. If the tax tables stayed the same, however, your tax would grow by more than 3.8 percent because all of that $1,900 in additional income would be taxed at the rate of your highest tax bracket. Back in the 1970s and 1980s, high inflation would often push up people's incomes so much that they'd get bumped into higher tax brackets even if they had little or no increase in their "real" income. This so-called "bracket creep" was extraordinarily unpopular. Starting in 1985, tax brackets were automatically adjusted for inflation so people would not pay higher average tax rates simply because of inflation.

One group liked bracket creep: politicians. Inflation generated automatic real tax increases year after year, which allowed Congress to convey "tax cuts" on a regular basis—giving back part of the tax bonanza generated by inflation. Once brackets were indexed, the golden era ended. Although real income growth also tended to increase revenues, it wasn't anywhere near as fast as during the rampant inflation of the 1970s. In that environment, tax cuts required real spending cuts or higher deficits, a much less pleasant trade-off for politicians.

Even though many income tax parameters, including the tax bracket thresholds of the regular income tax, are automatically adjusted for inflation, the tax system is far from neutral. As noted, the AMT exemption level is not automatically adjusted for inflation, although it's been adjusted on an ad hoc basis for the last decade. And some parameters affecting eligibility for credits, deductions, and exclusions are fixed in dollar terms. For example, the Child Tax Credit has phased out starting at $110,000 of income for couples since it was created in 1997, affecting more and more families every year.

Inflation causes another problem for the income tax—capital income and expense are mis-measured because they are not adjusted for inflation. This can result in a large overstatement of income and expense. For example, if the interest rate is 6 percent but inflation is running at 3 percent, half of interest simply compensates for inflation, and does not comprise real income. But the tax code includes the whole 6 percent in taxable income, effectively doubling the tax burden on interest income. For example, someone who has $1,000 in the bank earning 6 percent interest would report $60 of income. At a 25 percent tax bracket, that generates $15 in tax. But the *real* interest is only $30 (half was simply inflation), so the $15 in tax corresponds to a 50 percent tax rate on real income. A similar problem occurs with other kinds of capital income—dividends, capital gains, rents, royalties, etc.

By the same token, inflation also causes interest expense to be overstated. Thus, when there's inflation, the tax system subsidizes debt and penalizes saving. When inflation is substantial, this can cause havoc in financial markets, severely distorting the incentives to save, lend, and borrow. Some countries with persistent, high inflation tried to adjust taxable capital income and tax-deductible expense to include in taxable income only the parts not reflecting inflation, but these adjustments can get very complicated, and are probably not worth the trouble as long as inflation stays as low as it has recently been in the United States. But if higher inflation starts to rear its head, as some people fear, this might become an important tax policy issue.

What are payroll taxes and how are they different from income taxes?

Payroll taxes are taxes on wages and salaries. The largest payroll taxes are the 12.4 percent tax (technically, but not substantively, 6.2 percent collected from employers and employees) to fund Social Security and the 2.9 percent tax (half collected from each) to fund Medicare. States also collect smaller taxes to fund unemployment insurance and sometimes other programs. Some local governments (notably New York City and Philadelphia) impose a wage tax to collect revenue from workers who live outside the city. This kind of tax is sometimes called a commuter tax.

The earnings base for Social Security tax is capped at $106,800 in 2011. That cap is adjusted every year for increases in average wages. Because of the cap, the Social Security tax is a much smaller share of earnings at the top than for low- and middle-income earners. However, in contrast to the income tax (where higher tax liability does not earn free passes to national parks or Platinum-grade anti-missile defense), Social Security benefits are tied to payroll taxes remitted during one's working life. Because these benefits are also capped and the benefit formula is highly progressive, the program overall—taxes and benefits together—is not especially onerous on the poor.

Social Security and Medicare taxes are examples of *earmarked* taxes. The funds raised are dedicated to providing benefits under these two programs. To the extent that revenues exceed benefit payments, as they have for the past several decades, the surplus is invested in a special Treasury account and earns interest. In principle, the money set aside in the trust fund will allow benefits to be paid long after benefits exceed revenues, which due to demographic changes will soon be the case. Economists would say that such earmarking is purely symbolic because money is fungible, but many advocates for the programs believe that the earmarking is an essential factor in their political success. People support spending money on Social Security and Medicare because they think they have earned the benefits by contributing payroll taxes.

Another difference between payroll taxes and the income tax is that payroll taxes have traditionally only applied to wages plus earnings from self-employment. Income from capital had been exempt. Also there are no deductions and there's only a single tax rate, as compared with the graduated tax rate schedule that applies under the income tax.

Aren't other taxes also dedicated to Medicare and Social Security?

Yes. To help secure Social Security's finances in 1983, a portion of Social Security benefits was included in taxable income for higher-income recipients and the revenue collected dedicated to the trust fund. In 1993, a second tier of tax was added and

"DO AWAY WITH ALL THE TAX LOOPHOLES YOU WANT, BUT DON'T MESS WITH MY ENTITLEMENTS!"

Figure 2.6 www.CartoonStock.com

the additional income tax revenue earmarked for Medicare. The thresholds are not adjusted for inflation—a deliberate choice intended to phase in the taxation of a larger and larger share of benefits over time.

More recently, a new provision in the Patient Protection and Affordable Care Act of 2010 (health care reform) will apply a 3.8 percent tax on investment income for individuals with income (actually AGI with some slight modifications) of over $200,000 and couples with income greater than $250,000, earmarked to bolster Medicare's finances starting in 2013.

And in 2011 and 2012, the individual portion of the Social Security tax was reduced by 2 percentage points (out of 6.45 percent) in an effort to stimulate the economy. However, the revenue lost from this temporary provision was made up from general revenues (that is, other taxes or borrowing).

Thus, over time, payroll taxes have comprised a smaller share of Social Security and Medicare's finances. This trend concerns program advocates who think a large part of their political popularity comes from the perception that recipients have earned their benefits by virtue of their payroll tax liability. As the connection between payroll taxes and benefits becomes more and more attenuated, the programs might come to seem more like welfare and less like insurance.

Is it true that most taxpayers owe more payroll than income tax?

Yes. The Tax Policy Center estimates that 54 percent of tax units with earnings owe more payroll tax than income tax, even when counting only the half of payroll tax technically levied on the employee.[13] Economists believe that the employer share is also borne by employees in the form of

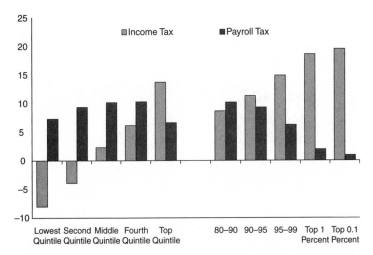

Figure 2.7 Average income and payroll tax burden, by income group, 2010. *Source*: Tax Policy Center, Table T11–0099, available at: http://taxpolicycenter.org/T11–0099

lower wages. Counting both the employee and employer share, 82 percent of taxpayers owe more payroll tax than personal income tax. Only within the top 10 percent of tax-paying households do a majority of households owe more income tax (figure 2.7).

3

BUSINESS INCOME TAXES

How do we tax corporations' income?

In principle, under an income tax all income is subject to taxation. Moreover, no kinds of income are subject to exceptionally high tax and no kinds are subject to exceptionally low tax. This principle applies to labor income, the income from savings (i.e., capital income), and business income. In reality, the U.S. income tax diverges from this ideal in many important ways. For just one example, capital income can be shielded from tax if it is earned within a pension account or an IRA.

The taxation of business income earned by corporations also deviates from this principle because, except for those mostly small corporations that can opt out, corporate income is subject to a separate tax. Net income is calculated the same way as it would be for any other business, receipts minus the costs of doing business—that's not the issue. But corporate income is taxed according to a graduated tax schedule: the first $50,000 of taxable income is subject to a 15 percent rate, the next $25,000 is subject to a 25 percent rate, and all taxable income over $18.333 million is taxed at a 35 percent rate, with income between $75,000 and $18.333 million being subject to a jumble of rates between 34 percent and 39 percent. Thus, the tax rate depends on the amount of the corporation's income and has nothing to do with the tax bracket of the company's owners. High-income owners of small corporations have their income taxed at the lower corporate tax rate, while low-tax-rate owners of big, profitable corporations (individuals with low income or nontaxable investors, like pension funds) have their income taxed at higher corporate tax rates.[1]

The corporate income tax rate schedule means that most corporations are subject to rates of 15 or 25 percent on their income, but most corporate income is subject to a 35 percent corporate tax rate. Both statements can be true simultaneously because, while most corporations are fairly small, the bulk of corporate income is earned by the small fraction of big corporations that, in most years, have enough income to be in the top 35 percent bracket. In 2008, 537,000 corporations had positive income tax after credits. About 380,000 of them faced the 15 percent rate and owed $752 million of corporate income tax; just 6,900 corporations faced the 35 percent rate, but remitted almost 200 times as much tax, $147 billion.

But this is not the end of the story. Not only does corporate income trigger corporate income tax, it may also generate a tax liability for the owners of the corporation—the shareholders—on their personal income tax. The personal tax liability depends on what the corporation does with its money. If it pays money out in the form of dividends, the dividends are taxed as income of the shareholders. Since 2003 dividends are taxed at substantially lower rates than other income—no higher than 15 percent—but before that dividends were usually taxed like other income. What if the corporation keeps the profits in the company and uses them to make further investments? To the extent that this increases the value of the corporation, its stock price rises and if a shareholder sells any of these shares, the appreciation in value since the time the stock was purchased is also subject to tax as a capital gain.

Why do economists say that we "double tax" corporation income?

Double taxation in this context refers to the fact that the income earned by corporations may be taxed at the business level by the corporate income tax and also at the shareholder level by the tax on dividends and capital gains (or both).

The two-layered nature of the tax is an indisputable fact, but the label of double taxation is a bit misleading because it suggests the tax rate is "twice as big" as is levied on other income. But twice as big as what? Does the *number* of separate taxes matter, or just the combined effective tax rate? To answer that question, consider a retail sales tax. Say you had a choice of being subject to one of two sales tax regimes. Under the first, there is a single retail sales tax levied at a rate of 6 percent. In the other, retail sales trigger two separate taxes—say a regular tax and a surtax—but both the regular tax and surtax rates are 1 percent. You would, of course, prefer the double tax regime, because the total tax of 2 percent is lower than the single tax of 6 percent. The same reasoning applies to the double taxation of corporate income; we need to inquire into the total rate of tax and the consequences of the two layers of tax and how they operate—rather than fixate on the fact that there are two layers rather than one layer of tax.

What are the others ways business income is taxed?

Most businesses, especially smaller ones, do not operate as corporations. Most small businesses are sole proprietorships, with one owner. Others are partnerships, which have explicit rules about how the profits of the business are split among the partners. In 2008, there were 3.1 million partnership returns, 4 million S corporation returns, 22.6 million nonfarm sole proprietorships, and 1.8 million (regular or C) corporations.[2] In the first three cases, there is no tax that applies to the business per se. Instead the owners, or part owners in the case of partnerships, must include their business income as part of their individual taxable income. Sole proprietor income must be reported on Schedule C of the Form 1040, and partnership income shows up on Schedule E. Thus for noncorporate business income, there is just one layer of tax at the owner's personal level, and the applicable tax rate depends on the owner's total taxable income—not the amount of profits of any one business. For tax purposes these businesses are called *pass-through* entities, because there is no business-level tax at all, but instead the business income is subject to the owner's personal taxable income. This means that the losses of pass-through entities are also passed through to the owners and are subtracted from any other income the owners have. In contrast, if a corporation has negative taxable income, it cannot be subtracted against other income of its owners. Instead, it can be carried back for up to two years to offset previous profits, or carried forward (without interest) to offset future profits. Because of the disparate treatment of losses, many businesses operate as pass-through entities in their start-up phase, when losses are common, and then switch to C corporation status later.

"First the good news -- we don't have to pay any corporate taxes this year."

Figure 3.1 www.CartoonStock.com

For two reasons, the line between the tax rules that apply to corporate and noncorporate businesses is not as hard and fast as the previous discussion suggests. Many businesses that are legal corporations can elect to be exempt from the corporate tax and be taxed much like partnerships, where each owner's share of the corporation's income becomes part of their taxable income. These businesses are known as S corporations, or S corps, because their tax treatment is spelled out in Subchapter S of Chapter 1 of the Internal Revenue Code (and not because S corporations are usually "s"mall). Several restrictions limit which corporations qualify for this election, the most important of which is that there can be no more than 100 shareholders. This eligibility restriction makes S corporation status infeasible for the big, public corporations that have millions of distinct shareholders. In fact, most S corporations have only a few shareholders. In 2008, there were 4 million S corporation returns, with a total of only 6.9 million shareholders. Only 3,800 S corporations had more than 30 shareholders, while 2.4 million had only 1 shareholder and another 1.2 million had just 2.[3]

The dividing line is also not clear-cut because of the growth of hybrid forms of business organization, in particular, the limited liability company, or LLC. An LLC is not a corporation but does, like a corporation, provide the owners with limited liability—no matter how badly the business does, the owners' assets not invested in the business are safe from creditors. For tax purposes, an LLC gets pass-through treatment—it escapes the corporate income tax and instead each owner's share of the business profits adds to their individual taxable income. When business owners are deciding on the type of business entity, they look at both the legal ramifications and the tax treatment.

Why tax corporations?

To many people, taxing corporations is a no-brainer. A recent *New York Times*/CBS News Poll found that when individuals were given a choice between raising taxes on corporations and raising taxes on households making more than $250,000 a year, two-thirds wanted to tax corporations. Moreover, most Americans say corporations do not pay their fair share of taxes. A 2009 survey by Harris/Tax Foundation found that 49 percent of individuals characterized corporate income taxes as not at all fair. To these people, the reason is obvious—corporations are big, rich, and maybe even evil. Are these things true, and if so, do they justify taxing them as separate entities?[4]

Let's start with big. Corporations as a whole are certainly a big part of the U.S. economy.[5] In 2010, nonfarm corporate businesses accounted for about 75 percent of the economy's net output.[6] So how we tax corporations and their profits affects a major chunk of the U.S. economy.

Are corporations rich? Some corporations are huge, and in good times make enormous profits. In 2011, Wal-Mart Stores was the world's biggest company, with profits of $16.4 billion and revenues of $421.8 billion and in 2009 was the world's largest private employer with 2.1 million workers.[7] Exxon Mobil had over $30 billion in profits in 2011.[8] Because they comprise such a large share of the U.S. economy, when times are good corporations as a whole make lots of money. But corporate profits are quite cyclical, and in recessions corporate profits tumble, as do corporate tax collections. Corporate profits peaked at $1.6 trillion in 2006 and fell to $1.2 trillion (in 2006 dollars) in both 2008 and 2009.

Not all corporations are huge, though, and not all huge businesses are corporations. For example, despite each having over 100,000 employees, the accounting firms PricewaterhouseCoopers and Ernst & Young are both partnerships (and therefore not subject to the corporate income tax).

Are the people who own corporations rich? Certainly well-to-do people own the lion's share of corporations. In 2007, the top 10 percent of income earners owned 75 percent of stocks and the wealthiest 10 percent of households owned over 90 percent. When indirect holdings through retirement accounts are included, the distribution becomes slightly less skewed, with the top 10 percent of income earners owning 66 percent of stocks and the wealthiest 10 percent of households owning 84 percent. Nevertheless, not all the people who own shares in corporations, directly or indirectly through their pension funds, are rich.[9]

So the corporate sector is hugely important, and some—but not most—corporations are enormous. Are they bad? Ascribing an ethical judgment to a legal entity is tricky. The overriding objective of corporations is to maximize the profits earned by their owners. It was Adam Smith who over 200 years ago clarified the connection between, on the one hand, people and businesses seeking their own private interests and, on the other hand, the greater good of society. Smith argued that, in the appropriate setting, society's goals would be served by harnessing the talents, energy, and information of people and businesses, as if by an "invisible hand." He was right, for the most part. Corporations seeking profit is generally a good thing. It encourages them to be innovative and efficient. At the same time, corporations (and people, too) may take actions that harm others and, to address this, such actions often need to be regulated.

Some people believe that big corporations have acquired too much political power and financial resources, using these resources to influence legislation they favor at the expense of consumers and workers, bargaining for favorable tax treatment and other policy favors. Some worry that giant businesses can become "too big to fail," which make them prone to take inappropriate risks believing that taxpayers will bail them out if things go badly. We don't mean to diminish these issues, but we don't think the corporate income tax is the appropriate policy instrument for dealing with them.

Another reason why lots of people think taxing corporations is a good idea is that they think that the burden is borne by somebody else, and not them. It's borne by rich CEOs and shareholders, but not *them*. Are they right?

Which people bear the burden of the corporate income tax?

As we discussed in chapter 2, the fact that money is transferred to the IRS from the corporation's bank accounts to settle a corporation's tax liability gives no clue as to who bears the tax burden. Because who actually bears the burden is not apparent, in an important sense the corporation income tax is a hidden tax.[10]

Economists are divided on the answer to the question. In the short run, an unanticipated increase in the corporate income tax rate would depress share prices, and thus be borne by stockholders. But most economists also believe that, over time, the burden will be spread beyond the shareholders. Some economists maintain that in the long run the corporate income tax falls mainly on labor, rather than on the somewhat wealthier owners of capital, because the tax reduces capital investment and lowers workers' productivity—and ultimately their wages. Other economists believe that the burden of the corporate tax ultimately rests mainly on the owners of capital, but not just shareholders. The burden is spread as investment flees the corporate sector to other sectors, which drives down the rate of return that can be earned in these sectors. This has been the operative assumption of the Congressional Budget Office, the Treasury, and other agencies when they analyze the distributional impact of changes in the corporate income tax.[11]

What are the impacts of double-taxing corporate income?

This system causes inefficient incentives for corporations to raise capital by borrowing and thus to become excessively leveraged and susceptible to bankruptcy in bad times. This happens because, although interest payments are deductible as a business expense (and are taxable income to the lender), corporations cannot deduct anything in recognition of the cost of attracting equity financing, even though the equity providers (i.e., the shareholders) are taxed to some degree on the income they receive.

Finally, the two levels of tax, corporate and individual, generally cause the tax rate on business income to be higher than it is on other income and the cost of capital for corporate businesses to be higher than it is for other businesses, neither of which is justifiable. Mitigating the double taxation of income flowing through corporations would lower the cost of equity capital to domestic corporations, reduce the tax bias toward debt finance, and at the same time move the tax system in the direction of a comprehensive income tax that taxes all income once and only once, at a uniform rate.

What would happen if we just eliminated the corporate income tax?

Simply eliminating the corporate tax without other changes is a bad idea. It would make the effective tax rate on the income earned by corporations less than on other income, so it would provide an artificial, purely tax-driven preference for income earned by corporations. It would also make operating a corporation a tremendous tax avoidance opportunity. People like us would find it tremendously attractive to incorporate ourselves; the corporation would owe no tax, and our accountants would devise ways for us to enjoy the fruits of any profits in untaxed, or lightly taxed, ways, such as driving a company car for our weekend errands. This would apply not only to existing businesses but also to new "businesses" because it would now become attractive for people to incorporate themselves and thereby make their labor income tax-exempt. If the corporation tax were to be abolished, taxpayers could shift what is essentially labor income to the corporate sector and receive it free of tax, while financing their consumption via loans from their companies. Policymakers could try to write laws to stem this kind of abuse, but that would just add to complexity (and create more jobs for smart tax lawyers and accountants). Thus, one function of the corporate income tax is a "backstop" to the individual income tax because in part it applies to the labor income of corporations' principals.

How can some companies get away with paying no income tax despite billions in profits?

It's not surprising, or troubling, that when a company has a bad year and has no income, it owes no income tax. More troubling is the case of a corporation that reports to the world in its financial statements that it is phenomenally profitable and still remits no income tax. For example, the *New York Times* reported that General Electric, one of the largest companies in the world, paid no income tax in 2010 despite worldwide profits of over $14.2 billion and U.S. profits of $5.1 billion.[12] How can that happen?

For one thing, the IRS definition of corporate income subject to tax differs from the definition of income for public financial

Figure 3.2 © Tribune Media Services, Inc. All Rights Reserved. Reprinted with permission.

statements. The rules have different objectives. Generally Accepted Accounting Principles, known by the acronym GAAP, are designed to constrain corporations from painting too optimistic a picture of how well the company is doing in an effort to attract investors. The accounting rules governing taxable income, on the other hand, should, in principle, be designed to keep corporations from low-balling their income to minimize their tax liability.[13]

Based on this logic you might think that taxable income is generally higher than earnings on financial statements. You'd be wrong—very wrong. Academic researchers have estimated that in the late 1990s the total book income of firms with more than $250 million of assets was consistently higher than their total taxable income, as much as 60 percent higher in 1998.[14]

In the last half century, the Congress has often altered how business taxable income, and business tax liability, is calculated in an attempt to stimulate business investment. Between 1962 and 1986, investment tax credits (ITC) were the preferred policy instrument of choice. Under an investment tax credit, a business could get a credit of usually between 7 and 10 percent of the purchase price of qualifying capital goods. The 1986 tax reform eliminated the ITC, and it has not returned since. But the idea of defining income more generously for tax purposes as a way to make investment more attractive did not perish. Since 1981 the most popular approach has been to accelerate how quickly depreciation allowances, used to allocate the cost of long-lived capital goods over their useful life, can be taken for particular investments. These accelerated depreciation allowances explain much of the difference between taxable income and income calculated under GAAP. Other items that intentionally have different accounting treatment for GAAP and tax purposes (such as stock options) also explain why corporations may have higher book income than taxable income. In any given year, taxable income may fall short of accounting income for corporations that in previous years suffered big losses; because the losses may be carried forward to offset the tax on profits earned later.

Why is it troublesome that some companies view their tax departments as profit centers?

Surveys of corporate tax departments document that they are often evaluated by—and compensated on the basis of—how much tax savings they generate and how low the company's effective tax rate is. In one recent survey, two-thirds of corporate tax executives said that minimizing the effective tax rate is extremely or very important.[15]

The problem is that the tax department starts weighing in on business decisions. Companies alter the way they do business not because it makes them more efficient, but because it saves tax. Often these tax-driven decisions would make no business sense at all, but for the tax savings. (To be fair, in some cases the change in behavior is exactly what Congress intends.) An inefficient company with a great tax department can be more profitable than an otherwise efficient one that doesn't pay enough attention to tax strategies. The tax savvy business thus finds it easier to attract capital and may even drive its more efficient, but less tax-obsessed, competitor out of business. And, of course, the fact that some of the smartest people in the company are developing innovative tax strategies rather than innovative products is a pure waste of economic resources.

Income earned by corporations is double-taxed, and tax avoidance opportunities abound. Make up your mind—Is corporate income taxed too much, or too little?

Asking the right question is often a critical part of gaining insight into an issue. And here we have subtly changed the question from "should we tax corporations?" to "how should corporate income be taxed?" If we want to have an income tax (and we will come back to this question later), then we want to tax the income earned by corporations the same as other income, no more or less, and in a way that minimizes inefficient incentives.

Whether the tax liability triggered by corporate income is remitted by the legal entity called the corporation generally does not matter except if it facilitates the collection and monitoring of taxes. After all, we're not much concerned that most of the tax liability triggered by labor income is actually remitted by employers (via withholding) rather than the workers. It's easier for the IRS to keep track of a much smaller number of firms, many with sophisticated accounting systems, than the hundred-million-plus employees. In the same way, it is easier for the IRS to collect much of the tax due on corporate income from corporations. But there is one notable difference between employers' withholding and remitting tax for their employees and corporations withholding and remitting tax for their shareholders. With minimal information from their employees, employers can tailor the withholding amount to the approximate tax liability of the employee. But even then, the withholding is almost never exact. Thus, when the employees figure their own tax liability, they can credit the employer withholding against that liability, and so must remit only the difference between the two. As it happens, most households' tax liability is less than what has been withheld by their employer(s), so that they qualify for a refund. Either way—tax due or tax refund—the total tax owed doesn't depend on employer withholding.

Let's now carry the withholding analogy back to the case of the corporation income tax. With a large number of anonymous shareholders, often running into the millions, it is not realistic for public corporations to calculate their tax liability based on the appropriate tax liability of all of their shareholders. But one can imagine treating the corporate tax as a credit against the tax liability of the shareholders, and indeed many countries have operated systems with this basic structure. The

United States has never done this, with the result that the tax liability on corporate taxable income is effectively the same for all shareholders, about 35 percent, whether the shareholder would be in an individual tax bracket close to 35 percent or in a 0 percent bracket.

The slightly graduated tax on dividends and capital gains personalizes the tax burden somewhat, but it only adds to, and never subtracts from, the corporate level tax, so that the total tax on corporate income is often higher than that on other types of income and not closely related to shareholders' tax status.

What about corporate tax avoidance and evasion? One answer is to enforce the tax law optimally, which we discuss in chapter 9. Second, clean up the tax base to minimize opportunities for unintended tax sheltering. Finally, it makes sense to limit the preferred lower rate on dividends (and maybe capital gains) only to shareholders of companies that have remitted some minimal level of corporate tax. This was part of the original Bush administration proposal that led to the dividend tax reduction in 2003, but did not make it into the enacted legislation. Linking the tax on dividends to the corporate tax would recognize that the identity of the remitter is not critical and a sensible tax structure would recognize the two levels of tax and try to coordinate them.

What is depreciation?

At first blush, measuring business income is pretty straightforward—it's simply receipts net of the costs of doing business. Wages and salaries of employees and independent contractors are a cost of doing business, so these should be subtracted from receipts. (Even saying this glosses over some tricky accounting issues—should the wages be deducted when paid or when the products the workers make are sold, and what if the employees are compensated with stock options that cannot be cashed in for years?) Same with paper clips. In practice, some steps in this process can become quite complicated. Consider installment sales. For the measurement of taxable income, income occurs when the cash is received; for purposes of financial statements, it is recognized up front when the sale is made.

For long-lived capital goods the central issue is *when* a deduction can be taken for the cost. If a factory (or a machine) is productive over many years, measuring income accurately in each year requires allocating some fraction of the cost of the factory to each year it is in use. For many decades, the tax code dealt with this issue by grouping capital goods into broad categories based on their average productive lifetime, and then allowing businesses to deduct the purchase cost over these lifetimes according to a fixed schedule. Some deviation from these schedules was allowed, but the objective was to match the time pattern of depreciation allowances with the actual depreciation of the capital good due to wear and tear, as well as technological obsolescence.

This way of thinking about depreciation allowances changed in 1981. The Reagan administration was looking for a way to induce more business investment by tweaking the tax code. Cutting the corporate tax rate was deemed to be politically unattractive and, besides, would provide no incentive for noncorporate businesses. As an alternative, they hit on the idea of allowing businesses to deduct the cost of capital goods more quickly. This reduced tax liability and thus increased cash flow in the short term although, later in the life of the capital goods, taxes increase and cash flow falls. But remember, time is money. Getting deductions earlier is almost always valuable to a business.

Since 1986, when the investment tax credit was eliminated, tinkering with the tax depreciation schedules has become the preferred tax policy for kick-starting the economy by stimulating business investment. Compared to the corporate-tax-cut alternative, accelerated depreciation has two advantages. One that we've already mentioned is that it applies to all businesses (although more valuable to capital-intensive ones), and not just to those that are incorporated and subject to the corporate income tax. Second, it is easier to target the tax break from accelerated depreciation rules to new investment, which is what you would want to do to maximize the "bang per buck," where here the bang is the kick to investment and the buck is the tax revenue foregone. Cutting the tax rate produces a lower bang per buck because it applies to all income, including income produced by past investments. Indeed, at any time, current corporate profits are almost entirely the result of past investments, so that an across-the-board tax cut increases after-tax profits without stimulating much additional investment. Thus, a rate cut largely rewards past investments and does not effectively target new investments.

Many corporations, however, would prefer lower tax rates to accelerated depreciation. As Tom Neubig, an economist for the accounting firm Ernst & Young has pointed out, a lower corporate rate would lower the effective tax rate corporations report on their financial statements, and therefore would increase their book net income.[16] In contrast, under current accounting rules, accelerated depreciation offers only a timing benefit and does not reduce the effective tax rate shown on the financial statement or increase book income. This is a problem with the accounting rules, because accelerated depreciation does reduce the tax burden on corporations. This problem arises because the GAAP accounting rules do not allow corporations to discount future tax payments to take into account the time value of money, presumably because the use of discount rates introduces additional ways corporations could manipulate their accounting numbers. But, regardless of why these numbers are problematic, much evidence suggests that reported book income matters to financial analysts and investors, and so corporate CFOs pay close attention to it, making it plausible that they favor tax rate cuts to accelerated depreciation.

What is "bonus depreciation"?

Bonus depreciation is the name given since 2002 to the policy of accelerating depreciation by allowing firms to deduct immediately, or "expense," some fraction of the cost of capital goods while depreciating the remaining fraction over time. The fraction has varied, from 30 percent at its original enactment, to 50 percent for several years between 2003 and 2010. In the tax bill passed in 2010, 50 percent bonus depreciation was replaced by 100 percent bonus depreciation for capital purchases made in 2011. Of course, 100 percent bonus depreciation simply allows a business to deduct an asset's entire purchase and installation costs right away even though the income it generates usually flows over many years.

Why not let businesses write off their investments right away? It would make the process of determining taxable income easier, as businesses would no longer have to keep track of depreciation schedules for long-lived capital goods. The problem is that it would mean abandoning the attempt to tax business income, or at least part of it. Only a small fraction of the cost of a factory that will last twenty years is really a cost of earning income *this year*.

It turns out that if the tax system allowed a deduction for long-lived capital goods in the year of purchase, a capital investment that returned just exactly the normal rate of return in the economy would be subject to no tax at all. The government becomes essentially an equal, albeit silent, partner, in the business enterprise, sharing a fraction of all costs in the form of a tax deduction, and asking in return as tax the same fraction of all receipts. In technical terms, such an investment has a net present value of zero and, with expensing, the government shares in both the cost of investments and the return of the investments by exactly the same percentage. Thus, the present value of the tax on a flow of cost and returns with a present value of zero also has a present value of zero. For investments that end up offering better than this normal return, that is those with a positive net present value, the corporate tax would still collect some revenue.

Are there implicit spending programs run through the corporate income tax?

Indeed there are, and they come in several varieties. One type is the so-called "rifle-shot" provision, where special tax treatment is granted for the circumstances that apply only to one or a few companies. Because putting the company's actual name into the tax code would invite unwanted scrutiny, the circumstances are described very precisely but circumspectly. The classic example of a rifle-shot provision applied to an individual, rather than a company: a 1954 statute about the taxation of lump-sum distributions to employees was designed so only Louis B. Mayer, the retiring head of the Metro-Goldwyn-Mayer movie studio, qualified. In their wonderful book on the legislative origins of the Tax Reform Act of 1986 entitled *Showdown at Gucci Gulch*, Jeffrey Birnbaum and Alan Murray recount several examples. One benefited "an automobile manufacturer that was incorporated in Delaware on October 13, 1916" (viz., General Motors) or "a binding contract entered into on October 20, 1984, for the purchase of six semi-submersible drilling units" (viz., an Alabama firm called Sonat).[17]

Others are special tax provisions aimed at particular sectors, more or less explicitly. The subsidy to producing ethanol is an example of an explicit subsidy. Since 1978, producers of transportation fuels receive a tax credit for each gallon of ethanol that is blended with gasoline that now amounts to 45 cents.

For oil and gas drillers, the using up, or depletion, of the natural resource is a key cost of doing business. Depletion allowance is the term used for the tax deduction allowed to account for the reduction of reserves as a product is produced and sold; this is analogous to the depreciation allowance for

Figure 3.3 Henry Payne and Mackinac Center for Public Policy.

other capital investments. Producers can choose either of two depletion allowance regimes: cost depletion and percentage depletion. Many experts believe this deduction scheme is way too generous if the goal is to measure income accurately rather than subsidize oil and gas production.

A recent example is the domestic production activities deduction, which allows a special tax deduction to qualified taxpayers involved in certain domestic production activities. In general, the deduction equals a percentage of the net income derived from eligible activities—9 percent since 2009. This provision effectively reduces the tax rate on income earned in domestic production, and at the same time provides an incentive to account for a company's receipts and expenses so as to maximize the portion of total income that can be counted as subject to this lower tax rate.

Other provisions of the tax code provide subsidies to certain industries even though these industries are never mentioned. For example, accelerated depreciation favors those sectors that tend to utilize the kind of capital that qualifies for the most accelerated write-offs.

Are multinational corporations taxed differently than domestic companies?

Most big corporations operate not only in the United States but also in many foreign countries. For example, Nike has over 700 factories worldwide and operates offices in 45 countries, and McDonald's has restaurants in 118 countries.[18] Operating in many countries allows them to seek low-cost places to produce their products and profitable places to sell them.

The global nature of corporations raises a number of complex and contentious tax issues. Both the home country (where the company has its legal residence) and the host country (where the operations are) generally claim the right to tax the income of the company. If both countries tax the income at their full rates, then the total tax rate can become so punitive that few cross-border commercial operations would ever happen, and that is generally not a good outcome for people in either country. Governments recognize the possibility of this kind of double taxation and design their tax codes to avoid punishing corporations that operate across national borders.

What is a foreign tax credit?

The foreign tax credit is the centerpiece of this system in the United States. In principle the United States taxes the worldwide income of its residents, both individual and corporate. But, to alleviate the potential double taxation, a U.S. corporation is entitled to a credit against its income tax liability for the income taxes its foreign subsidiary remits to the foreign government. To see how this works, first consider what happens if a U.S. corporation has a wholly owned subsidiary in a country, call it Fredonia, which has the same corporate tax rate as the United States—35 percent. The subsidiary makes one dollar of profit, and owes 35 cents to Fredonia. The dollar is also part of the U.S. parent company's taxable income, so the dollar of profit earned in Fredonia triggers 35 cents of U.S. tax.

But, because the United States allows a foreign tax credit of 35 cents, there is no net U.S. tax owed (and no double taxation).

The story gets more complicated, and more interesting, for a U.S.-based company operating in a country with a low effective tax rate. As an example, we'll consider that the "host" country for the investment is China, which has a corporate tax rate of 25 percent. The basic U.S. rate exceeds the Chinese tax rate, and thus the foreign tax credit, by 10 percentage points. Under our tax rules, this extra, or residual, tax is not due to the United States until the profits are returned, or repatriated, back to the United States as dividends paid to the parent. So the residual tax can be deferred for a long time. Moreover, by careful (and generally legal) tax planning, the U.S. parent corporation may be able to get access to the foreign subsidiary company's profits without ever remitting the 10 percent residual tax.

Why do we try to tax corporations on their worldwide income? Why not follow the practice in most of Europe and simply exempt foreign income from tax?

Many recent proposals for corporation tax reform include moving from our current worldwide system of taxing income to a territorial system. Simply put, under the former system the worldwide income of U.S. individuals and corporations is subject to U.S. taxation no matter where it is earned and a credit is allowed against income taxes paid to foreign countries. Under the proposed territorial system, the United States taxes only the income earned within its borders, and not foreign income. In recent years, developed countries have been moving toward territorial systems, but that in and of itself is not a reason for the United States to follow suit.

At first blush moving the base of taxation from worldwide income to income earned within the United States seems like a narrowing of the tax base rather than a broadening. But we should be seeking the best broad base, not *any* broader base. The principal argument for moving to a territorial system is that it would improve the *business competitiveness* of U.S.-headquartered multinational corporations operating in low-tax foreign countries. For example, if a U.S. and German company are both considering setting up a subsidiary in Ireland, both companies would owe the (low) Irish income tax, but only the U.S. company would owe, upon repatriation, a residual tax to its home country. The German company, in contrast, governed by Germany's territorial tax system would not owe any taxes to the German government irrespective of what it chooses to do with profits from its Irish subsidiary—invest them back in its Irish operations or repatriate them to Germany.

From a global perspective, this combination of policies seems capriciously inefficient: Why should multinational companies based in countries with worldwide systems face a tax-related disadvantage in low-tax countries relative to multinationals based in countries with territorial tax systems? This seems to be no more justifiable than facing companies with different tax rates depending on the first letter of their company name.

Granted that this leads to an inefficient allocation of resources from a global perspective, is it also inadvisable for the United States? That is a trickier question. Some research has suggested that cross-border synergies might redound to make investment of U.S. multinational companies more profitable elsewhere, including in the United States, perhaps leading them to expand their operations here. But it's not obvious that prosperity in the United States is better served when U.S.-based multinational companies invest in the United States relative to investment by foreign-based multinationals. U.S. workers employed by Toyota, Royal Dutch Shell, or Nestlé USA have learned that a job is a job. Indeed, for a U.S. multinational company a territorial tax system improves the relative attractiveness of investing in (low-tax) foreign countries compared with investment in the United States, and so it might discourage domestic investment and hiring.

Another problem with a territorial system is that, as long as the United States has a higher statutory corporate rate than many other countries (including tax havens), moving to a territorial system would greatly increase the incentive for shifting taxable income overseas, as we discuss below. Under a worldwide system like the one that exists today, shifting taxable income from the United States to a low-tax country merely postpones the residual U.S. tax liability until repatriation; in contrast, under a territorial system it would be lost forever.

Figure 3.4 www.CartoonStock.com

Defending our revenue base would require vigilant enforcement and more onerous rules than those now in place.

What is transfer pricing? Why is it important to multinational corporations (and taxpayers)?

Most other countries have lower statutory corporate tax rates than the United States does. Moreover, different countries calculate taxable income differently than we do. The hodgepodge of tax rates and base definitions creates tax planning opportunities for multinational corporations, and headaches for revenue authorities of countries with relatively high tax rates.

When tax rates differ, the multinational corporation has an incentive to shift its taxable income from a country with a high tax rate to a country with a low tax rate. For example, say a U.S. car company has a manufacturing subsidiary in Ireland. The United States has a corporate tax rate of 35 percent, while the tax rate in Ireland is 12½ percent. If the company can somehow reduce its U.S. taxable income by a dollar and increase its Irish taxable income by a dollar, its worldwide tax liability falls by 22½ cents (35 cents minus 12½ cents) per dollar shifted.

Transfer pricing is one way to shift income from a high-tax country to a low-tax country. When the U.S. parent company sells something to its Irish subsidiary, it "charges" an artificially low price; when an Irish subsidiary sells something to its U.S. parent, it charges an artificially high price. This increases taxable income in Ireland and increases deductions—and therefore lowers taxable income—in the United States. Because the transfer prices are between two parts of the same multinational company, they have no effect on its overall pre-tax profits, but do shift taxable income from the high-tax country to the low-tax country, and thus reduce the company's worldwide tax burden and thereby increase its worldwide after-tax profits. The high-tax country often objects and requires that the transfer prices of products be close to the prices that would be charged among parties in "arm's-length" commercial transactions. But this is very difficult to enforce, especially when intangible goods change hands, such as the license to make use of technology developed by the parent company. This is because such intangibles are rarely exchanged between two unrelated parties, so valuing the asset is very difficult.

What is formulary apportionment? Would that be a better option than trying to enforce transfer pricing rules?

U.S. states face a similar problem.[19] They are allowed to tax only income earned in their state, while most big companies operate in many states. Again take Wal-Mart as an example. Imagine how difficult it would be, and ripe for tax-minimizing schemes, if to determine taxable profits each state tried to check on the prices Wal-Mart charged as it shipped goods across state boundaries. But then how do the forty-three states that have a state corporate income tax determine how much income was earned in their state if they don't calculate and keep track of inter-state prices?

Here's how they handle this issue. They all use a formula that estimates the fraction of a company's total U.S. income that is taxable within the state. For about twenty states, that fraction is determined by the ratio of in-state sales to U.S. sales. Other states also factor in the ratio of in-state employment to total U.S. employment and the ratio of in-state assets to total U.S. assets. Eight states rely on an equal weighting of the three ratios. Using a "formulary apportionment" scheme for determining how much of a multi-state corporation's total income is taxable by one state eliminates the need for companies to calculate, and the tax authority to monitor, inter-state prices. But it does not eliminate the payoff to tax avoidance schemes to reduce state income tax liability, and such schemes proliferate.

Some experts have argued that the U.S. government should adopt for worldwide taxation of U.S. corporations a formulary apportionment system like that used by the states. But implementing this system for countries, rather than states within the United States, runs into some very difficult problems. In the case of formula apportionment by U.S. states, there is an unambiguous place from which to start the formula calculation—total U.S. income. Compare that to how a formula apportionment system would work for the United States in determining the U.S. share of income of a multinational company. It would certainly be possible to calculate the ratio of U.S. sales—or employment or assets—to worldwide sales, employment, or assets. But then what? There is no global tax authority that is defining, monitoring, and auditing such a concept. Moreover, countries have very different methods of calculating taxable income, so implementing formula apportionment as a basis for calculating tax liability of U.S. multinational corporations is likely to present thorny issues of its own. And unilaterally adopting formulary apportionment would abrogate tax treaties we have established with many nations. For these reasons, it is unlikely that a worldwide formulary apportionment system will be implemented any time soon.

What are tax havens?

Tax havens are jurisdictions—often small, island, nations—that levy no or only nominal taxes and offer themselves as a vehicle for nonresidents to escape taxation in their country of residence. To facilitate tax evasion, tax havens often refuse to share information about the activities of foreign taxpayers in their countries. A U.S. company might funnel enormous amounts of taxable income into such countries even though it has very little real economic activity there. For example, the profits of U.S.-controlled foreign corporations equal 340 percent of GDP in the Marshall Islands, 355 percent in the British Virgin Islands, 547 percent in the Cayman Islands, and an astonishing 646 percent in Bermuda. This compares to 0.2 percent of GDP in Germany and Italy, 0.4 percent in France and Japan, and 1.3 percent in Britain, even though U.S. corporations conduct much, much more real economic activity in those European countries than in their tropical post office box operations.[20]

There is considerable concern that tax havens are "parasitic" on the tax revenues of the non-haven countries, inducing them to expend real resources in defending their revenue base and in the process reducing the welfare of their residents. One report in 1998 by a respected multilateral organization, the Organisation for Economic Co-operation and Development (OECD), concluded that "governments cannot stand back while their tax bases are eroded through the actions of countries which offer taxpayers ways to exploit tax havens [and preferential regimes] to reduce the tax that would otherwise be payable to them."

In sharp contrast to this long-standing concern about their deleterious effects, some economists have recently argued that tax havens are a device to save high-tax countries from their own bad policies. In a global economy, goes their argument, countries should avoid taxing highly mobile capital (business

"RON CHOATE, OFFSHORE TAX HAVEN CONSULTANT, SPEAKING..."

Figure 3.5 www.CartoonStock.com

or investments that could easily move to another country) because it just drives capital away and is ineffective at raising revenue from capital owners who have many alternative investment opportunities. Looking the other way as corporations make use of tax havens allows countries to move toward the non-distorting tax regime they should, but for some reason cannot, explicitly enact. On the other hand, though, tax havens induce wasteful expenditure of resources, both by firms in their participation in havens and by governments in their attempts to enforce their tax codes. And they certainly siphon off tax revenues from the non-haven countries. In addition, tax havens worsen tax competition problems by causing countries to further reduce their tax rates below levels that are efficient from a global viewpoint. The same economic logic that underlies the call for lower statutory rates to address taxable income shifting suggests that there should be substantial attention paid—unilaterally and multilaterally—to defending a country's revenue base.

How does the U.S. corporate tax rate compare to the rate of other countries?

The United States has the highest statutory corporate tax rate among developed countries. We won this dubious title on April Fools' Day, 2012, when Japan cut its rate by 5 percentage points to nudge its rates (38 percent) below our average federal and state rate of 39.2 percent.

The U.S. rate is substantially lower than it was thirty years ago, but corporate tax rates have been falling throughout the world at a faster rate than in the United States. Perhaps surprisingly, in most other countries the amount of corporate tax revenue relative to total tax has *increased* over this period, the main exceptions being Germany, Japan, and the United Kingdom (figure 3.6).[21]

Both domestic determinants of corporate taxation and increases in international pressures for tax competition seem

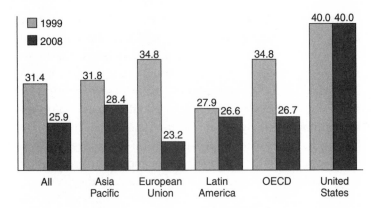

Figure 3.6 Statutory tax rates have been falling worldwide, except in the United States. Average statutory central, state, and local government taxes on corporations, 1999–2008. *Source*: http://economix.blogs.nytimes.com/2011/04/08/the-logic-of-cutting-corporate-taxes/

to be behind this trend. There is clear evidence that the corporate tax rate is insulated from a country's revenue needs: across countries, there is no association of the expenditure–GDP ratio with the corporate statutory rate and only weak evidence of a positive association with the average rate. There is suggestive, but not definitive, evidence that the domestic role of the corporate tax as a backstop to the individual income tax is important: across countries, there is indeed a strong association between the top individual rate and the top statutory corporate rate. Finally, there is intriguing evidence about the role of international competitive pressures on corporate taxation. Measures of openness are negatively associated with statutory corporate rates, although not with revenues collected as a fraction of GDP. Strikingly, larger, more trade-intensive countries do collect more corporate tax revenues, but this may be because these countries are more attractive venues for investment.

As we have already discussed, the statutory rate is only one component of the tax disincentive to business investment and may be outweighed by the definition of the business tax base, in particular, but not limited to the tax depreciation schedules. Calculating the net tax disincentive, called by economists the marginal effective tax rate on investment, is much more difficult than calculating the statutory rate and is especially difficult to do in a way that is comparable across countries. One careful, but certainly not definitive, study concluded that in 2008 the marginal effective tax rate on capital due to the corporate tax for the United States was just 16.2 percent, which ties for forty-sixth out of the eighty countries in the survey and eighteenth out of the thirty-one countries then in the OECD.[22]

Does our relatively high corporate tax rate hurt our companies' competitiveness and the country's competitiveness?

We've slipped in one of the most prominent policy buzzwords—competitiveness. The terms "compete" and "competition" have a special resonance and specific meaning to economists. But competitiveness does not have a clear meaning, and the term has been the source of much miscommunication. Because competition is an essential element of most athletic endeavors, sports analogies often crop up. But what is the right analogy? A running race, where each nation is an entry? A race where the prizes depend on the order of finish or one where the prizes depend only on how fast one runs? If the runner is a country, and the runner's time is income per capita, then surely the latter analogy is more apt. The benefits of prosperity are not diminished by another nation's greater prosperity. This is nothing more than what Adam Smith said over 200 years ago—global commerce allows every country to enhance its prosperity by concentrating on doing what it does best and taking full advantage of what other countries do best.

In the past, competitiveness has been associated with the relative size of a nation's export sector, or its trade surplus. This is dangerous because maximizing either of these quantities is not a defensible policy goal. A declining trade balance may be a symptom of a problem, but it is not a reliable indicator of economic health. One can easily conceive of a declining economy

Figure 3.7 By permission of Chuck Asay and Creators Syndicate, Inc

with a thriving export sector—if, for example, the export sector is propelled by a favorable exchange rate caused by the drying up of attractive domestic opportunities. Conversely, the discovery of natural resources, while a boon to prosperity, often causes a decline in the manufacturing trade balance.

In some debates competitiveness of a country is associated with the success of its resident multinational companies, sometimes measured by profitability share, sometimes by market share. But high multinational corporation profits could be achieved simply by a transfer from taxpayers to domestic corporations, a policy which most would agree is not appropriate and would not improve the fundamental soundness of the economy. With government subsidies, domestic firms could gain market share even in cases where the revenue gained is less than the additional cost of production, which again is not in the national interest.

Properly interpreted, competitiveness is not a substitute goal for prosperity. Its value as a policy buzzword is to remind us that the conditions under which we strive for prosperity have changed as the integration of national economies into the world economy has progressed. Just as the training regimen for a race at high altitude is different, it may be that how to achieve prosperity is different in a globally integrated economy. In a global economy the objective of policy is to maintain (and preferably grow) the real incomes of our citizens in the face of global international markets and the policies of other countries, which vary in trade policy from a free-trade orientation to aggressive promotion of exports and in tax policy from domestically oriented and open to international cooperation to aggressive courting of foreign investment to the beggar-thy-neighbor behavior of tax havens.[23]

The bottom line is that there is no compelling evidence that high corporate tax rates inhibit economic growth or suppress a nation's prosperity. This is not to say that our corporate tax system—rate, base, double taxation features, and so on—do not need reform. They do.

How do recent corporate tax reform proposals work?

In the past year the Democrats and Republicans unveiled competing corporate tax reform proposals. In February 2012, President Obama offered a plan that would reduce the top corporate tax rate from 35 percent to 28 percent and would eliminate dozens of special provisions, while giving new preferences to manufacturers that would set their maximum effective rate at 25 percent. Notably, it would maintain the worldwide system of taxation and indeed strengthen it by establishing a 15 percent minimum tax on multinational corporations' foreign earnings to discourage "accounting games to shift profits abroad" and relocation of production overseas. Obama's proposal is meant to be revenue-neutral, so that all revenue raised by eliminating special tax provisions would be used to lower rates or offset the cost of new or existing tax breaks favoring manufacturing, clean energy, and research and development activities. Note, though, that the largest source of revenue offsets comes from popular tax breaks—such as accelerated depreciation of businesses' capital investments and write-offs of research and experimentation costs—that provide incentives for investment, so that the net positive effect on the incentive to invest is unlikely to be large overall and would be negative for sectors that currently benefit disproportionately from special tax provisions. Note also that the base broadeners apply to all businesses' taxable income, not just corporations' taxable income, so that noncorporate businesses, a large and fast-growing fraction of all business income, would unambiguously face higher taxes and a decreased incentive to invest, as their tax base is broadened but they receive no tax rate cut.

In October 2011, Dave Camp (R-MI), the chairman of the House Ways and Means Committee, proposed a 25 percent corporate rate. Like President Obama's plan, it would broaden the corporate tax base rate to limit the revenue loss but did not specify exactly which base-broadening policies would accompany the lower tax rate. The key difference between the Camp plan and the Obama plan is that the former would effectively abandon the current worldwide tax system for something very close to a territorial system. While under a pure territorial system foreign-source income would be exempt from U.S. taxation, the Camp plan would exempt 95 percent of dividends paid by a foreign subsidiary to its U.S. parent company from tax, thus levying a 1.25 percent effective tax rate on repatriated earnings (5 percent of the 25 percent rate). Three anti-abuse rules were suggested as a way to limit the much larger incentive for U.S. multinational companies to shift taxable income to low-tax foreign countries.

Thus, both plans generally embrace a lower-the-rate, broaden-the-base philosophy but the Camp plan shies away from specifying the base broadeners (par for the tax reform course, as they actually raise somebody's tax burden) and the Obama plan retains a difficult-to-defend preferentially lower tax rate on manufacturers and subsidies for alternative energy. They differ sharply, however, in their treatment of foreign income. Obama is more concerned with clamping down on the shifting of taxable income and real activity outside our borders, while Camp focuses on ensuring that U.S. multinationals can compete with foreign corporations in low-tax foreign countries.

4

TAXING SPENDING

What is a consumption tax?

A consumption tax is a tax on spending. In the United States, the most common form of consumption tax is the retail sales tax administered by most states and some local governments. There are also specific consumption taxes called excise taxes that apply to items such as gasoline, alcohol, and cigarettes. In the rest of the world, the value-added tax (VAT) is a common form of consumption tax. A VAT is just a sales tax that is collected from businesses at all stages of production and distribution, not just the retail stage.

Why tax consumption rather than income?

People argue for a consumption tax on the grounds of fairness and efficiency; although, as we shall see, perceptions of fairness vary dramatically. Philosopher Thomas Hobbes made the fairness argument thus: "It is fairer to tax people on what they extract from the economy, as roughly measured by their consumption, than to tax them on what they produce for the economy, as roughly measured by their income."[1] Many economists think a consumption tax is more efficient than an income tax because an income tax discourages saving while a consumption tax does not. (See box 4.1.)

BOX 4.1 **Why an Income Tax "Double Taxes" Saving and a Sales Tax Does Not**

Imagine a world without an income tax. (Yes, it is fun, but this is just make-believe.) If you earned a dollar, you could choose to spend it now or save it for a year, in which case you'd have a dollar plus interest to spend. Suppose that you can earn 4 percent interest. Your choice is between spending $1.00 now and spending $1.04 in a year. At the prevailing interest rate, you will decide to save (or borrow) until a dollar more of current consumption is worth the same amount to you as $1.04 of consumption a year from now. The interest rate is "a return to waiting."

Now suppose you have an income tax at a flat rate of 50 percent. (This makes the math easy.) If you earn a dollar, you get to keep $0.50 after tax. You could spend it now or let it earn interest for a year. However, you wouldn't get to spend $0.50 plus interest in a year because you also pay tax on the interest. So, even though you'll get two cents in interest (at a 4 percent rate), you only keep one cent after tax. Your after-tax return to waiting is cut in half, to 2 percent, by the income tax. The income tax cuts your current consumption possibilities by half, but it cuts your future consumption possibilities by even more. Instead of having $1.04 to spend next year, you have $0.51. The original—say labor—income is taxed; subsequently any return on the part of that income that is saved is taxed as well. This is the sense in which the income tax is said to "double tax" saving. More accurately, deferred, or future, consumption is taxed more heavily than current consumption.

And the longer you defer consumption, the bigger the effective tax rate on future consumption. For example, if you wanted to save long enough for your money to double—about eighteen years at a 4 percent annual interest rate—your dollar would grow to $2.00 without tax. Every dollar saved provides one extra dollar—two dollars in total—to spend eighteen years in the future. With the income tax, you would earn 2 percent after tax, so your $0.50 would grow only to $0.72. Future consumption would be reduced by 74 percent (from $2.00 before tax to $0.72 after the income tax).

Now suppose we had a sales tax at a rate of 100 percent. (Note that a 100 percent sales tax rate is equivalent to a 50 percent income tax rate in terms of its effect on current consumption possibilities.) You could take the $1 you earned and buy something for $0.50, plus tax. (There'd be $0.50 in tax just as in the income tax example above.) Or you could put the dollar in the bank (there's no tax until you spend money) and hold it for about eighteen years until it doubles. At that point, you could afford to buy something for $1.00. That plus the $1.00 in sales tax would add up to the $2.00 you'd have in the bank. The tax reduces deferred consumption by exactly the same percentage as current consumption—50 percent. Thus, the sales tax does not distort the choice between current and future consumption.

A consumption tax sounds great. What's the catch?

The main drawback of a consumption tax is that most versions of it seem very regressive. This is because in a given year most lower-income people spend all their income and more—people on the bottom rungs get help from friends, relatives, and government transfer programs like food stamps. Higher-income people spend only a small fraction of their income (see figure 4.1). Thus, a flat-rate tax on consumption amounts to a much larger share of income for poor people than for those with high incomes. For that reason, some argue that consumption taxes are fundamentally unfair.

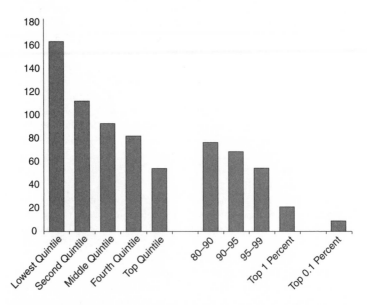

Figure 4.1 Consumption as a percentage of income, by income group, 2010. *Source*: Tax Policy Center, Table T09–0403

In fact, consumption taxes are rarely flat taxes on all pur-chases. They often exempt necessities like food and medi-cine. And some have other features designed to offset the tax's regressivity, which we'll discuss later.

More important, a snapshot of one year's spending and income overstates the regressivity of a flat-rate consump-tion tax. Many people with low income in a year have low income only temporarily, either because they are young or retired, or they're just having a bad year financially. These people generally choose a spending level more in line with their long-term income rather than their current income. If we redrew figure 4.1 to represent a lifetime of income and consumption, the height of the bars would not fall as fast. Another way to put it is, over a lifetime, most people spend about what they earn.

What is a retail sales tax?

It is a tax on final sales collected from retail businesses. All but five states levy retail sales taxes. The rates ranged from 2.9 percent in Colorado to 8.25 percent in California in 2011.[2] Many local governments and other jurisdictions also col-lect sales taxes.[3] The combined state and local tax rate can be as high as 12 percent (Alabama). Tuba City, Arizona, in the Navajo Indian Reservation, assesses the highest sales tax rate in the United States—13.725 percent.[4] Retail sales taxes are relatively simple, at least from the perspective of the average citizen. Retailers simply remit a fixed percent-age of their taxable sales volume to the tax authority. At the cash register, the tax due is separately reported from the pre-tax price. A complication is that some consumer goods and services are exempt from the sales tax (e.g., prescrip-tion drugs are exempt in almost all states) and some taxed at lower rates. However, modern cash registers make calcu-lating and reporting the tax a straightforward operation for most retailers.

Retail sales taxes do have some drawbacks, however. In some situations they're relatively easy to evade. Some unscrupulous sellers do not remit the tax due on cash transactions. (Do you wonder why your house painter offers a lower price for payment in cash than by check? It's probably *not* because he or she thinks cashing the check will be particularly burdensome.) Some buyers will cross state lines to avoid a high state sales tax—that is why people in Washington State (sales tax rate as high as 9.5 percent) like to shop in Oregon and Philadelphians (sales tax of 8 percent) will drive 30 miles south to Delaware. Oregon and Delaware are sales tax havens—they levy no sales tax at all. And Internet vendors often do not remit tax on out-of-state sales.

A final drawback of a retail sales tax is that the tax can "cascade" because business purchases of materials and services from retailers might trigger sales tax and then their sales trigger the tax again. Although every sales tax has measures to exempt "business-to-business" transactions—and in principle tax only sales to consumers—they have to be fairly restrictive to limit evasion. In consequence, some intermediate inputs end up being taxed twice or more.

What is a use tax?

When you live in a state with a sales tax, what you buy is generally taxable. But that's also true for purchases made over the Internet or in states without a sales tax. In that case, the tax is called a use tax and must be remitted by the consumer, or at least it's supposed to be, as long as the good is consumed in the consumer's state of residence. Many states include lines on the state income tax return where taxpayers can report out-of-state sales and add the use tax to their income tax bill. There's typically a credit against this levy for taxes already paid in other states. Compliance with voluntary use taxes is very low. California has estimated that $1.1 billion in use tax owed annually is never paid—a 1 percent compliance rate.[5] Nationwide, uncollected sales tax is estimated at $23 billion in 2012.[6] Owners of "brick-and-mortar" retail stores complain that this gives online retailers an unfair (and, from a social perspective, inefficient) advantage. And they have a good point. Online retailers reply that calculating the tax due for each purchaser, which can vary by state, locality, and type of good, is unreasonably onerous; however, software could be made available that would facilitate compliance.

What is a luxury tax?

While general sales taxes are regressive, some specific sales taxes are intended to be highly progressive. For example, Omnibus Budget Reconciliation Act of 1990 included a 10 percent excise tax on yachts, furs, and jewelry and, at first, high-end cars, as part of a legislative compromise that limited the increase in the top income tax rate. The theory was that the excise tax would hit the well-heeled who could afford it. In fact, industry made the case that the tax caused demand for expensive boats to plummet, ultimately costing thousands of jobs. That is, at least part of the burden of the tax fell on owners of yacht retailers and their workers rather than just on the rich consumers. (See page 22, "Who really bears the burden of tax?") As far as we know, there was never any careful economic analysis of the actual effects of the tax, but Congress was nonetheless persuaded to repeal it in 1993.

Luxury taxes, familiar to Monopoly enthusiasts, have a long history. The telephone excise tax was originally a luxury tax used to help finance the Spanish-American War in 1898.[7] Back then, only the very well off had telephones in their homes. The tax was introduced as a temporary measure, but it was continually extended and modified. In the 1960s, it was increased—on a temporary basis—to finance the Vietnam War. Some war protesters refused to pay the tax. It now applies to cell phones, as well as land lines, and there are still protesters.

What is an excise tax?

An excise tax is just a consumption tax on a particular item. An excise tax has a narrow base, while sales taxes tend to be broad-based. There are currently federal excise taxes on beer and wine, alcohol, gasoline and diesel, tires, airline tickets, telephone service, and cigarettes. Some excise taxes are dedicated to paying for particular activities. For example, the airline ticket tax revenue is designated for spending on airports, air traffic control, and other aviation-related infrastructure. Taxes on gasoline and diesel are earmarked for highway and transit projects.

What is a sin tax?

Sin taxes are excise taxes intended to discourage behavior deemed undesirable, at least in excess. Taxes on cigarettes, alcohol, beer, wine, and gambling are usually put in that category. Ronald Reagan liked to say "if

---

SIDEBAR 4.2 **The First Excise Tax and the Whiskey Rebellion**

The first excise tax in the United States didn't work out well.

In 1791, to pay off debt accumulated during the Revolutionary War, the new American government imposed an excise tax on distilled spirits (i.e., whiskey). The tax varied from 6 to 18 cents per gallon, with smaller producers bearing more of the tax burden than large distillers. The small producers were mostly farmers west of the Appalachian and Allegheny Mountains who relied on whiskey sales as their primary source of income. They protested this tax by tarring tax collectors, burning houses, and other acts of violence. President Washington sent troops to quell the tax-motivated rebellion.

The excise tax on spirits was repealed in 1802.

Source: http://www.ttb.gov/public_info/whisky_rebellion.shtml

you tax something, you'll get less of it." For a lot of taxes, that's an undesirable side effect. For example, we don't want people working less to reduce income taxes. However, sin taxes are explicitly intended to discourage the taxed activity.

What is a Pigouvian tax?

Sometimes markets don't work well. For example, people and businesses pollute too much if they see clean air and water as a free resource. The pollution that is a byproduct of economic activities is an example of an externality, in this case a negative externality. The polluter's activity adversely affects others who breathe the air or drink the water. Pigouvian taxes, named after the British economist A. C. Pigou, are designed to reduce externalities like pollution. The logic is similar to that behind sin taxes. The tax is intended to discourage the taxed activity, but not eliminate it. Ideally, the tax rate should be set equal to the social damage caused by the externality; in this way, the tax induces

SIDEBAR 4.3 **Cigarettes Kill People. Is that a Positive Externality?**

In 1999 the Czech Republic was considering raising excise taxes on tobacco. In an effort to dissuade the government from raising this tax, Philip Morris financed a study that estimated that, while smoking costs the Czech Republic $403 million per year due to death and disability, the excise tax collected from cigarettes is $522 million—far greater than the direct costs of smoking. Moreover, the government saved $31 million on public pensions and medical care because smokers die younger and thus collect fewer benefits. Thus, smoking creates a kind of positive pecuniary externality that would diminish if excessive excise taxes caused the smoking rate to plummet.

Perhaps, not surprisingly, the public found the argument that killing people saves money kind of immoral. The story did get the Czech Republic and Philip Morris a lot of international attention.

Note: NPR's Planet Money podcast has an entertaining discussion of the Philip Morris debacle, available at: http://www.npr.org/blogs/money/2010/07/16/128569258/the-friday-podcast-death-saves-you-money people and businesses to consider the extra social cost when they decide to undertake the taxed activity. The gasoline excise tax is a Pigouvian tax designed in part to encourage people to drive less, which leads to less highway congestion, road wear and tear, air pollution, and emissions of greenhouse gases. Some have rationalized the cigarette excise tax as a Pigouvian tax, although that is controversial. Pigouvian subsidies can be justified to encourage activities with positive externalities or spillover effects. Basic research and development activities are the most prominent example of this, and externality arguments are cited to justify the U.S. research and experimentation tax credit.

What is a VAT?

A VAT—or value-added tax—is a consumption tax that is collected in stages from producers and distributors all

"That must stand for Very Annoying Tax!"

Figure 4.2 www.CartoonStock.com

along the supply chain in proportion to their contribution to the final value of a product—their value-added. It sounds complicated, but there are good practical reasons for assessing a consumption tax in this way, and almost every country collects a VAT. The United States is a very rare exception.

There are two main ways to implement a VAT: the "subtraction method" and "credit-invoice" method. In the subtraction method, each producer calculates value-added by starting with their receipts and then subtracting the cost of inputs purchased from other firms. The quintessential example is the production process for a loaf of bread. To vastly simplify, suppose the farmer grows wheat using only his own labor and sells it to the miller for 10 cents. He'd owe a penny in VAT at a 10 percent rate on his sale to the miller. The miller grinds up the flour and sells it to the baker for 40 cents. His value-added is 30 cents (40 cents minus the 10 cents cost of buying the wheat from the farmer), on which he'd owe 3 cents in tax. The baker makes the bread and sells it to the grocery store for 80 cents, owing 4 cents in tax on her value-added. And the retailer sells it to the consumer for a dollar, owing 2 cents in tax on the final value-added. All told, 10 cents in tax is collected—the same amount as under a 10 percent retail sales tax—but it's collected in stages all along the line rather than all from the final retailer. One advantage of this arrangement is that even if one party along the supply chain doesn't remit the tax, the government still gets tax from the other producers.

The credit-invoice VAT is the more common type. Sellers all up and down the supply chain are subject to a tax on gross receipts, but they get a credit for the tax paid by suppliers so long as they receive a tax invoice verifying the tax was indeed remitted. So, in the example above, the baker would owe 8 cents in tax on the loaf of bread, but could credit against it the 4 cents in tax paid by the miller so long as she receives an invoice indicating that he'd remitted the tax. Her net tax bill would be 4 cents, just as under the subtraction method.

The credit-invoice VAT sounds really complicated. Why do it that way?

Countries use a credit-invoice VAT because it's easier to enforce. Taxpayers have a strong interest in doing business only with tax-compliant suppliers. To see why, think about the baker in the example above. If the miller doesn't provide an invoice, she owes the whole 8 cents in tax herself. So she's going to insist that the miller give her an invoice (or demand a price discount to reflect the extra tax that she'll owe). Thus, the miller has a strong incentive to be tax-compliant in order to attract business from other tax-compliant firms.

And the invoice method isn't as complicated as it sounds. A lot of the invoice tracking and reporting can be and is done by computers.

Are small businesses subject to the VAT?

Not usually. Most VATs exempt small businesses (such as street vendors). An advantage of the VAT over the retail sales tax is that exempting small retailers doesn't cost much revenue. Tax is still collected along the other parts of the supply chain. In some countries, small producers may opt out of the VAT, but if they sell a lot of goods to other tax-compliant businesses, they often voluntarily choose to register and remit the VAT because purchasers want an invoice.

Why doesn't the United States have a VAT?

Despite its prevalence in the rest of the world—every developed country has one—the United States has never come close to enacting a VAT. Al Ullman, Chairman of the powerful House Ways and Means Committee, proposed a VAT in 1979 and was promptly voted out of office in the next election.

While other factors clearly played a role (he disliked meeting with constituents and was widely seen as arrogant and aloof), Ullman's advocacy of the VAT while sitting in a position where he might have made it happen was perceived as an important element in his undoing.

SIDEBAR 4.4

"Liberals think it's regressive and conservatives think it's a money machine.

If they reverse their positions, the VAT may happen."

—Larry Summers, former Secretary of the Treasury (1988)

Source: http://www.nytimes.com/1988/12/19/business/tax-watch-the-likely-forms-of-new-taxes.html

One reason that we don't have a VAT is that—news flash—Americans really dislike taxes (e.g., "Tea Party"). The idea of adding a new one that could raise hundreds of billions of dollars per year doesn't sit well with a lot of people. Some also worry that a VAT would be *too* efficient, in the sense that it could easily raise hundreds of billions of dollars per year in additional revenues, which would fuel expansion in government. They point to evidence from Europe that increases in VAT revenues are followed by increases in government spending as a share of the economy. (This doesn't prove that the VAT revenues *caused* the increase, but VAT critics are convinced that the VAT would fuel an explosion in government spending. Grover Norquist, head of Americans for Tax Reform, has said that "VAT is French for big government.") A distinct set of critics object to a VAT because it is regressive—just as with a retail sales tax, its burden would comprise a larger share of income for poor families than rich ones. And some worry that a VAT would interfere with states' ability to administer their own sales taxes—the largest source of revenue for state and local governments.

How much money would a VAT raise?

It depends on how broad the base is. A very broad-based VAT, like the one in New Zealand, could annually collect over $50

billion per percentage point. So a 10 percent VAT could collect as much as $500 billion per year. If there are exemptions
for food, medicine, housing, and other necessities, as is common almost everywhere else in the world, the tax would raise
much less. A typical European-type VAT would raise about
$32 billion per percentage point.[8]

There would, though, be considerable costs to administer-
ing and enforcing a VAT that don't depend on the tax rate
chosen, which is why a VAT would probably not be worth
doing unless the rate were at least 5 percent or so (because the
administrative and compliance costs would be a large fraction
of revenues raised if the tax is small).[9]

A very broad-based VAT would almost surely require some
type of offsetting subsidies to mitigate its effect on lower-
income families. One option would be to offer a flat refundable
income tax credit designed to offset the amount of VAT paid by
the average family at the poverty level. A very broad-based VAT
with such a tax credit would raise about as much revenue (net
of the subsidy) as the typical narrow-base European model.

What is the typical VAT rate in other countries?

They range from 5 percent for Canada and Japan to 25 percent
or more in the Nordic countries (figure 4.3). The average rate
is 18 percent.

How would a federal VAT interact with state and local sales taxes?

States worry that a VAT could undermine their primary source
of revenue—the sales tax—for several reasons. First, a VAT at
rates common in the rest of the world would make the combined federal, state, and local retail sales tax rate quite high.
(State and local retail sales taxes averaged 9.6 percent in 2010.)
At such high rates, tax evasion could be a serious problem.
Second, the base and computation method for the VAT could
vary significantly from those used to calculate sales taxes.

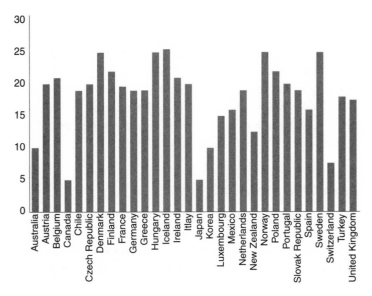

Figure 4.3 VAT rate for OECD countries, 2010. *Source*: http://www.oecd.org/dataoecd/ 12/13/34674429.xls

This could seriously complicate compliance for businesses and undermine support for state and local sales taxes.

There are, however, some potentially offsetting factors. If there were a federal VAT, the state and federal government could share information for purposes of monitoring and enforcing compliance—as they do currently for the income tax. States could also choose to enact their own VATs using the same tax base as the federal tax. This would simplify compliance for businesses. Potentially more important, conforming to the federal VAT might make it possible for states to require out-of-state vendors to remit the VAT for them. Currently, out-of-state sellers who don't have a meaningful physical presence in a state are not required to remit sales tax because the Supreme Court has ruled that the wide disparity in tax rules would put an undue burden on out-of-state vendors who might have to make sense of the rules of thousands of taxing jurisdictions. However, the Court said the federal government could authorize such a tax if the states conformed their tax bases—an effort that is underway right now. Following the federal VAT rules would certainly qualify. Tax avoidance on Internet and mail order sales is currently the biggest threat to the sales tax base: the projected sales tax loss for 2012 on e-commerce sales is $11.2 billion.[10] The revenue gained from improving compliance on this dimension might well offset the losses from increased evasion.

Does a VAT promote exports?

No. Some people think that a VAT is an export subsidy because it applies to imports, but not exports. (VAT already remitted—as verified by invoice—is rebated at the border.) But this treatment is exactly the same as would apply under a national retail sales tax, where the tax would apply to goods sold here, regardless of where they were produced, and would not apply to exports. Exports would have U.S. VAT rebated, but foreign consumption taxes would be applied when the goods are sold there. The "border tax adjustment" simply maintains a level playing field between exports and imports.[11] That is why this tax treatment is allowed under international trade agreements that proscribe export subsidies, whether explicit or implicit in tax rules.

SIDEBAR 4.5 **Streamlined Sales Tax**

The National Governors Association and the National Conference of State Legislators created the Streamlined Sales and Use Tax project in 1999 to simplify sales tax collection and ease administrative burdens for retailers. The Streamlined Sales Tax standardizes tax definitions, exemption administration, and source rules. Twenty-four of the forty-five states with a retail sales tax abide by the Streamlined Sales and Use Tax agreement. Legislatures in nine other states have introduced legislation to conform their sales taxes.

The goal is to simplify the tax enough that the federal government can enact legislation allowing states to require out-of-state vendors to remit sales tax to consumers' states of residence.

Source: http://www.streamlinedsalestax.org/index.php?page=faqs

What is the flat tax?

Many proponents of tax proposals featuring a single rate of tax have named their plans a flat tax. To economists, *the* flat tax is a design first outlined by Alvin Rabushka and Robert Hall of Stanford University in 1980.[12] Their flat tax is a VAT split into two parts, a tax on labor income and a tax on businesses. Recall that a subtraction-method VAT allows businesses a deduction for all purchased inputs except labor. Under a flat tax, companies would deduct wages, too. (This kind of tax is sometimes called a modified cash flow tax.) Workers are subject to a tax on wages (at the same rate as the business tax), typically after deducting an exemption. The wage tax isn't really flat because there are two brackets—zero and the single tax rate—but wages above the exemption are taxed at a flat rate.

The advantage of the flat tax is that it is a consumption-based tax—a modified VAT, really—but is more progressive because of the exemption in the labor income tax base. To

Figure 4.4 www.CartoonStock.com

achieve that, the flat tax exempts all capital income from its individual tax, and allows businesses to write off their purchases of capital goods in the year purchased.

Wouldn't a flat tax be super simple and fair?

A really comprehensive flat tax would be considerably simpler than our current system because there would be no deductions or credits, and only the one exemption. But the current income tax would also be a lot simpler under those circumstances. It's true that calculating tax when there's only one rate is simpler than calculating tax when there are multiple rates, but most people look up their tax in a table or use software or a paid preparer, so the value of this simplification is negligible. Because capital income (interest, dividends, etc.) would be exempt from tax, that would simplify reporting and recordkeeping for most taxpayers. On the business side, depreciation accounts could be dispensed with because capital purchases are expensed, and financial flows no longer have tax consequences; interest

Figure 4.5 Cagle Cartoons, Inc.

payments are not deductible, nor are interest receipts taxable. Overall, a flat tax would be substantially simpler than a similarly comprehensive income tax.

Another practical advantage is that, with a flat tax, taxpayers would be more likely to know their marginal tax rate than under a more progressive schedule (such as current law). Armed with better information, in principle, they would be able to make better economic decisions.

Fairness is another matter. It would be hard to make a flat tax as progressive as our current income tax. (See page 163, "What makes a tax system fair?") For one thing, you would need not just an exemption but also refundable tax credits, because low-income people on average get refunds under our income tax. Second, a flat tax would surely reduce tax liability at the top of the income distribution. To raise the same amount of revenue as our current income tax, middle income households would inevitably owe a lot more.

There are flat taxes all over Eastern Europe. Are they the same as the flat tax advocated for the United States?

No. The flat taxes common in Eastern Europe are flat-rate income taxes, not consumption taxes. That is, the base includes capital income, not just wages and other compensation. That makes the European flat taxes more progressive than the consumption-style flat tax just discussed.

What is the X Tax?

David Bradford was a brilliant economist who taught at Princeton University and an outspoken consumption tax advocate. He was intrigued by the flat tax but was very concerned about its regressivity and proposed a more progressive alternative that he labeled the "X Tax," reportedly to distract attention from whether it is a consumption tax or an income tax.[13] It is basically a flat tax with multiple tax rates applying to the labor income base where the top labor income tax rate equals the flat business tax rate. It can also have refundable tax credits. At least in principle, the X Tax could be made as progressive as the current income tax while still offering many of the economic advantages of a consumption tax.

The Treasury Department developed a variant of the X Tax for President George W. Bush's tax reform panel. They concluded that, with a very broad base, an X Tax with a top rate of 35 percent and refundable tax credits to protect workers with low incomes would collect about as much revenue as current law (circa 2005) and have a similar distribution of tax burdens. The Treasury model also predicted that the "progressive consumption tax" (their name for the X Tax) would increase economic output (GDP) by 6 percent over the long run; although, as we discuss later, such predictions are by no means airtight.[14]

What is a consumed income tax?

Under a consumed income tax, individuals would file a personal tax return, but the taxable base is income minus saving (which equals consumption).[15] Taxpayers are allowed unlimited deductions for their net contributions to savings and retirement accounts, essentially an unlimited (traditional) IRA. Loan proceeds must be added to the tax base. Like the X Tax, this approach allows for much more progressivity than a VAT or flat tax, because a graduated rate schedule can be applied to this tax base. Former senators Sam Nunn (D-GA) and Pete Domenici (R-NM) proposed a version called the Universal Savings Account (or USA) Tax in 1995, but it never garnered much support because it was perceived as too complex.

Are tax breaks for saving and retirement indirect steps toward a consumption tax?

Sort of. For most Americans, who have limited savings, the income tax is very much like the consumed income tax discussed above. They can save as much as they want tax-free so

"I used to get toys as birthday gifts but now that I'm in pre-school, all I get is money for my college fund."

Figure 4.6 www.CartoonStock.com

long as they put the money in one of a variety of tax-free savings accounts. There's a catch, though—the savings accounts are all earmarked for particular activities. There are several types of tax-free retirement accounts, the most common of which are Individual Retirement Accounts (IRAs) and 401(k) plans. There are also tax-free accounts to pay for education and health expenses. Typically, contributions are deductible and withdrawals are taxable, although some more recent accounts like Roth IRAs and "529" (college savings) plans do not allow a deduction up front but don't tax withdrawals. In both kinds of accounts, earnings accrue tax-free. However, there are penalties if the money is withdrawn for non-designated purposes. This is a key difference with the tax treatment under a consumed income tax, which would allow tax-free savings for any purpose.

Because a significant fraction of saving is tax-free under our "income tax," many analysts believe that our tax system is more properly viewed as a hybrid between an income tax and a consumption tax.

Do these tax breaks actually encourage saving?

This question is the subject of much debate in the economics literature. Most, but not all, empirical research suggests that saving is not very sensitive to its rate of return. This might sound surprising because you'd expect people to be more likely to save when the after-tax rate of return is higher than when it is lower. There's a bigger reward to waiting to consume one's wealth in the former case. However, there's another offsetting factor at work. When the rate of return increases, you have to sacrifice less current consumption to achieve any particular level of future consumption. Most people don't save because they like saving per se but because they want a higher level of future consumption. This motive can actually cause people to save *less* when the rate of return increases. Effectively, the higher rate of return makes it possible to consume more both now and later.

Empirical evidence suggests that these two effects roughly balance out. When the rate of return increases, some people save more and some save less. Overall, there doesn't seem to be much effect; more precisely, research has not yet compellingly demonstrated such an effect.

Based on that evidence, you might expect tax incentives for saving to be pretty ineffective, as all they do is raise the after-tax rate of return. Actually, it's even worse than that for high-income people who account for most of the saving. They often save much more than the amount they can put in limited tax-free accounts. When they're deciding whether to save more or less, that is all done in taxable forms, unaffected by the tax subsidy. All the subsidies do for them is lower their tax liability without affecting the return to additional saving. Because the tax break increases their after-tax income, they're likely to consume more now, which means that aggregate saving goes down.

However, tax-free retirement accounts or education accounts might encourage people to save through other mechanisms. For one thing, by tying up people's money for many years, these accounts can help them to follow through on their savings plans. Also, to the extent that the accounts run through employers, they make it easier to set aside saving in small palatable pieces. Payroll withholding turns out to be a more effective way to get some people to save than relying on them to set aside money on their own.

So these accounts can be somewhat effective in increasing saving for some people. However, there has been a massive expansion in retirement savings incentives while the personal saving rate has plummeted. Before the recession, it stood near zero, although it has crept up since then. So these incentives don't appear to have been hugely effective (or they've been more than offset by other saving disincentives).

If the economy runs on consumption, why would we want to encourage saving?

A New Year's Eve, 1965, *Time* magazine article quoted iconic free-market economist Milton Friedman as saying, "We are all Keynesians now."[16] Friedman later explained that the quote was taken out of context. He meant that even though the language of John Maynard Keynes—famous for recommending fiscal policy as a tool to manage the economy—had pervaded popular consciousness, most people had no idea what this meant.

We have thought of Keynesian misunderstandings many times in discussing tax policy with reporters and others. For example, critics sometimes complain that a flat tax or consumption tax would hurt the economy because "The economy runs on consumption..." President George W. Bush urged the nation to visit Disney World as our first response to terrorism. Clearly, the public, our political leaders, and at least some members of the press have decided that spending is a civic virtue.

That is a dangerously misguided view of macroeconomics. Sure, a sudden drop in spending could bring on a recession, and more spending (and investment) is the tried and true Keynesian prescription for a downturn. But when the economy is performing well, inadequate consumption is not a problem we have to worry about. Instead, too little saving is the real threat.

Experts debate how to measure personal saving, but by any reckoning it has been trending south for a long time. By some measures, the saving rate approached zero in the last decade. It increased somewhat during, and since, the Great Recession, but is still low by historical standards. Lower interest rates and the rapid rise in stock market prices in the 1990s followed by soaring house prices until 2007 likely contributed to the decline in saving. But part of the problem may be that we have gone from believing that thrift is a virtue—a lesson learned the hard way during the Depression—to thinking that it is a vice.

Spending beyond our means—both privately and publicly (through deficits)—is a big problem. To start, when we spend more than we produce the difference has to be made up by imports. There's a direct connection between our spendthrift ways and our massive trade deficits and the shrinking dollar.

Second, at the household level, people need to save to buffer themselves against financial shocks—an unexpected layoff or medical expense, for instance—and to finance retirement. The baby boomers should have been saving like crazy during their peak earning years instead of spending like there's no tomorrow.

Third, baby boomers' retirement and the continuing rise in medical costs will impose unprecedented demands on the government. Our best option would be to put entitlement programs—Social Security, Medicare, and Medicaid—on a secure financial footing. But there's no sign of that happening any time soon. Next best would be to leave our children and grandchildren enough financial resources to cover the hefty taxes needed to pay for the promises we've made to ourselves.

Bottom line: Saving is still a virtue.

What's the difference between Roth and traditional IRAs?

Roth IRAs are named for former Senate Finance Committee Chairman William Roth (R-DE). Contributions to traditional IRAs are deductible and earnings accrue tax-free, but withdrawals are fully taxable. Roth IRAs reverse the tax breaks: contributions are not tax-deductible and withdrawals are not taxable, while earnings accrue tax-free. (Both kinds of accounts assess penalties for withdrawals before the age of 59½.) Under certain circumstances, the tax breaks under the two kinds of accounts end up being equivalent. Suppose you're in the 25 percent tax bracket and contribute $1,500 to a Roth IRA. Alternatively, you could contribute $2,000 to a traditional IRA. The after-tax cost of the contribution is the same in both cases. In retirement, you can withdraw the $1,500 plus interest in retirement from the Roth and it's all tax-free. For the traditional account, you'll have to pay tax, but if the tax rate stays at 25 percent, you'll still get to net ¾ of the $2,000 plus interest for retirement consumption. That is, you end up (after tax) with $1,500 plus interest—the same as with the Roth.

Obviously, this example makes several assumptions. The key ones are that you contribute the same amount after tax under each plan, and that the tax rate stays the same. In fact, if the limits on contributions to Roth and traditional IRAs are the same, you can squirrel away more tax-free income in the Roth. And if you expect tax rates to go up in the future, then a Roth becomes a much better deal, because the higher tax rates you'd face when withdrawing your funds from a traditional IRA don't apply. Also, you have to start withdrawing funds from a traditional IRA at a certain age, but you can hold onto a Roth until you die, which is especially valuable for people who don't really need the money to pay for retirement. And there are estate tax advantages of the Roth.

Finally, Roth IRAs can turn out to be a bad deal for the federal budget because, if they really became popular, they could significantly reduce revenues in the future. Recall that withdrawals from traditional IRAs are taxable, whereas Roth

BOX 4.2 **Stupid Tax Tricks: Roth IRA Conversions**

As part of a bill raising the limits on retirement plan contributions, Congress allowed high-income taxpayers, starting in 2010, the option to convert their traditional IRAs into Roth IRAs in exchange for remitting tax on the balance at the time of conversion. (People with moderate incomes were always allowed to do this.) To sweeten the deal further, tax due on conversions done in 2010 could be postponed and remitted in two equal installments in 2011 and 2012. Even though most taxpayers would only take advantage of this option if they expected to save taxes over the long run, the official estimators scored this as a short-term revenue raiser because they expected many taxpayers to take advantage of this option and remit extra tax in 2010, 2011, and 2012.

Here's why Roth rollovers were so good for taxpayers and so bad for the Treasury. By pre-paying tax on accumulated IRAs, rich folks could effectively increase their tax-free savings by close to half. And the rollover option is worth most to people who don't actually need retirement accounts to finance their old age.

The policy didn't serve any valid goal, other than to further enrich the already wealthy. It didn't encourage saving (or work for that matter). And, although it brought revenue into the Treasury coffers for a few years, it meant that billions of dollars of future tax revenues would never be collected because the accounts, once converted, were forever exempt from income tax.

In fact, the rollover gambit is really borrowing on very unfavorable terms to the government. We estimate that the implicit interest rate in 2010 was about 14 percent compared with an interest rate on long-term government bonds of about 4 percent.

If CBO and Joint Committee on Taxation (JCT) had scored the rollover provision as borrowing rather than revenue, Congress probably would not have enacted it. The revenues produced from the conversions would have been disregarded and the implied interest arising from the substantial and growing revenue losses would have been scored as a multi-billion dollar cost over the budget period.

Note: Converting a traditional IRA into a Roth increases the amount of tax-free savings because in a traditional IRA, a portion of the account will go to pay off tax on the eventual withdrawals. On a Roth IRA, the entire account is tax-free. At a 35 percent tax rate, that means more than 50 percent more tax-free retirement income ($1/0.65 = 1.54$, so the Roth produces 54 percent more tax-free savings). The 14 percent implicit interest rate on government borrowing via Roth IRA conversions is derived from the revenue estimates in Leonard E. Burman, "Roth Conversions as Revenue Raisers: Smoke and Mirrors," *Tax Notes* (May 22, 2006): 953–956. At an interest rate of 14 percent, the stream of small tax revenue gains in the short term and large revenue losses in the long run just balance out in present value. (Put differently, 14 percent is the internal rate of return.)

IRAs are tax-free forever. Given that our long-run budget situation is very bleak because of an aging population (and their expensive Social Security benefits) and rising health care costs (which impacts Medicare and Medicaid), reducing future tax revenues seems like a dubious policy (box 4.2).

Do consumption taxes disproportionately burden the old?

While spending is a very large share of income for the elderly, they are somewhat insulated from consumption taxes because most old people get most of their income from Social Security, which is indexed for inflation. If consumption taxes translate into higher prices, Social Security benefits automatically increase.

However, for older people with large pensions and other capital income, the transition from an income tax to a consumption tax may be quite burdensome. Consider a couple on the eve of retirement. The couple has been subject to income tax on their earnings and expected to live off their savings during retirement without facing much more tax. If, though, we were to switch to a consumption tax, say a retail sales tax, there is a tax hit as they draw down their savings to live the good life they've planned during their working years.[17]

That said, a lot of high-income elderly people continue saving a fair amount well into their retirement, and they continue to benefit from the fact that saving is exempt from consumption tax. A broader point is that taxes should properly be looked at over a lifetime. Over the life cycle, savers benefit more from a consumption tax than an income tax, even if they end up paying high taxes as a share of income in retirement.

5

OTHER KINDS OF TAXES

What is the estate tax?

The estate tax is a tax on the wealth held by people who die. (The "estate" is the legal entity that holds assets between time of death and payment of any tax and distribution to heirs of the remaining assets.) The federal tax only applies to people with considerable assets—at least $5 million as of this writing. At present, the tax applies to an estimated 0.13 percent of decedents. There is also a parallel gift tax, which is "unified" with the estate tax to prevent avoidance of the estate tax by giving away one's money while still alive. This means that gifts made before death are also subject to the estate tax to the extent they exceed the exempt threshold. However, annual gifts below $13,000 per recipient are exempt from estate and gift tax.[1]

The estate tax has generated an intense political controversy. Opponents call it the "death tax" and paint a macabre picture of the grim reaper (played by the IRS) snatching from their grieving families the hard-earned wealth of the most productive members of society. They see the tax as a complex, unfair, and inefficient levy that violates every norm of good tax policy.

Supporters see it as a pillar of a progressive tax system, because it only applies to the very richest Americans, discourages large concentrations of wealth (which some people

Figure 5.1 © The Seattle Times Co.

believe are undesirable), and one that has the added virtues of plugging income tax loopholes and encouraging charitable contributions. In attempting to reconcile these divergent views, politicians have debated three estate tax options: live with it, reform it, or throw it out. Remarkably, in 2001 they chose all three! The 2001 tax bill (the first of the Bush tax cuts) changed the estate tax rules, phased in lower tax rates and a higher exempt threshold, and ultimately repealed the tax—but for only one year, 2010. In 2011, along with the rest of the Bush tax cuts, the estate tax was supposed to return from the dead like Freddy Krueger with the old rates, exemptions, and rules back in force.

Back in 2001 and the subsequent decade, few observers thought that the U.S. Congress would allow the estate to expire for just one year. People respond to incentives, and the incentives created by a one-year estate tax holiday provoked a lot of gallows humor about keeping Grandma alive until 2010 and "Throwing Mama from the Train" at the end of the year.

GLICK

"With all the uncertainty surrounding the repeal of the federal estate tax, I will need your advice -- should I be planning to die this year or shouldn't I?"

Figure 5.2 © Arnie Glick

Astonishingly, the U.S. estate tax actually did "die" for one year. Billionaires like New York Yankees owner George Steinbrenner who died in 2010 were admired for their tax savvy. As far as we know, there's no evidence of heirs deliberately hastening the demise of their loved ones (although it seems to have happened in earlier estate-tax change episodes in the United States and some other countries!), but there certainly was a powerful financial incentive to do so for some rich families.[2] The Joint Committee on Taxation estimated that the one-year hiatus from the estate tax cost the U.S. Treasury $14 billion in 2010 compared with the revenue that would have been raised if the 2009 rate and exemption had been extended. Had Congress done nothing, the estate tax would have returned for all estates larger than $1 million at rates up to 55 percent. Ultimately, Congress and the President agreed to a temporary extension of the Bush

Figure 5.3 By permission of Chip Bok and Creators Syndicate, Inc

tax cuts. The estate tax was reincarnated with a $5 million exemption and a 35 percent rate, but only for two years. It's likely that the whole drama will replay in 2012, although with a smaller incentive to throw mama from the train than in 2010.

How is estate tax liability calculated?

At present, it's basically a flat tax on taxable estates larger than $5 million. To calculate the taxable estate, various deductions are subtracted from the gross value of assets held at death. The largest is an unlimited marital deduction— any transfers to a spouse are tax-free. Gifts to charity are deductible, as are state and local transfer taxes (inheritance and estate taxes). There are some tax breaks for farmers and small business owners; most notably, the taxable estate may often include less than the full value of a farm or closely held business. Farmers may value land based on the value of what it produces rather than the market value. This can substantially reduce the estate tax value of land held close to a city (which might be worth much more as a housing development or an office park than as a farm). People who own a large share of a family business may claim "valuation discounts" on the logic that the business would be worth much less if broken into pieces than as a whole. The argument is that a partial share of a business is worth less because of a lack of marketability and the drawbacks of minority ownership such as less say in making business decisions. All told, researchers have estimated that these discounts can reduce the taxable value of farms and businesses by up to 59 percent.[3]

The estate tax can be extremely complex, mostly because it accommodates many sorts of complicated trusts and other legal arrangements. Most of these reduce the ultimate amount of tax liability. Some are designed to protect the interests of spouses or other heirs while minimizing tax liability. (For example, to take advantage of the $5 million exemption available to one's spouse, estates can include a "credit-shelter trust" that is treated as if it were owned by a child or other heir, but the surviving spouse may draw funds from the trust if needed to pay her expenses. Through such arrangements, couples effectively benefit from a $10 million exemption if at least that much is ultimately passed to heirs, but the surviving spouse has access to the money if she needs it.)[4] Some also allow deductions for gifts of income-generating assets to charities before death with the understanding that the donor will receive the income generated by the donated asset and full control only passes to the charity after the donor dies.

Critics of the estate tax bemoan the complexity of the tax, but every one of the complex provisions has a powerful constituency of estate lawyers and wealthy people who benefit financially from it. Proposals to simplify the estate tax have a poor track record in Congress.

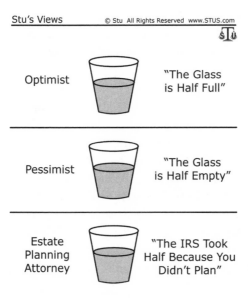

Stu's Views   © Stu All Rights Reserved www.STUS.com

Optimist — "The Glass is Half Full"

Pessimist — "The Glass is Half Empty"

Estate Planning Attorney — "The IRS Took Half Because You Didn't Plan"

Figure 5.4 http://www.stus.com

Why tax estates when the assets that went into them were already subject to plenty of tax?

Critics of the estate tax argue that it amounts to double, or even triple, taxation. Consider the following example: Someone builds a business from scratch and pays tax on the income it produces every year and saves enough of the income (after tax on the return to saving) so as to accumulate substantial wealth. Doesn't an estate tax on that wealth amount to double (or triple) taxation? That sounds unfair and inefficient (because it penalizes hard work and thrift).

Supporters of the estate tax respond that a lot of income is never taxed, that it is an important backstop preserving the integrity of a loophole-ridden income tax, and that it makes important contributions to the progressivity of the federal tax system. The most obvious example of income that may never be taxed is capital gains, which can escape individual income tax entirely if an asset is held until death. (See page 40,

"What is the 'Angel of Death' loophole?") Recognizing that fact, the "Angel of Death" loophole was partially rescinded (on very large capital gains) for the one year when estates were tax-free. More generally, there are thought to be numerous ways that wealthy individuals can accumulate income and wealth and owe little or no income tax. (Even income that is eventually taxed as capital gains is only subject to tax at a 15 percent rate, while the top ordinary income tax rate is 35 percent.)

For sure, the estate tax is the most progressive tax in the federal tax system. The Tax Policy Center estimates that, in 2011, 97 percent of the tax will be collected from the estates of households in the top 5 percent of the income distribution, and 78 percent from the richest 1 percent. By comparison, only 58 percent of personal income tax revenues are collected from the top 5 percent and 34 percent from the top 1 percent.[5]

What are the estate tax's effects on work and saving?

Some are concerned that the estate tax discourages work, saving, and entrepreneurship—all activities that contribute to society. For those people rich enough that extra income would be mostly passed on to their heirs, an estate tax reduces the return—leaving a bigger bequest—to earning and saving income. Some economists have tried to measure how big this discouragement effect is, and our reading of the empirical evidence suggests that the overall effects are fairly modest. The full picture must, though, also consider how an estate tax affects the heirs, as well. Heirs expecting an inheritance would have less incentive to work and save. As Andrew Carnegie noted in 1891, "The parent who leaves his son enormous wealth generally deadens the talents and energies of the son and tempts him to lead a less useful and less worthy life than he otherwise would." Indeed, empirical evidence suggests that heirs work and save less if they expect to receive a large bequest. To the extent that the estate tax diminishes inheritances (both because the tax reduces the after-tax estate and also because it encourages gifts to charity to avoid the tax), it would be expected to raise the energy and productivity of potential heirs.

How does the estate tax affect small businesses and family farms?

How the estate tax impacts small businesses and family farms has been an especially contentious issue. Critics complain that it forces heirs to break up family businesses in order to be able to afford the tax. In fact, very few small businesses and farms appear to be affected by the tax, mainly because the threshold is so high. Small businesses rarely are worth $5 or $10 million. The CBO has calculated that only 1,137 (2.1 percent) of small farms and 8,291 (2.4 percent) of small businesses would be affected by the estate tax at 2009 levels.[6] The higher exemption in 2011 would reduce that number further. The Tax Policy Center estimates that only 120 taxable estates would have farm and small business assets comprising at least half of the estate value. Moreover, the valuation provisions mentioned above often reduce tax liability, and special provisions are available to help heirs pay the tax without dissolving the business, including interest-free and reduced interest loans to defer the tax. Finally, any competent accountant would advise the owner of a family business to purchase life insurance to cover the estate tax liability; this doesn't eliminate the tax burden—the policy premiums comprise the tax—but this simple bit of planning keeps the estate tax from being a devastating cost to the next generation of owners.

What is the difference between an estate tax and an inheritance tax?

Many people think these are the same, but they're different. An estate tax is assessed on the estate, rather than heirs, and applies to the entire value of the estate. An inheritance tax, levied by several states, applies to heirs, and the tax liability could depend on how much is inherited, the heir's other income, as well as the relationship of the heir to the decedent.

Many states and some foreign governments impose inheritance taxes. Inheritance taxes can be stand-alone taxes or integrated with the income tax. One particularly simple option would be to have heirs include in taxable income any gifts and bequests they receive above a threshold amount—say $1 million per heir.

There are several arguments in favor of this approach versus an estate tax. One is that it gives donors an incentive to break up large estates and therefore to some extent discourages large concentrations of wealth. A second argument is that, while donors might be very wealthy, their children and grandchildren might have much more modest incomes. A progressive inheritance tax can account for that by taxing the bequest based on the circumstances of the heir.

Finally, some advocates argue that replacing the estate tax with an inheritance tax would offer political advantages by shifting the focus of the debate away from the tax treatment of the people who accumulated the wealth toward those who will receive a bequest (Paris Hilton rather than Conrad Hilton). And it would be harder to call an inheritance tax a "death tax" as it would apply to the living heir.

It would, though, be more complicated to administer an inheritance tax, because it requires that each heir calculates his or her tax liability separately. One administrative virtue of an estate tax is that it is levied at the same time that probate rules require that the estate be valued.

What is a financial transaction tax?

A financial transaction tax is a tax on the gross value of certain financial transactions such as bank withdrawals or stock sales. It is fairly common in less developed countries because it can collect a lot of money from a small number of well-heeled financial institutions.

Recently, some have proposed a financial tax in the United States as a way to recoup some of the costs of the financial crisis that led to the Great Recession. A few well-known economists—most notably, the late James Tobin, a Nobel Laureate from Yale University—proposed it as a way to discourage "noise trading." The idea is that investors often buy or sell based on rumors and misinformation—what economists call noise. Noise can prevent asset prices from accurately reflecting their fundamental or long-term value so, at least in theory, discouraging noise trading might make markets work better.

There are, though, some serious problems with financial transaction taxes. One is that they are as likely to discourage trading based on real information as on noise. Thus, they can exacerbate inefficiencies by preventing markets from responding to news. Second, the taxes can cascade. For example, banks make numerous bond transactions to balance their portfolios, meet reserve requirements, and satisfy customers' demands for funds. This can result in a relatively large burden as a share of financial institutions' income.

Finally, people may avoid dealing with financial institutions subject to the tax and instead conduct transactions using cash or barter. There is an incentive to come up with an alternative means of exchange, such as IOUs, that become a de facto sort of currency. There is an incentive to try to move transactions offshore so that they are done using financial institutions not subject to the tax. Because financial intermediation is generally quite efficient, allowing safe financial transactions to occur at low cost, this kind of disintermediation is inefficient. It is also sometimes unsafe (see box 5.1).

What is the property tax?

The property tax is an annual wealth tax that applies to particular kinds of property, usually homes, commercial property, and sometimes automobiles. Typically, state or local governments assess these taxes. Overall real estate property taxes are the largest source of tax revenue for local governments and are often earmarked to finance schools.

BOX 5.1 **Stupid Tax Tricks: The Bank Debit Tax in Colombia**

Colombia has a bank debit tax, which applies to all financial transactions. In particular, it applies to check transactions. The tax rate is low, only 0.2 percent of the check amount, but that can still be a significant share of profit margins when they are small (as in retail or financial services). People have reacted to the tax in a number of ways. Instead of cashing checks at a bank and triggering the tax, check recipients endorse the check over to their suppliers or other creditors, and the supplier endorses the check to another business or person, and so on, until the back of the check was covered with lots of tiny signatures. If 20 signatures could be squeezed onto the back of the check, the tax as a share of the transaction volume was cut by 95 percent. That is, if a 100 peso note changed hands 20 times, it is financing 2,000 pesos in transactions. The ultimate tax of 0.2 peso is 0.2 percent of the note value, but only 0.01 percent of the total transaction amount.

The Colombian authorities ultimately banned multiple endorsements and thus squashed this form of tax avoidance. However, a more straightforward way to avoid the tax exists, which is to conduct transactions in cash. At the time both of us were studying the Colombian tax system, it was one of the most dangerous countries in the Western Hemisphere, and the financial transactions tax was encouraging people to carry around brief cases full of currency to avoid the tax. This gave new meaning to the economic concept of "deadweight loss."

Note: See María Angelica Arbeláez, Leonard E. Burman, and Sandra Zuluaga, "The Bank Debit Tax in Colombia," in *Fiscal Reform in Colombia*, ed. Richard M. Bird, James M. Poterba, and Joel Slemrod (Cambridge, Mass.: MIT Press, 2005), 225–246. Thornton Matheson assesses financial transaction taxes in "Taxing Financial Transactions: Issues and Evidence," International Monetary Fund Working Paper, 2011.

Some economists question whether property taxes should even be considered taxes rather than a fee for services provided by local governments. For example, if a town invests in excellent public schools, that will make the town more attractive to current and potential residents, who would be willing to pay more to live there. If the property tax revenues are well spent, the increase in property values should at least offset the higher tax burden. And, alternatively, if a community underinvests in key public services, citizens will vote with their feet and property values will fall, negating the tax savings from having an underfinanced public sector. Because people have different willingness to pay for public services, the mix of property taxes and services will vary among communities. Households that place a relatively high value on, say, excellent public schools, will be attracted to communities with high taxes and very good schools, while others will tend to gravitate to low-tax, low-service communities.

This view is less prevalent these days. Public choice theorists have put forward an alternative hypothesis, called ominously the Leviathan hypothesis. The idea is that citizens will never have as much incentive to monitor and control their governments as bureaucrats have in perpetuating and expanding public spending. In this sense, the public sector is like an ever-growing leviathan, or monster. Over time, its activities can substantially diverge from the needs and desires of citizens. There is some empirical evidence in support of this theory.

Figure 5.5 www.CartoonStock.com

Interest in taming leviathan has been one motivation behind property tax and spending caps that have spread around the country.

What is a lump-sum tax?

On one dimension a lump-sum tax is an economist's dream tax system. Everyone is assessed a tax bill that does not depend on how much they earn or any other economic activity. For example, the tax might be $10,000 per adult per year. In 2011 this would raise about $2.37 trillion, enough to replace the revenue collected from both the individual and corporation income taxes, plus some payroll tax revenue. Such a tax is sometimes called a "poll tax" because it used to be common for local governments to require a flat payment before someone could vote. Of course, this tax could be avoided by not voting, so it could still distort behavior (and, indeed, in many places it was intended to discourage low-income people—and especially people of color—from exercising their franchise, which is why the Supreme Court ultimately struck the poll tax down). In principle a lump-sum tax could also vary from individual to individual, so long as it doesn't depend on anything that people can voluntarily change.

Such a tax is in theory quite efficient. It collects revenue without changing any prices. As a result, it doesn't favor any activity over others and therefore does not, in economists' jargon, "distort" behavior. Of course, in the real world, some people simply wouldn't be able to afford to pay the tax and it is hard to convince voters that it is fair that Mark Zuckerberg owes no more tax than a single mother just getting by on a minimum-wage job. In the United Kingdom, Margaret Thatcher, who was a big fan of economics, got a small lump-sum tax enacted.[7] It was enormously unpopular and is thought to have been a significant factor in the Tories' defeat in the next parliamentary election.

Do economists have other goofy ideas about ideal tax systems?

Why, yes, we do. One idea is a tax based on innate ability. In principle, if you could measure income-earning ability, the government could assign tax bills based on that, regardless of what people actually earned. In theory, this could be a very progressive tax, as high-ability people could be assigned much higher tax bills than those of modest abilities. And so long as the tax can be collected, it doesn't distort workers' decisions about, for example, how much and how hard to work, as one's actual income—and anything else other than ability—does not affect tax liability.

In practice, this is a nonstarter for several reasons. One is that ability is impossible to measure accurately, in part because if people suspected that a test would be used to determine tax burden, they'd have a strong incentive to produce a low score. (Ideally, the test would be administered after earning ability is to some extent observable, but before a child could fathom why her parents were telling her, "Annie, on *this* test you should always give the WRONG answer.") Second, are you really going to assess a tax burden of $100,000 per year on high-ability Annie because she *could be* a Wall Street hotshot even though she has chosen to be a journalist (earning $25,000 per year)? Even if ability could be measured, collecting the tax might appear unseemly.

Gregg Mankiw and Matthew Weinzierl put forward as a parody our favorite theoretically brilliant (goofy) idea: a tax on height. Research shows that height is correlated with lifetime income. Tall people earn more than shorter people on average so a tax based on height would be progressive and efficient—as people are extremely unlikely to try to alter their height in response to tax rules. Even a small tax on height could allow cutting back on progressive, but distorting, income taxes.[8]

Certified offbeat economist Joel Slemrod (winner of the Ig Nobel Prize for Economics) and coauthor Kyle Logue have gone further to suggest that, in the future, when each person's genome can be charted and its effects on likely lifetime income prospects understood, a genome levy could tax people who have the "most-likely-to-invent-the-next-Facebook" genes and subsidize those prone to debilitating diseases, thus achieving some progressivity with no disincentive to work, save, or invent.[9]

Do these ideas explain why people don't like economists?

No comment.

"There's a thin line between thinking outside the box and a caffeine-induced wacko idea."

Figure 5.6 © Steve Smeltzer

PART II

THE COSTS AND BENEFITS OF TAXATION

6

TAXES AND THE ECONOMY

How do taxes affect the economy?

In many, many ways. They reduce the reward to working, saving, and investing and so diminish the incentives to undertake these activities, which can lower GDP and hamper growth. When they discriminate among different activities, they affect how the economy's resources are allocated and may direct them to wasteful uses. People and businesses spend real resources complying with the tax system and trying to avoid or evade taxes. Those resources could otherwise be spent on activities that would make us happier, so that also represents a cost to society. Although economists are divided on the efficacy of Keynesian fiscal policy, many, including us, think that enlightened tax policy can help an economy recover from a severe economic downturn and poorly chosen tax policies can exacerbate a recession. (There's a near consensus among economists that monetary policy is the better tool to manage economic fluctuations during normal times.) At all times taxes affect the distribution of well-being because they are the principal means by which the cost of government is assigned to the citizens.

Of course, the uses to which tax revenues are put may boost the economy by supporting such things as a legal system, productive infrastructure, education, and health care. And, putting the abstraction of an "economy" aside, tax revenue funds the Social Security and Medicare systems and provides income support for tens for millions of low-income households.

Why do economists think that raising funds costs much more than the tax sticker price?

Because the act of raising taxes hampers the economy. Consider a bridge that costs $100 million to build. Raising $100 million extra in taxes will exacerbate all the adverse incentive effects caused by taxes: the disincentive to work, the disincentive to save, the incentive to engage in unproductive tax sheltering, and so on. Raising $100 million more in a $15 trillion plus economy means that the extra disincentive caused will be a tiny fraction of the existing distortions, but it will not be tiny relative to the $100 million price tag for the bridge. Because of this, the true social cost of building the bridge is the dollar cost plus the extra cost of the distortion caused by the higher tax. For technical reasons, it is hard to accurately measure the economic cost of taxation, and estimates vary widely, although a majority of economists would probably put the number at about 30 cents on the dollar, in which case the bridge should provide at least $130 million worth of benefits to make it worthwhile. While economists are far from consensus on just how much distortion high tax rates cause, there is near-unanimous agreement that the total economic cost exceeds the sticker price.

Do some taxes help the economy?

Earlier in chapter 4 we discussed Pigouvian taxes, which are designed to induce people and businesses to consider the cost their activities impose on other people. (See page 97, "What is a Pigouvian tax?") These sorts of taxes, of which carbon taxes are an example, help the economy in the sense that they improve the allocation of resources. Indeed, they could be justified even if the government needed to raise no revenue at all.

What is the Laffer Curve?

It's something that UCLA economist Arthur Laffer drew on a napkin showing the relationship between tax revenues and tax rates. Laffer asserted that tax revenues would be zero at a zero tax rate (not surprisingly) and at a 100 percent tax rate because people would choose not to report any income to the tax authorities if it would all be taxed away. We can imagine scenarios where the tax authorities might still be able to collect tax revenue, since there would likely be rampant tax evasion at a 100 percent tax rate and the authorities could probably catch some cheaters, but we will avoid delving into the implications of this dystopia. The basic insight is that at sufficiently high tax rates, revenues would fall substantially. Thus, there must be a revenue-maximizing tax rate beyond which further rate increases would be counterproductive.

Even accepting the hypothesis that revenues are zero at the end points, the rate at which revenues are maximized— the peak of the Laffer Curve—could in principle be anywhere between 0 and 100 percent. A recent survey by economists Peter Diamond and Emmanuel Saez estimated that the revenue-maximizing federal income tax rate was "conservatively" 48 percent assuming the existing tax base and could be as high as 76 percent if the tax base were much broader (because there would be fewer avenues for tax avoidance). Evidence from other studies also suggests that current tax rates are safely below the unproductive level.

Which is a better economic stimulus, cutting taxes or spending more?

Bringing up the word "stimulus" reminds us that tax policy can play another role—altering the length and severity of a cyclical downturn. The use of tax cuts and increased government spending policy to ward off or dampen recessions is sometimes called Keynesian policy, after the British economist John Maynard Keynes who in the 1930s championed the notion that active fiscal policy can minimize the effect of recessions. Although the belief in the potential efficacy of fiscal policy was widespread among economists in the 1950s, 1960s, and 1970s, by the end of the 1970s many economists had soured on the notion of active countercyclical fiscal policy, in part because of the late-1970s phenomenon of stagflation—high unemployment combined with high inflation—which was not easily explained within the framework of Keynesian economics. These days it remains a controversial and divisive topic among economists.

What is certain is that, since 2001 and especially since 2008, activist fiscal policy has made a comeback in the United States. Major tax cuts were part of the stimulus bills passed in 2008 and 2009, and even in 2012 the debate about whether to extend cuts in payroll taxes revolved around Keynesian issues such as whether—and to what extent—it would boost aggregate spending. All of these stimulus programs contained both tax cuts and additional government spending. Although tax cuts provide an instant, visible boost to people's disposable income, most economists believe that the "bang-per-buck" of direct government purchases exceeds that of tax cuts, because tax cuts are effective in stimulating economic activity only to the extent the extra disposable income is spent. Especially in light of recent evidence, discussed below, that people often save a significant portion of any tax cut (either directly or by using the money to pay down credit card and other debt), direct government spending seems like the more effective stimulus.

The problem with direct spending as stimulus is that it's much better if the direct spending creates something of value, and it is not easy to have a large list of worthwhile projects that are ready to go as soon as Congress gives the word. In the parlance of the day, the projects should be "shovel-ready," as well as of intrinsic value. If there is a long lag before the projects can get underway, the stimulus might arrive too late, when the economy is back on track, when the hurdle for such projects is higher because the projects will use less idle resources and are more likely to draw resources away from valuable competing uses.

What kinds of taxes provide the most stimulus?

Tax policy can provide a short-term boost to the economy in at least two different ways. One way is to increase taxpayers' income, in an attempt to get them to spend more. Because most consumers generally base their spending not only on their current income but also on their expected future income, how effective this will end up being depends on how temporary or permanent the tax cuts are perceived to be. Tax cuts that are perceived to be long-lasting will increase consumption more (as long as the taxpayers don't think too far ahead, to when the deficits caused by tax cuts will leads to higher taxes and lower after-tax income). How much spending rises with higher income depends on that term famous from Economics 101, the marginal propensity to consume (MPC)—how much extra spending an additional dollar of income induces. This will in general vary by taxpayer characteristics. For those who live paycheck to paycheck, spending everything they get, the MPC will be close to one—even for a very short-lived tax cut. It might also be high for people who try to maintain a target level of saving per pay period. Until recently the conventional wisdom had been that, on average, low-income people will have a higher MPC than high-income folks, because they are more likely to have unmet immediate spending needs. If this is true, tax cuts aimed at lower-income households would have a bigger bang-per-buck, producing more stimulus through higher spending per dollar of tax cut. But recent evidence based on taxpayer surveys has called this received wisdom into question. When asked how the stimulus checks sent out in 2009 affected behavior, the percentage of people who said it would mostly increase spending was no higher for low-income people than high-income people; it was low—under 20 percent—for both groups.[1] There are reasons to question how much people's actions track such self-reports, but the responses suggest that even well-targeted temporary tax cuts may be less effective than previously thought.

Another kind of stimulus works by inducing consumers and businesses to change the timing of their spending and investment, respectively—to move it forward to when times are bad. Recent examples in the United States abound. In 2009 businesses were allowed to immediately write off for tax purposes (rather than deduct over the course of many years) their expenses for investments made before a certain date. Households were offered a tax credit for buying a house, or trading in their old clunker for a new car, for a limited time only. In some cases this type of policy might induce more total investment, but its primary effect is often to accelerate planned future economic activity to the low-tax period, without much increasing total spending. This doesn't sound very helpful, but it can make sense to shift economic activity into a period where there is an exceptionally large amount of idle resources, people, and capital. It does, though, require a very high degree of foresight by policymakers. Otherwise, the expiration of the tax break and the resulting drop-off in spending can hurt a still-weak economy.

The United Kingdom cut its value-added tax rate for one year with the hope of stimulating consumption due to the temporarily low tax rate. It seems that Americans are not the only people who love a sale. In contrast to a disposable-income-increasing stimulus, a retiming stimulus works best when it is perceived to be temporary, for only that provides an impetus to consume or invest now, before the tax sale ends.

What are built-in stabilizers?

Taxes tend to fall and spending increases automatically when the economy falters, even without explicitly enacted stimulus programs. When the economy slows, incomes decline, which automatically reduces income tax liability. Drops in earnings often result in larger Earned Income Tax Credits (although some may have earnings so low that their EITC is reduced or eliminated). Certain non-tax spending programs, such as unemployment compensation and food stamps, also increase during a recession. All of these "built-in stabilizers" tend to dampen the decline in after-tax income and soften the resultant decline in consumer spending.

Why do smart, serious people disagree about optimal tax policy?

For at least two reasons. The first is that even smart, serious people can disagree about how the economy works. For example, whether higher tax rates dampen the incentive to work a lot or a little is a critical input into optimal tax policy, but even after decades of research there is still substantial disagreement. Second, what is appropriate tax policy also depends on noneconomic values, most importantly what priority to put on reducing economic inequality. For any given set of beliefs about how the economy works, people with more egalitarian values will favor more progressive tax systems. No economic arguments can resolve differences in values. For that we need ethicists, philosophers, theologians, and deep introspection, but not economists.

For outsiders trying to make sense of disagreements among economists about policy prescriptions, this creates a dilemma. If Economist X says she favors shifting the tax burden toward high-income people, is that because her professional expertise has convinced her that the economic costs—in terms of disincentives to work, invest, and so on—are low, or because her own values are more egalitarian, or some of both? Economists should have some claim to expertise about the former, but we have no claim to be heard about values. A citizen who wished to be enlightened by experts must try to sort out the path that leads an economist to the policy prescriptions, or else ignore them entirely and try to make sense of the evidence about how the economy works.

Actually, it's even worse than that. If economics were a purely scientific venture, then we would expect that economists' judgments about such things as the magnitude of disincentive effects would bear no relationship to their values. After all, do we expect that physicists' views about the nature of black holes are correlated with their political party affiliation? Of course not. We expect that it depends on how they assess theory and evidence about the universe. But this doesn't work in economics. Most economists with conservative values believe that the economic costs of taxation are high, which leads to conservative policy prescriptions (low taxes and small government). Liberals tend to believe that taxation entails much smaller costs—a view consistent with liberal policies. A careful study of the policy preferences and values of economists in the top 40 academic departments found not only considerable disagreement among economists about policy proposals in their areas of specialization (probably no surprise) but also that policy positions are usually more closely related to differences in values than to differences in estimates of relevant economic parameters.[2] The same study found a statistically significant correlation between values and reported economic parameters. That could be because economists' scientific conclusions about how the economy works influence their attitudes toward such matters as income distribution, or alternatively that their estimates of economic parameters may be influenced by their values—which is very unsettling for economics as a science. To be clear, we are not arguing that most economists fudge the numbers to conform to their values, but there may be subtle biases at work that can move us to more readily accept evidence that comports with our worldview (box 6.1).

It may be that the same phenomenon arises in other politically charged scientific disciplines where values or personal dispositions end up influencing research design or interpretation of research so that experts' apparently scientific claims are correlated with their nonscientific worldview.

Where does that leave the citizen looking for professional expertise from economists? Forewarned. In an ideal world economists would describe what they think they know about

BOX 6.1   The Liberal–Conservative Divide on
the Cost of Government

Nick is a conservative economist and Adam is a liberal
   "People like free services and monthly checks in the mail, but people don't realize the true cost—not just in terms of higher taxes, but in lower productivity. And slower growth will hurt our kids a lot more than deficits."
   "There's no compelling evidence that taxes at the level we pay—just about the lowest in the industrialized world—have much effect on work, savings or investment," Adam said. "Besides, why assume away the positive role that government can play in fostering economic growth? Think of all the government dollars shelled out to protect property rights, provide infrastructure and support education."
   I found my chance to intercede. "Why is it that so many liberals believe the effect of taxes on incentives is small, while their conservative counterparts believe that taxes create huge distortions? Since this is an empirical question, you'd expect the conclusions to be independent of one's politics."
   "Not necessarily," Nick responded. "Some conservatives are skeptical about government because we view the costs of paying for it as very high."
   "Do any Republicans believe that taxes don't affect behavior much?" I asked. "Do any Democrats believe that taxes are costly?"

Source: Leonard E. Burman and Joel Slemrod, "My Weekend with Nick and Adam: Tax Policy and Other Willful Misperceptions," *The Milken Institute Review* (September 2003): 50–58. Reprinted by permission.

how the economy works, and, if asked about what policy they favor, would be clear about how their answer depended both on what they think they know and on what values they hold. The reality is that this rarely happens.

How do taxes affect prosperity and growth?

We've just cautioned against accepting the value judgments of economists that are usually implicit in their policy pronouncements. We argued that as economists our professional expertise is to understand the consequences of alternative tax policies, which are crucial—but generally not dispositive—inputs into the policymaking process.

We have now reached the point where we can declaim about the consequences of taxation—how tax systems affect the level of GDP per capita, overall and by income group, as well as on future growth in these measures of how prosperous we are. This, after all, is our expertise as economists.

And now the painful truth—we don't know for sure. Luckily (for us), it is too late to return this book and get a refund.

One reason for this somewhat embarrassing state of affairs is that getting a definitive answer is inherently difficult. Say we would like to know how the 2009 stimulus tax rebates affected the economy. We have great statistics on what happened after the rebate checks were sent out. We also have great statistics on what was going on with the economy before the rebate checks were sent out. What we don't know is how the economy would have performed *without* the rebate program—what economists call the counterfactual. And we can never know for sure. Economists have all sorts of ingenious methods to make educated guesses about the counterfactual. We have statistical methods for estimating the counterfactual, and thereby estimating the effect of the policies actually implemented. Recently many economists have tried to learn from randomized field experiments, where different versions of a policy are implemented in different places, and the differential impact is studied. This method works well for small, localized policies, but it is useless for big, macroeconomic policies like tax policy changes. What government would allow, for the sake of learning how policies work, a big tax cut in some regions and a small tax cut elsewhere? The people who get the small tax cuts would be (understandably) outraged, and it would be difficult to control for any spillover effects of the policies across regions. For all of the ingenuity and statistical sophistication of researchers, these methods remain inexact and, as a result, substantial uncertainty persists about the central questions that inform policy.

However, the evidence is good enough for us to say with a lot of confidence what kinds of claims are *not* true.[3] It is not true that cutting taxes by itself will guarantee a spurt of growth. We know this by observing that some countries with substantially higher tax takes are doing quite well, thank you. We know that higher tax rates on the rich do not guarantee economic disaster, because in the 1950s and 1960s, when the U.S. top individual tax rates exceeded 90 percent, the U.S. economy performed very well indeed. Better than in decades since, on the whole, in the rate of growth of GDP and productivity. We know that lowering tax rates will not boost the economy so much that revenues will go up rather than down. We know this by observing that recent tax cuts in the United States and in other countries were inevitably followed by bigger deficits.

But we also know that taxes can blunt the incentives that people and businesses have to do the things they must do to be successful: work hard, educate themselves, invest in physical capital, and so on. These disincentives must be taken seriously in the formulation of tax policy.

How do taxes affect working and saving?

Two decades ago the conventional wisdom was that the labor supply of prime-age males hardly budges when tax rates changed; these men, often family bread-earners, have to work regardless of what their labor brought in. Some recent research has found a greater responsiveness, suggesting that a tax cut from 30 percent to 25 percent might raise labor supply as much as 2 percent, still fairly small but enough to suggest significant economic costs from sharp increases in taxation. Most economists believe that the labor supply decisions of women are much more sensitive than men are to the after-tax wage, especially with regard to the decision of whether to be in the labor force at all.[4] This is especially troubling given the household-based income tax system we have, where a spouse considering working faces a marginal tax rate determined by the earnings of their spouse, so there may be as much as a 35 percent tax rate imposed even for small amounts of income.

We know much less about the responsiveness of saving to the real after-tax rate of return, in part because it is much more difficult to measure savings than hours worked. Over time there seems to be no clear correlation between this rate of return and aggregate personal savings rates. This doesn't necessarily mean that there is no relationship, as it could be that so many other factors affect savings that it is not possible to identify the effect of taxation alone. Thus, the economic argument against taxing the return to saving, as a pure income tax does but a consumption tax does not, rests on a theoretical, not empirical, argument that any such effect is especially harmful to the long-run growth prospects of the economy.

How do taxes affect entrepreneurship?

Some research has suggested that one aspect of progressive tax systems in general, and capital gains taxes in particular, inhibit risky entrepreneurial activity. It is that they levy a higher tax on successful ventures than they rebate on unsuccessful ones. This is an unavoidable outcome of a graduated rate schedule, under which higher returns push one into the higher tax brackets, while losses push one into lower tax brackets. Thus, the government is an unequal and unhelpful business partner; it takes more from a business in good times than it does during bad times. Furthermore, there are several limitations on the tax benefits of losses. Only a limited amount of capital losses can be deducted from other positive income. Offsetting this is the preferential tax rates levied on capital gains; indeed, the asymmetric treatment of gains and losses is one argument made for the preferentially lower tax rates. (See page 39, "What are the arguments for and against lower capital gains tax rates?")

There are, however, some valuable tax benefits for entrepreneurs.[5] Perhaps most valuable is the fact that they can effectively write off much of the labor they contribute to the business, often called "sweat equity." Entrepreneurs often toil for years earning low wages, and therefore having low tax liability, while they build their business. If all works out, they will earn back their labor contribution with a fair return (more if the business is especially risky) and that return will often be taxed as a capital gain at low rates. This is even better than the tax treatment of IRAs or 401(k) plans. In that case, they can deduct the up-front investment—just as they do for sweat equity—but the ultimate return is fully taxed as ordinary income rather than capital gain. Moreover, for very talented (high-earning) people, the contribution of labor may far exceed the limits on contributions to retirement accounts.

How do taxes affect research and innovation?

Like many countries, the U.S. government subsidizes basic research and development (R&D), both via direct funding (mostly dedicated to defense and health) and, since 1981, through tax credits related to R&D activity. The support is motivated by the belief that basic R&D has important spillover effects that benefit not just the businesses that do it, but other businesses as well—it generates positive externalities (as opposed to the negative externalities that pollution-generating activity does), which suggest a Pigouvian subsidy. The tax law provides a credit of 20 percent of a taxpayer's qualified research expenditures that exceed an amount based on past activity. Although the basic form of the credit hasn't changed much since it was first enacted, the credit has expired eight times and has been extended thirteen times, making it difficult for businesses to make long-term commitments based on its continued existence and bringing to mind what President Lyndon Johnson once said: "The most damaging thing you can do to any businessman in America is to keep him in doubt, and to keep him guessing, on what our tax policy is."

Most studies conclude that the credit does in fact stimulate more R&D. One credible study estimated that a 10 percent fall in the after-tax cost of R&D induces just over a 1 percent rise in the level of R&D in the short run, but almost a 10 percent rise in the long run.[6] This and many (but not all) other studies suggest that the credit is effective in the sense that each dollar of forgone tax revenue causes businesses to invest an additional dollar in R&D. In other words, the credit stimulates about as much R&D activity as direct spending would.

What is "trickle-down" economics?

This term is generally applied in a pejorative way to policies that heavily feature tax cuts for the most well-to-do, but which are defended on the grounds that they will eventually benefit everyone through job creation and investment. The term has been attributed to the humorist Will Rogers, who said during the Great Depression that "money was all appropriated for the top in hopes that it would trickle down to the needy." In modern terminology, tax cuts for the 1 percent help the 99 percent.

One careful recent study casts doubt on that proposition.[7] It first makes the point that income growth for the 99 percent was highest in the United States from 1933 to 1973 when top income tax rates were high and has slowed down since the 1970s when top tax rates came down. A statistical analysis of the data shows that, other things equal, lower marginal tax rates for the 1 percent are associated with lower, not higher, real income for the 99 percent.

Why not run deficits forever?

The United States can run a structural deficit (meaning noninterest spending is greater than revenues) forever so long as the debt doesn't rise faster than GDP. If debt rises slower than GDP, the debt/GDP ratio will fall over time.

Whether we *should* run deficits is a much more complicated question. We should borrow to finance investments that will pay off over time. That includes obvious things like many roads and dams but also spending on wars and homeland security if those investments make us safer over the long run.

But we should save (that is, run surpluses) if we have large underfunded future obligations. The enormous projected shortfalls in Social Security, Medicare, and Medicaid may outweigh the returns on public investments, so the optimal policy might be to run surpluses right now.

A further complication is that the optimal policy depends on future economic growth. Running deficits is a way to smooth our aggregate consumption over time if we know that the economy will be growing. Basically, we're sharing in our grandchildren's good fortune. If future and current generations care equally about each other, this sort of makes sense.

There is, though, tremendous uncertainty about future economic growth. Historically, the economy has grown at an average rate of around 2 or 3 percent per year. If that continues, then our grandchildren will be much richer than we are. However, there are many risks. For example, what will climate change do to the economy? Will resource constraints (e.g., finite fossil fuels, clean water, etc.) become binding, slowing growth? Will a new era of innovation stimulate productivity gains?

On balance, it's not at all clear what the optimal deficit policy is, but there's a pretty good chance that it's *not* to run structural deficits forever.[8]

One final caveat, there's a very strong argument for running a temporary structural deficit when the economy is operating far below capacity (as it is at the time we wrote this).

If people care about their children, won't they just save more to make up for any deficits? That is, do deficits matter at all?

Former vice president Dick Cheney once famously said that "Ronald Reagan proved that deficits don't matter." His comment attracted scorn and derision, but some very smart and thoughtful economists have made a similar argument—without the reference to President Reagan.

The basic idea is this: If people care about their children and grandchildren, then they will, as private citizens, take steps that completely offset government's actions that have long-term negative consequences. To the extent this occurs, then if the government borrows, citizens know that will just translate into higher future taxes on their children and grandchildren, so they will save more to offset these consequences and smooth out consumption. If taxpayers are infinitely farsighted and perfectly rational, private saving will completely offset any public borrowing.

David Ricardo, the brilliant political economist of the early nineteenth century, was the first to make this hypothesis, which is often called "Ricardian equivalence" in his honor. Long considered an interesting but implausible scenario, Ricardian equivalence was resurrected in the 1980s by Harvard economist Robert Barro.[9]

Although there is certainly something to the idea that individual saving and borrowing can be affected by deficit policies, we think full Ricardian equivalence does not hold in practice for many reasons. To start, people obviously do not live forever (Ricardo's scenario). Barro replies that all that matters is that people care about their kids and, by a kind of transitivity property (economists call it the "overlapping generations model"), that means that they care about all their future descendants. Critics have pointed out that, in the limit, this implies that everyone cares about everyone else's descendants because given enough time, everyone becomes related. Other problems include that the argument assumes that everyone borrows when the government is running a surplus, which isn't plausible given that most people face borrowing constraints. More fundamentally, we don't know how future tax burdens and spending cuts will be distributed, so it is unclear how much (if at all) to save to offset the consequences of future policies on our descendants.

And—this is a hard thing for economists to say—there's a lot of evidence that people aren't ultra-rational (and sometimes

" SINCE IT'S FALLING ON ME TO HELP PAY
OFF THE BUDGET DEFICITS WHEN I GROW UP,
I THINK YOU NEED TO INCREASE MY ALLOWANCE,
DAD! "

Figure 6.1 www.CartoonStock.com

aren't even slightly rational). If they were, you'd expect to see substantial boosts in private saving when deficits soar. But if there is a relationship, it's a very subtle one. The government has been running large and growing deficits for the past dozen years and until the Great Recession, savings were very close to zero.

7

THE HIDDEN WELFARE STATE

Are a trillion dollars in middle-class entitlement programs really hidden in the tax code?

Yes, give or take...The actual amount is in dispute for reasons we'll get to, but many spending programs are run through the income tax.[1]

When policymakers want to support or penalize a certain activity or group of people or businesses, they have a choice about whether to do it through traditional spending agencies— like the Department of Housing and Urban Development—or through the tax code. One would like to think that the choice of delivery vehicle depends only on how the program can most effectively be administered, but there are good reasons to think that our political system is biased in favor of the tax delivery mechanism.

Economists and lawyers call spending programs run through the tax code "tax expenditures." No doubt this sounds like an oxymoron—"jumbo shrimp" comes to mind— but bear with us. Congress's nonpartisan Joint Committee on Taxation counted 202 different tax expenditures in 2009, a 50 percent increase from 1986. There are tax expenditures in every budget category. For example, military officers and soldiers get free housing on base or an allowance to help pay for off-base housing. These benefits are tax-free, saving recipients $12 billion of tax liability in 2011. The tax savings on the housing allowances are equivalent to a boost in pay—albeit one that depends on the soldier's tax bracket—but, unlike a direct increase in salary, they don't show up as Department of Defense spending. Instead, the extra compensation is counted as a reduction in taxes.

To take a better known example, taxpayers who itemize deductions can deduct charitable contributions, which provide a tax saving proportional to the taxpayer's rate bracket. But, rather than allow a deduction for charitable donations, the government could directly subsidize qualified charities by sending them a check related to the amount of private donations they receive; this is how it's done in the United Kingdom. Under either method, charity is subsidized, but in the first case it appears to be a cut in taxes, while in the second case it appears to be an increase in spending.

The biggest tax expenditures are the tax exclusion for employer-sponsored health insurance, the mortgage interest tax deduction, and the tax break for 401(k) retirement plans (table 7.1). (If pensions and 401(k) plans were grouped together as retirement breaks, they'd be the second largest tax break.) An obvious aspect of the big tax expenditures is that they affect a broad swath of the population (unlike the military housing allowance exclusion) and are enormously popular. Even though some of them have dubious merit as public policy, changing them would be politically difficult if not impossible.

What exactly is a tax expenditure?

The broad definition of tax expenditures—spending programs run through the tax code—is not in dispute, but there is far from consensus about what exactly belongs in that category. The Office of Management and Budget uses the definition proposed by Treasury Assistant Secretary Stanley Surrey, who invented the concept in 1967, and his coauthor, Paul R. McDaniel:

The tax expenditure concept posits that an income tax is composed of two distinct elements. The first element consists of structural provisions necessary to implement a normal income tax, such as the definition of net income, the specification of accounting rules, the determination of the entities subject to tax, the determination of the rate schedule and exemption levels, and the application of the tax to international transactions. The second element consists of the special preferences found in every income tax. These provisions, often called tax incentives or tax subsidies, are departures from the normal tax structure and are designed to favor a particular industry, activity, or class of persons. They take many forms, such as permanent exclusions from income, deductions, deferrals of tax liabilities, credits against tax, or special rates. Whatever their form, these departures from the normative tax structure represent government spending for favored activities or groups, effected through the tax system rather than through direct grants, loans, or other forms of government assistance.[2]

The controversies all revolve about what constitutes the "normal tax structure." The most important one is whether tax expenditures should be defined with respect to an income tax or a consumption tax. If the normal tax were taken to be a consumption tax, which does not tax the return to saving, then the tax breaks related to pensions, 401(k) plans, capital gains, and the exclusion of net imputed rental income on homes would not be on the list. Nonetheless, many items would be included regardless of the definition of "normal tax." Economists Donald Marron and Eric Toder have estimated that 70 percent of tax expenditures (by dollar amount) would be classified as such under either benchmark.[3]

Measuring the value of tax expenditures is also challenging. By convention, the estimates simply reflect how much the relevant tax breaks reduce taxpayers' liability in a year, without accounting for how taxpayer behavior, and

Table 7.1 Largest Tax Expenditures in Fiscal Year 2011, in Billions of Dollars

	Provision	Amount
1	Exclusion for employer-sponsored health insurance	294.3
2	Mortgage interest deduction	100.9
3	401(k) plans	72.7
4	Lower rate on capital gains	62.0
5	EITC	55.7
6	Pensions	52.3
7	State and local tax deduction (excluding property tax)	46.3
8	Tax deferral for multinational corporations	41.8
9	Child Tax Credit	40.8
10	Charity deduction (other than education, health)	39.8

Note: The health insurance estimate includes $113.7 billion in payroll tax expenditure (because employer contributions toward health insurance are exempt from both income and payroll taxes); the EITC and Child Tax Credit estimates include the refundable parts—$52.6 and $22.4 billion, respectively—which are considered outlays (spending) rather than tax cuts under the budget rules.

Source: U.S. Budget, Analytical Perspectives, FY2013, and authors' calculations.

therefore tax liability, would change if the tax breaks were repealed. Longtime Ways and Means Committee tax counsel, John Buckley, has argued that repealing or scaling back tax expenditures could raise far less revenue than the conventional method suggests because taxpayers would change their behavior to avoid paying more tax.[4] For example, if the mortgage interest deduction were repealed, some taxpayers would sell taxable assets and use the proceeds to pay down their mortgage. Tax revenue would then decline by the amount that otherwise would have been due on the diverted assets' income.

Why do we call tax expenditures entitlement programs? They're tax cuts.

Many tax expenditures are similar to mandatory spending programs (commonly called entitlements) because they provide subsidies to everyone who is eligible and they are not subject to annual appropriation. Like entitlements, they continue forever unless Congress makes an explicit decision to modify or repeal them. This isn't true of every tax break. For example, most of the tax cuts enacted in 2001 and 2003 were originally scheduled to expire at the end of 2010 (and have since been extended through 2012). The low-income housing tax credit is actually allocated by state housing agencies and subject to a state-by-state cap. They're not appropriated, but they are not open-ended entitlement programs either.

Like entitlement programs, tax expenditures are large, growing, and hard to control.

Who benefits from tax expenditures?

Most taxpayers qualify for at least some tax expenditures. Whether they benefit or not compared to a world with no tax expenditures at all is a much more difficult question to answer, as tax rates could be lower—or explicit expenditure programs increased—if there were not so many exclusions, deductions, and credits, but exactly how tax rates would be cut is not obvious.

Leonard E. Burman, Eric Toder, and Chris Geissler estimated the distribution of tax expenditures by income groups (see table 7.2).[5] Tax expenditures are a significant share of income for households at all income levels. Strikingly, they are most significant for high-income people—worth about 13.5 percent of income for the richest 1 percent, and 11.4 percent of income for the richest 20 percent, compared with 9.6 percent overall.

Higher-income people benefit most from exclusions and deductions, whereas low- and middle-income people benefit more from tax credits. This isn't surprising. In a progressive income tax, deductions and exclusions from taxable income are most valuable per dollar to taxpayers in high tax brackets. Credits typically are at the same rate for everyone, and some

Table 7.2 Major Tax Expenditure Categories as a Percent of Income, Selected Income Groups, 2007

Type	Bottom 20 percent	Middle 20 percent	Top 20 percent	Top 1 percent	All
Exclusions	0.5	3.8	4.7	2.9	4.2
Above-line deductions	0.0	0.1	0.1	0.1	0.1
Capital gains, dividends	0.0	0.0	2.1	5.9	1.3
Itemized deductions	0.0	0.4	2.9	3.2	2.0
Nonrefundable credits	0.1	0.3	0.1	0.0	0.1
Refundable credits	5.5	2.2	0.3	0.0	1.1
All	6.5	6.8	11.4	13.5	9.6

Note: Column totals may differ from the sum of components because of interactions.

Source: Leonard E. Burman, Christopher Geissler and Eric J. Toder, "How Big Are Total Individual Income Tax Expenditures, and Who Benefits from Them?" *American Economic Review Papers and Proceedings* 98, 2 (May 2008): 79–83.

phase out at higher income levels. Low-income households benefit most from the refundable EITC and Child Tax Credit, which are akin to vouchers in the sense that families can benefit even if they do not have income tax liability.

Why has the use of tax expenditures been growing in recent years?

Income tax expenditures have been proliferating since the mid-1990s (figure 7.1). As already mentioned, according to data from the Joint Committee on Taxation the number of individual income tax expenditures increased by 50 percent between 1996 and 2007—from 130 in 1996 to 202 in 2007.[6]

It is not entirely clear why, but we suspect that politics is a big part of it. Taxpayers dislike paying taxes, but they like getting help from the government. In the recent antitax environment, a politician who proposes a new spending program is open to attack for being a "tax and spend" liberal. In contrast, if a nearly equivalent program can be run through the tax code as a tax expenditure, it can be defended as a tax cut rather than a new spending program. Its cost does not appear in calculations of the cost of government (although it obviously does affect the deficit

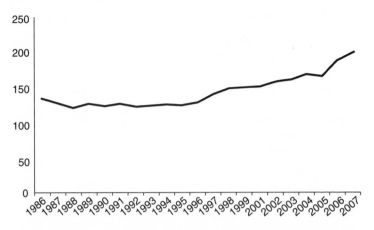

Figure 7.1 Number of individual income tax expenditures, 1986–2007. *Source*: Joint Committee on Taxation, annual tax expenditure compilations back to 1985. Recent reports are available at https://www.jct.gov/publications.html?func=select&id=5.

or tax rates that households face). In that way, it may appear more benign and more affordable than direct spending programs.

How should policymakers decide whether to run a subsidy through the tax system?

Some tax purists would argue that most subsidies should be delivered through program agencies rather than the IRS because, they argue, the only role of the tax system is to collect revenue. But there are cases where the tax system is the more efficient delivery mechanism. This is especially true if eligibility can easily be determined using information already on tax returns or that tax authorities can easily obtain—via information reporting of third parties such as employers. There are also issues about the timing of tax subsidies. Usually, tax subsidies are claimed when filing a tax return, potentially long after the qualifying activity occurs. This can make the subsidy less effective if taxpayers are very short on cash. On the other hand, establishing eligibility for cash transfer programs can be difficult and time-consuming, and there can also be a welfare stigma associated with applying for a benefit. Tax subsidies have the advantage of being relatively easy to claim and completely anonymous so there is no welfare stigma.

Many potential subsidy programs have been derailed because there is no plausible way for the IRS to enforce them without an audit. Ideally, an independent third party would report eligibility to the IRS. Often, however, there is no such entity.

For example, employers may exclude up to $20 per month for "qualified bicycle commuting" expenses if "the bicycle is regularly used for ... a substantial portion of travel between" home and work. We like bicycling (one of us is a bicycle nut), but this policy is completely unenforceable. How could an employer verify that employees qualify? By counting how many times a month they show up in spandex? Who's going to scrutinize employees' bike shop receipts to be sure that the expenses are for the employee's bike and not her kid's?

How should tax expenditures be designed?

Many choices arise in the design of subsidies. First, there's the question of whether the subsidy should be delivered by way of a tax credit, an exclusion, or a deduction from taxable income. Exclusions are often used for fringe benefits. For example, if your employer offers health insurance at work as part of your compensation, the value of that insurance is not included in your taxable income; alternatively, the government might tax all employee compensation—cash and fringe benefits—and then provide subsidy payments to those who receive fringe benefits. The big advantage of the exclusion is that it's very simple from the point of view of the recipient. But here's the rub: the rate of subsidy is larger for taxpayers in high brackets than those in low tax brackets. A deduction is similar except that the taxpayer subtracts it from income on the tax return rather than simply excluding it from income in the first place. Why we would want to offer a higher rate of subsidy for charitable donations to higher-income people is beyond us.

Figure 7.2 Cartoon © Mark Parisi. Permission granted for use, www.offthemark.com

Exclusions and deductions make more sense when the objective is not to subsidize an activity but rather to adjust taxable income to be a better measure of a taxpayer's standard of living. In that case, excluding the item from income results in a better measure of the taxpayer's true economic status. This argument justifies the deduction for extraordinary medical expenses, which reduce a family's well-being below what their pre-deduction income suggests.

A tax credit is more like a voucher. It reduces tax liability by the same amount for all households with sufficient tax liability to use the credit. However, a tax credit may be of little or no value to households that don't have much tax liability. For that reason, a few tax subsidies are offered as refundable tax credits and available even if the taxpayer has no tax liability, so that net tax liability becomes negative—the household gets money from the government. In addition, policymakers have to choose the credit rate, whether there is a limit on the total credit, and whether the credit phases in or phases out with income. The advantages of phasing out a credit (or deduction) are that the revenue cost of the subsidy is lower and that the benefit is targeted to those with lower incomes. The disadvantages are that the phase-out complicates tax compliance and can create undesirable incentive effects. Phasing out a credit as income rises is tantamount to a marginal tax on income. (See page 46, "What are hidden tax brackets?") Thus, policymakers have to trade off the incentive effects caused by the phase-out and the efficiency costs of raising more tax revenue to make up for a more widely available credit.

Are all tax expenditures run through the income tax?

No. Several large fringe benefits are exempt from payroll tax, as well as income tax. The Joint Committee on Taxation estimated that the exclusion of the value of employer-sponsored health insurance from the payroll tax base cost the Treasury $100 billion in 2007, not that much less than the income tax expenditure ($145 billion). The payroll tax savings are partially offset by reduced

SIDEBAR 7.1 A Tax Credit for People Who Don't Get Tax Credits?

One April Fool's Day many years ago, a Treasury economist who shall remain nameless (it wasn't either of us) proposed a tax credit for people who don't get other tax credits. His memo was in standard format for new proposals. He noted that, under current law, a minority of taxpayers do not qualify for any tax credits. The reason for change was that the credit-deprived thought this was unfair, with some justification. His proposal was to create a new tax credit that would only be available for taxpayers who are not eligible for any other tax credits.

Although this proposal never made it into legislation, or even a public legislative proposal, it illustrated one of the key drawbacks of the proliferation of tax expenditures. Surveys show that most taxpayers think they are not getting their fair share of tax benefits.

Social Security benefits, so it is not entirely clear how to measure this kind of tax expenditure, but it is surely significant.[7]

The late Treasury economist Bruce Davie pointed out that there are also excise tax expenditures.[8] For example, different kinds of beer are subject to different levels of excise taxes, conveying an effective subsidy for microbrews. (Davie questioned the wisdom of this tax expenditure on both equity grounds—microbrews are generally favored by those with higher incomes—and efficiency grounds.) The Treasury published a list of tax expenditures under the estate and gift taxes until 2002.

And, arguably, the many preferences given to particular goods and services under state and local sales taxes constitute tax expenditures.

Is the whole concept of tax expenditures based on the fallacious assumption that government owns all your money?

One recurring critique of the tax expenditure concept is that it rests on the assumption that all income belongs to the government unless government deigns to refund it in the form of tax breaks. Interestingly, neither this argument nor the concept of tax expenditure is a new one. Canadian economist Neil Brooks reports that in 1863, William Gladstone, then a Tory member of the British parliament, railed against the exemption from income tax of charitable contributions. He complained that the charitable deduction would make no sense as a direct expenditure, conflicting as it would with efforts to bring "the whole expenditure of the State...within the control, and under the eye, of the House of Commons. If this money is to be laid out upon what are called charities, why is that portion of the State expenditure to be altogether withdrawn from view...and to be so contrived that we shall know nothing of it, and have no control over it?" The rebuttal from Sir Strafford Northcote would be familiar to modern critics of tax expenditures: "'The right hon. Gentleman, if he took £5 out of the pocket of a man with £100, put the case as if he gave the man £95.'"[9]

BOX 7.1 Len Burman Takes on Jon Stewart, Host of "The Daily Show," on Tax Expenditures

Dear Jon,

"The Daily Show" is my favorite TV show. I think you're the smartest policy analyst on television. (Okay, as you prove time after time, that's a really low bar, but, seriously, you're brilliant.)

Last month, however, your satire missed the mark. You had a lot of fun with President Obama's pledge to make "spending reductions in the tax code":

What??? The tax code isn't where we spend. It's where we collect.... You managed to talk about a tax hike as a spending reduction. Can we afford that and the royalty checks you'll have to send to George Orwell?

Jon, meet me at camera 3.

I know you say it's fake news, but when you riff on policy, people take you seriously. And, with respect, in this case, you don't know what the hell you're talking about.

For 40 years, tax geeks like me have been trying to explain that there's a boatload of spending programs masquerading as tax cuts, and they're multiplying. Their number increased by almost 60 percent between 1987 and 2007.

The fact that pols can claim credit for "tax cuts" (good) rather than "spending" (bad) has made them irresistible to legislators of both parties. Never mind that the IRS doesn't have the budget or expertise to effectively administer a couple hundred spending programs (sorry, tax cuts) or that many of them make no sense. The tax code's cluttered with this junk.

Finally we get the president of the United States to acknowledge this and you drill him a new one.

You don't believe there's spending in the tax code??? Here's a real life example: the chicken-s**t tax credit. Really, section 45 of the Internal Revenue Code. You can look it up. The late Senator Roth of Delaware (home of lots of chickens and "poultry manure," as it's euphemistically called) put this little goody into our tax laws. Here's the backstory: the EPA said that enormous chicken farms could no longer put their poultry waste in pools or bury it because it poisoned the ground water. One of the best options to meet the new requirement was to dry the vile effluent and burn it to make electricity, but that was still costly. Roth didn't want chicken farmer profits to plummet or chicken and egg prices to rise just because farmers couldn't use the earth as a giant toilet, so he pushed through the chicken s**t tax credit to create a profitable market for that (as well as all sorts of other crap).

There are lots of chicken s**t tax subsidies. The mortgage interest deduction is basically a housing voucher for rich people. Those who really need help get bupkes. The tax-free health insurance you get at work is heavily subsidized by the tax code, but those with low incomes rarely get health coverage and, if they do, the subsidy is worth little or nothing. The ethanol tax credit is a farm price support program that is literally starving people. It's spending, Jon. Often really dumb spending. And when we're talking about cutting food stamps, nutrition programs for mothers and infants, and environmental protections to save money, those spending programs in the tax code should be on the table too.

Tax subsidies add up to more than $1 trillion per year. That's not chump change, but, until recently, it's been off limits in any bipartisan budget negotiations in Congress because Republicans have been unwilling to consider anything that might be labeled a tax increase.

But there's a glimmer of hope. The president, his bipartisan debt commission, the bipartisan Domenici-Rivlin task force that I served on, and even Paul Ryan want to slash tax subsidies. Arch-conservative Oklahoma Senator Tom Coburn, leader of the bipartisan "gang of six," has said that he'd support tax increases so long as they didn't include rate increases. That is, he wants to rein in subsidy programs run by the IRS.

This is important. Coburn was willing to take on Grover Norquist, who has very effectively prevented any sensible compromise on the budget by insisting that cutting tax subsidies would violate the taxpayer protection pledge that he strong-armed most Republicans to sign. Now Grover can use your laugh line to reinforce Republican intransigence and doom any chance of bipartisan cooperation.

In all seriousness, Jon, this is not helpful.
With respect,
Len Burman

Source: Originally published on Forbes.com.

The fact is that tax expenditures have the same effect on incomes and allocation of resources as direct spending programs. Arguably the whole distinction between taxing and spending is artificial, so maybe the spending program shouldn't be labeled an expenditure either, but tax expenditures and direct expenditures are functionally equivalent—whatever they are called—and should be subject to scrutiny both by those who care about efficient delivery of public services (and small government) and by those who care about the integrity of the tax system.[10]

8

THE BURDEN OF TAXATION

What makes a tax system fair?

The issue of tax fairness is highly contentious and, unfortunately, economics provides little guidance. For example, some people think that a flat tax on wages is fair because it taxes everyone at the same rate; to those who believe in tax progressivity, that epitomizes unfairness.

Defining fairness is tricky. One notion of fairness— so-called horizontal equity— is the idea that, other things equal, the tax burden should not vary much among people at about the same standard of living; in other words, the tax system should not discriminate on the basis of irrelevant characteristics or tastes. That means, for example, that the tax system shouldn't discriminate between owners and renters, people with health insurance and people without, or those who choose to drive a hybrid car and those who drive an old clunker. Of course, the tax system does discriminate in each of those cases, always with the rationale that a higher policy goal is being advanced: building community (mortgage interest deduction), encouraging health insurance coverage (health insurance exclusion), and improving the environment and reducing reliance on foreign oil (hybrid vehicle tax credit). Thus, even when we have an apparently reasonable standard of fairness such as horizontal equity, other goals may trump it and often do. The consequence is that neighbors with identical standards of living might often bear very different tax burdens.

A more controversial notion is that of vertical equity—how should the tax burden vary across people of different levels of well-being. Most, but not all, people accept the idea that higher-income people should owe a larger share of their income in tax than those less able to pay—but how much more? This concept underlies our progressive federal income tax, but many of the loopholes and preferences in the tax system can undermine progressivity. Also, an income tax violates horizontal equity in the sense that it taxes people who choose to save more than otherwise similar people who prefer to spend all of their incomes and those who choose to work more than otherwise similar people who prefer to lie on a beach. (See page 90, "Why tax consumption rather than income?")

What is the benefit principle?

The benefit principle is another notion related to fairness— the idea that tax burden should be related to how much one benefits from what government provides, that is, taxes are a quid pro quo. This principle suggests that, if you can identify the people who benefit from a particular government service, they should pay for it. So, for example, people pay a fee for visiting many national parks and local governments often charge a fee for water use and trash collection.

This principle is fairly straightforward and unobjectionable in the cases mentioned, but measuring the benefits of *all* of what government provides to citizens is practically impossible. Adam Smith argued that the value of services such as national defense, police, and courts increases with income, and suggested that a proportional income tax would be the appropriate levy. Bill Gates, Sr. (father of Microsoft's Bill Gates) has argued that very wealthy people owe an enormous debt to their country because the educated populace, investment in research, robust legal institutions, and so on create an environment especially conducive to wealth creation. On those grounds, he defends both a progressive income tax and an estate tax as a kind of user charge.

Note, though, that the benefit principle more broadly applied would also conflict with other social objectives. For example, charging recipients for Food Stamps would completely undermine the objective of the program to provide a social safety net.

Do special fairness concerns come into play when tax laws change?

Yes. People often make decisions with long-lasting implications assuming a particular set of tax rules. If the rules change, some people can be hurt much more than others. For example, if the mortgage interest deduction were eliminated, existing homeowners would likely be hurt in two ways. First, their after-tax mortgage costs would increase. Second, the value of their homes might fall. A transition rule, sometimes called a grandfather clause, could be put in place fairly easily to protect homeowners from the first, but not the second, factor.

How is the tax burden distributed?

Using data from individual income tax returns, it is possible to estimate how tax burdens are distributed by income levels (figure 8.1). Typically, the tables are based on a single year of data, so they represent a snapshot of households' economic status. The calculations account for non-filers—including many elderly households and low-income households without children. To make such a table, one must make assumptions about what group of people end up bearing the burden of the tax, as distinct from who just writes the checks to the government. In the Tax Policy Center's tabulations, the individual income tax is assumed to be borne by the taxpayers, payroll taxes are borne entirely by workers (including the part technically levied "on" employers) and the Social Security and Medicare benefits tied to taxes collected are ignored, the estate tax is borne by decedents, and the corporate tax—whose ultimate burden is very controversial—is assumed to be borne by all capital owners (although the Tax Policy Center has recently changed that assumption). These are all reasonable assumptions based on evidence and economic reasoning, but they are not incontrovertible.

Under those assumptions, the federal tax system is fairly progressive overall. Taxes comprise about 6 percent of income for the poorest 20 percent of households, but 23 percent of income for the richest quintile. At the very top of the income distribution—the richest 1 in 1,000—federal taxes comprise more than 30 percent of income. At low income levels, the individual income tax burden is negative—meaning that refundable tax credits more than offset households' income tax liability. The payroll tax, however, is larger than the tax credits, so the combined income and payroll burden is positive. A small portion of the corporate tax is assigned to this group—mostly reflecting older families with a small amount of income from pensions and 401(k) plans but otherwise modest incomes.

At higher income levels, income taxes—both individual and corporate—become a larger share of income, while the payroll tax dwindles in importance, due to the cap on taxable payroll, for those with high incomes. The estate tax is a factor only for those with very high incomes, and even for them, it's a small percentage of income (mostly because few of them die each year).

Robert McIntyre at Citizens for Tax Justice (CTJ), a liberal advocacy organization, has pointed out that state and local taxes tend to be regressive, so that the total tax burden is less progressive than figure 8.1 suggests. States heavily rely on regressive sales and property taxes and even their income taxes tend to be much flatter than the federal income tax. CTJ has the only comprehensive model capable of estimating the

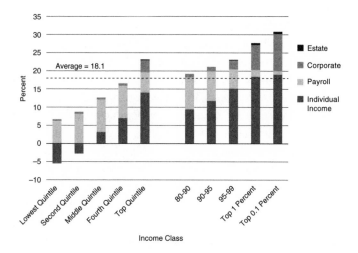

Figure 8.1 Effective federal tax rates by income class, 2011. *Source*: Tax Policy Center, http://www.taxpolicycenter.org/T11-0100.

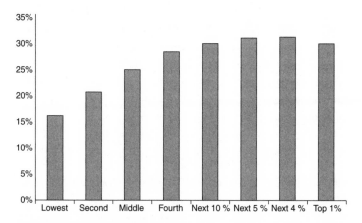

Figure 8.2 Combined federal, state, and local tax as percent of income, 2010. *Source*: Citizens for Tax Justice, "America's Tax System Is Not as Progressive as You Think," April 15, 2011. http://www.ctj.org/pdf/taxday2011.pdf

distribution of state and local taxes (figure 8.2). By their estimates, the federal, state, and local taxes together comprise a growing share of income, but only up to about the 95th percentile. The very wealthy actually experience a decline in tax burdens as a share of income.

What is the burden of deficits?

Typically distribution tables ignore the burden represented by deficits. For this reason, according to distribution tables such as figures 8.1 and 8.2, the Bush tax cuts made almost everyone seem better off. They provided a free lunch. If tax cuts paid for themselves because of more robust economic growth, then this assumption might be warranted. But, as we noted earlier, that is simply not true, so that current deficits imply higher taxes in the future, a lower level of government services, or some combination of the two. (See page 146, "Why not run deficits forever?")

Because it is impossible to know ex ante how the resulting deficits will be addressed, it is also impossible to determine the winners and losers when a tax cut is financed with borrowed money. For example, table 8.1 shows the distribution of tax changes by income percentile arising from the 2001–2006 tax cuts under different assumptions about who will eventually bear the burden that deficits create. The first column assumes that nobody pays—the standard assumption. This creates a tax nirvana in which every income class gets at least a small tax cut—averaging $74 for households in the bottom quintile and $11, 286 for people in the top quintile. The average family could expect a tax cut worth $2,483 in 2010.

If we consider that the tax cuts must ultimately be offset by spending cuts or tax increases (or some of both), the

Table 8.1 Average Estimated Income Tax Change in 2010 Due to the Bush Tax Cuts, under Different Financing Assumptions, in Dollars

Cash Income Percentile	Financing Method			
			Proportional	
	None	Lump-Sum	to Income	to Tax
Lowest Quintile	−74	2,409	278	105
Second Quintile	−642	1,841	276	−164
Middle Quintile	−1,149	1,334	554	−208
Fourth Quintile	−2,484	−1	413	−424
Top Quintile	−11,286	−8,803	−2,054	825
All	−2,483	0	0	0

Source: Tax Policy Center, Numbers, Distribution of the 2001–2008 Tax Cuts, Tables T08–0157, T08–0159, T08–0161, T08–0163.

story changes pretty dramatically. The last three columns show the distribution of tax changes under different assumptions. In the first, the tax will be offset by equal lump-sum tax increases of $2,483. This makes the plan revenue neutral, but now the bottom three quintiles come out much worse off and only the top 20 percent is significantly better off. While it is unrealistic to expect a future Congress to enact a large lump-sum tax to pay back the loans taken out to finance the tax cuts, it is certainly plausible that broad-based spending cuts might result. In that case, lower-income families could be much worse off than if the tax cuts had never been enacted. Tax cuts that favor the rich are offset later by cuts in expenditures that benefit the poor.

The last two financing options are more progressive. One option would be a surcharge set as a flat percentage of income (column 3). In that case, the bottom four quintiles are still made worse off than without the tax cuts, but the burden on low-income families is more modest. However, it is also possible that the high-income people who seem to be the big winners from the policy will ultimately end up worse off. If the tax cuts are ultimately financed with a tax increase proportional to tax liability, the top quintile's apparent $11,000 windfall turns into a tax increase of over $800. The message of this exercise is that deficit financing does not reduce the burden of government spending—on the contrary—but it certainly blurs which people will bear the burden.

It should also be noted that the efficiency effects of tax cuts also depend on how they are ultimately financed. But it is impossible to discern for sure either the effects on the economy or on the distribution of well-being without knowing how the tax cuts are financed.

Is progressive taxation class warfare?

No. All societies must determine how to assign the burden of how to pay for government and how much to weigh fairness in this determination. In the United States nearly everyone agrees that the tax burden should depend on how well off one is. Exactly how the tax burden should vary between the poor, the middle class, and the rich will always be contentious, but the resolution of this issue—which depends on economic matters, as well as values—should be confronted rather than dismissed by sloganeering.

9

TAX ADMINISTRATION
AND ENFORCEMENT

How much does it cost to run the U.S. tax system?

The easy part of answering this question is to add up the budgets of the various tax administration agencies across the country. At the federal level, that would be the Internal Revenue Service, or IRS. In fiscal year 2010 the IRS budget was $12.4 billion, which comes to just 0.53 percent of all the taxes it oversees.[1] Collecting revenue at a cost of just 53 cents per hundred dollars sounds pretty good, and indeed the IRS often trumpets this percentage as a sign of its great efficiency. Among developed countries, this is one of the lowest cost-to-revenue ratios.[2] But this percentage by itself is not particularly informative about the efficacy of our tax process or tax administration. For one thing, countries vary widely in the scope of responsibilities placed on the tax authority. More importantly, a low ratio could simply mean that the task of collecting taxes is carried out poorly on some important dimensions, such as deterring evasion, so that revenue is collected in a capricious and inequitable manner.

The biggest reason why the 0.53 percent is an inadequate and incomplete measure of the cost of collecting taxes is that the IRS budget is only the tip of that iceberg. The bulk of the iceberg is the value of the time and the out-of-pocket expenses incurred both by taxpayers themselves and by third parties such as employers who withhold and remit tax on behalf of their employees and provide information reports. These costs, known as compliance costs, greatly exceed administrative costs, and therefore comprise most of the cost of collection. Our best estimate for the U.S. income tax compliance cost, done for fiscal year 2004, comes to 14.5 percent of individual and corporation income tax receipts—almost 30 times larger than the administrative costs! Extrapolating the 14.5 percent figure to fiscal year 2012 receipts yields a compliance cost of about $215 billion.[3]

More than half of this cost is the value of the time individuals spend on their tax affairs—3.5 billion hours—including recordkeeping, researching the law, and completing the returns. Using a 2,000-hour work-year implies that there is the equivalent of 1.75 million "hidden" IRS employees—you and us—who are essential to operating the self-assessment income tax system.

How does tax remittance and collection work?

Everyone would like the tax system to collect revenue with a minimum of hassle and invasion of privacy. But everyone also knows that some people will seek any advantage and escape their tax liability when they can get away with it, leaving everyone else—the dutiful and those without the opportunity to evade—facing a higher tax burden than otherwise. Thus, no government can simply announce a tax system and then rely on taxpayers' sense of duty to remit what is owed. Some dutiful people will at first undoubtedly pay what they owe, but many others will not. Over time the ranks of the dutiful will shrink, as they see how they are being taken advantage of by the others. Thus, paying taxes must be made a legal responsibility of citizens, with enforcement and penalties for noncompliance. A tax administration, and substantial taxpayer involvement, is needed to operate the tax collection system and to ensure that it runs efficiently and equitably.

For tax liabilities to be legitimate—neither arbitrary nor capricious—they must be based on observable and verifiable information. For a tax system to be cost-efficient, the information must be obtainable at a relatively low cost. For an impersonal tax like a retail sales tax, the key information is the volume and nature of transactions between businesses and consumers. For a personal tax like the individual income tax, information about individuals—their total income, sources of income, marital status, and perhaps also information about their charitable donations, medical expenses, and so on—must also be provided to the tax authority and monitored.

There are three key components of tax administration and enforcement: audits, information reporting and matching, and withholding. Although the dreaded tax audit gets the most attention, and therefore we'll talk about it first, the other two are at least as important.

Who gets audited, and why? What's the DIF?

The IRS publishes the percentage of income tax returns that are audited in broad classes of taxpayers. Overall, in fiscal year 2010, 1.1 percent of individual income tax returns, 1.4 percent of corporation income tax returns, and 10.1 percent of estate tax returns were audited.[4] The audit rate is much higher for those who report higher income: 8.4 percent if your total reported positive income exceeds $1 million, 2.7 percent if your income is between $200,000 and $1 million, and less than 1 percent for returns with income less than $200,000. Among corporations, the bigger ones are more likely to be audited: about 1.1 percent of corporations with total assets of less than $10 million, 14.3 percent for corporations with assets between $10 million and $1 billion, and 98.0 percent for the largest category—the 447 corporations with assets over $20 billion. Indeed, most of the very biggest corporations are subject to a continual IRS audit, with the audit team given a more or less permanent office at corporate headquarters.

To economize on its resources, the IRS would like to target its audits to tax returns more likely to have some funny business going on. To do so, it uses a procedure known as the DIF, standing for discriminant function, that calculates a numeric score for each individual and some corporate tax returns that it receives. Getting a high DIF score increases the likelihood that an examination of your return will result in a change to your income tax liability and is an important—but not the only—factor in determining which returns are audited. A

Figure 9.1 Cartoon © Mark Parisi. Permission granted for use, www.offthemark.com

return may also be selected for audit if information received from third-party documentation, such as Form W-2 from your employer, does not match the information on your return. In addition, your return may be selected for audit—or you may be contacted about whether you should but didn't file a return—as a result of information the IRS acquires from a host of other sources, including newspapers, public records, and from other individuals. The IRS Whistleblower Office pays people who identify persons who fail to remit the tax that they owe. If the whistleblower provides specific and credible information that the IRS uses to collect taxes, penalties, interest, or other amounts from a noncompliant taxpayer, it may award the whistleblower up to 30 percent of the additional collections.

What is information reporting?

Certain transactions that trigger tax liability must be reported to the tax authority, even though the party that reports the information does not have statutory liability for the tax. This system provides the tax authority with information that can be compared against the amount of tax actually remitted, allowing suspect returns to be identified and followed up on. In this case, successful evasion requires coordination between the party providing the information report and the party responsible for remittance, but—and here's the key—their incentives and willingness to falsify the data are unlikely to be the same and may even work in opposite directions.

Thus, a working system of information reporting discourages noncompliance by increasing the risk of detection at low cost to the tax authority. It forms a central element of all modern tax systems. In common with all other OECD countries, the United States requires information reporting (and withholding—see below) by employers on wages and salaries. Information reporting, but generally not withholding, is also required of financial institutions that pay interest and corporations that pay dividends. The United States has among the most extensive information reporting of any OECD country. Information reports cover interest and dividend distributions, certain gambling winnings, mortgage interest, proceeds from sales of stock and homes, student loan interest, tuition payments, IRA and medical savings account information, as well as partnership and S corporation income and estate or trust distributions.

In FY 2010 the IRS received 2.7 billion information returns, 88 percent of them electronically. Discrepancies between information returns and tax returns generated 4.3 million contacts between the IRS and taxpayers, resulting in $7.2 billion of additional assessments. The IRS used information returns from third parties to identify non-filers and initiated another 1.2 million contacts that resulted in $13.4 billion of additional assessments.[5]

The Housing Assistance Tax Act, signed into law by President George W. Bush in July 2008, expanded the scope of information returns to credit cards. As of 2011, financial firms that process credit or debit card payments are required to send their clients and, more importantly, the IRS, an annual form documenting the year's transactions. The new 1099-K must be filed when a merchant has at least 200 payment transactions a year totaling more than $20,000, but applies to all payment processors, including PayPal, and others that service very small businesses.

Another expansion of information reporting, which was part of the 2010 health care reform bill, would have required that all business payments or purchases that exceed $600 in a calendar year be accompanied by a Form 1099 filing. But this requirement, which was scheduled to take effect in 2012, provoked protest from small businesses and was repealed in 2011 before it could take effect.

How far to expand information reporting involves a delicate policy trade-off. Certainly having more third-party information makes the job of the IRS easier. But it requires the reporting party to track information and to send this information both to the IRS and to the taxpayer.

What is tax withholding?

Withholding refers to the situation where some or all of a tax liability must be remitted to the tax authority by someone other than the party that nominally "owes" the tax. Withholding allows the tax authority to collect the bulk of personal tax liability from a much smaller number of larger entities—usually businesses—who have more sophisticated recordkeeping and accounting systems. It also acts as a revenue safeguard, ensuring that some tax is remitted even when the statutory bearer fails to file a return or otherwise disregards their tax obligations.

Withholding is usually restricted to businesses and government agencies. Individuals in their capacity as employers and consumers are usually excluded—they are too numerous, with too high fixed costs, to be suitable withholding agents. A common source of tension is the conditions under which an employer is required to withhold for someone who works for the company. It must withhold with respect to payments to workers deemed to be employees but not those deemed to be independent contractors. Which category a worker falls under depends on the degree of control the company exerts over working conditions and the worker's independence.

To be able to withhold the appropriate amount of tax, the withholding agent must have an ongoing relationship with the statutory bearer of the tax, or, alternatively, the withholding scheme must be sufficiently simple to avoid the need for such a relationship, as is true for impersonal, usually flat-rate, taxes.

Who ultimately bears the burden of the compliance costs associated with withholding and information reporting? In the short term, it falls on the owners of the businesses, although, like other business expenses, the costs can usually be deducted from taxable income (reducing tax liability), and so get partially transferred to the government. Who ultimately bears the burden of compliance costs depends on the same demand and supply forces that determine the incidence of taxes themselves—they may be passed on to customers, workers, or others.

A few countries provide explicit compensation to income tax withholding agents. Most (the United States included) do not, but effectively compensate withholding agents by allowing a time lag between when tax liability is triggered and when remittance is due, so interest can be earned on the tax withheld before being remitted in the intervening period. Some American states offer "vendor discounts" to retailers who remit retail sales tax, often justified as a recompense for the compliance costs incurred.[6]

Upon further reflection, though, employer withholding is just the most familiar example of the general irrelevance of who remits tax for the question of who bears the burden of tax. (See page 22, "Who really bears the burden of tax?" for the general rule, and page 24, "Are there cases in practice where it does matter who writes the check?")

Why do people cheat on their taxes? Why do they comply?

Tax evasion has been around as long as taxes have.[7] The history of taxation is replete with episodes of evasion, often notable for their inventiveness. During the third century, many wealthy Romans buried their jewelry or stocks of gold coin to evade the luxury tax, and homeowners in eighteenth-century England temporarily bricked up their fireplaces to escape notice of the hearth tax collector.

Economists have an instinctive answer to why people cheat on their taxes—people evade when they think they can get away with it. This is consistent with what humorist Dave Barry had to say about tax compliance—"We'll try to cooperate fully with the IRS, because, as citizens, we feel a strong patriotic duty not to go to jail." People consider the chances of successful evasion, the penalty if they are caught, and decide whether to evade in just the same way they would decide whether to make any other gamble. The cost-benefit story for tax evasion explains very well the broad facts about tax evasion. The IRS calculates that the rate of noncompliance is just 1 percent for wages and salaries. This is not surprising, because information reporting and withholding by employers means that the chances of getting away with this type of evasion are very small. In sharp contrast, the estimated noncompliance rate for self-employment income is an astounding 57 percent.[8] Self-employment income is subject to neither information reporting nor withholding, making evasion detection much more difficult.

Nonetheless, considerable experimental (and anecdotal) evidence suggests that for many people tax evasion involves more than amoral cost-benefit calculation. Some social scientists stress the importance of intrinsic motivation, under which taxpayers comply with tax liabilities because of civic virtue, or a sense of duty, and even suggest that more punitive enforcement policies can backfire by making people feel that they pay taxes because they have to, rather than because they ought to. They switch from thinking of taxpaying as a civic duty to thinking of it as a cost-benefit calculation. A field experiment conducted in Israel found evidence to support the importance of intrinsic motivation in another setting. In order to encourage parents to pick their children up from day care on time, the center implemented fines for parents who were late. To their surprise, this led to an *increase* in the number of parents arriving late, probably because parents stopped feeling guilty about late pickups and started viewing added minutes as a purchase like any other.[9] Others argue that tax evasion decisions may depend on perceptions of the fairness of the tax system or what the government uses tax revenues for: a person with some of the spirit of Henry David Thoreau may avoid taxes because that person thinks government policy is wrong. During the Vietnam War, a number of pacifistic opponents to the war argued that it was

immoral to pay income taxes that would go toward supporting an "imperialistic" American military machine, and either
refused to pay income taxes at all or the portion of their tax
that would go to the war effort. Such individual judgments
can be complex; for example, expenditures on warfare might
be tolerated in a patriotic period, but rejected during another
period characterized by antimilitarism. This idea that people
are more likely to comply with their tax obligations, even
against their short-term material interest, if they believe in
what government is doing is certainly plausible and intuitive,
but there is little hard evidence, for the United States anyway,
that this is a big part of the tax evasion story.[10]

Tax noncompliance seems related to some other observable
characteristics of taxpayers. On average, married filers and
taxpayers younger than 65 have significantly higher average
levels of noncompliance than others. There is some evidence
that men evade more than women. There also seems to be substantial heterogeneity in tax evasion. The IRS tax gap studies
concluded that, within any group defined by income, age, or
other demographic category, there are some who evade, some
who do not, and even a few who overstate tax liability.[11]

A recent study based on IRS audit data found that the percentage of true income not reported on tax returns rises with
income, while the ratio of underreported tax liability to true
tax owed is higher for low-income individuals. The latter is a
result of our graduated tax structure, which implies that the
same percentage reduction in reported income results in a
higher percentage of underreported tax for a low-income individual relative to a higher income taxpayer.[12]

How much cheating is there?

This is not an easy question to answer—would a cheater respond
honestly to a survey question about this? But the best estimates
of the extent and nature of tax noncompliance anywhere in the
world are the "tax gap" studies done for the federal taxes that the

IRS oversees. The IRS has, beginning in 1979, periodically estimated what it calls the "tax gap," meaning how much tax should be paid, but is not paid voluntarily in a timely way. These studies provide separate estimates of the failure to pay the proper amount of tax due to underreporting of tax due on tax returns, non-filing, and nonpayment or late payment of taxes owed. The IRS comes up with its estimates by combining information from a program of random intensive audits with information obtained from ongoing enforcement activities and special studies about sources of income—like tips and cash earnings of informal suppliers such as nannies and housepainters—that can be difficult to uncover even in an intensive audit.

The most recent tax gap estimates, published in 2012, pertain to tax year 2006. The overall gross tax gap estimate for 2006 was $450 billion, which comes to 16.9 percent of estimated actual (paid plus unpaid) tax liability. Of the $450 billion estimate, the IRS expected to eventually recover $65 billion, resulting in a "net tax gap"—that is the tax not collected—for tax year 2006 of $385 billion, or 14.5 percent of the tax that should have been paid (table 9.1).

Almost two-thirds of all underreporting of income happens on the individual income tax. For the individual income tax, understated income—as opposed to overstating of exemptions, deductions, adjustments, and credits—accounts for over 80 percent of individual underreporting of tax. Business income, as opposed to wages or investment income, accounts for about two-thirds of the understated individual income. Taxpayers who were required to file an individual tax return, but did not file in a timely manner, accounted for less than 10 percent of the gap. While the individual income tax comprises about two-thirds of the estimated underreporting, the corporation income tax makes up about 17 percent and the payroll tax gap makes up about one-fifth of total underreporting.

The extent of misreporting varies enormously by the type of income or deduction. Based on an earlier tax gap study, only 1 percent of wages and salaries are underreported and

Table 9.1 Tax Gap Estimates, Tax Year 2006 (Money amounts are in billions of dollars)

Tax Gap Component	
Total Tax Liability	2,660
Gross Tax Gap	450
Overall Voluntary Compliance Rate	83.1%
Net Tax Gap	385
Overall Net Compliance Rate	85.5%
Non-filing Gap	28
Individual Income Tax	25
Estate Tax	3
Underreporting Gap	376
Individual Income Tax	235
Nonbusiness Income	68
Business Income	122
Adjustments, Deductions, Exemptions	17
Credits	28
Corporation Income Tax	67
Small Corporations (Assets < $10M)	19
Large Corporations (Assets > $10M)	48
Employment Tax	72
Self-Employment Tax	57
FICA and Unemployment Tax	15
Estate Tax	2
Underpayment Gap	46
Individual Income Tax	36
Corporation Income Tax	4
Employment Tax	4
Estate Tax	2
Excise Tax	0.1

Source: http://www.irs.gov/pub/newsroom/tax_gap_map_2006.pdf

4 percent of taxable interest and dividends are misreported. (These percentages exclude underreporting associated with non-filing.) Of course, wages and salaries, interest, and dividends must all be reported to the IRS by those who pay them; in

addition, wages and salaries are subject to employer withhold-ing. Self-employment business income is not subject to infor-mation reports, and its estimated noncompliance rate is sharply higher. As mentioned earlier, an estimated 57 percent of non-farm proprietor income is not reported, which by itself accounts for more than one-third of the total estimated underreporting for the individual income tax. All in all, over one-half of the tax gap is attributable to the underreporting of business income, of which nonfarm proprietor income is the largest component.[13]

Given the difficulty of accurately measuring tax evasion, it's very hard to say whether it's been going up, down, or staying roughly the same. The estimated tax gap percentage for 2006 is not much different from earlier tax gap estimates. However, taking into account changes in methodology and the uncer-tainty of the estimating procedures, one cannot infer any sta-tistically significant trend in compliance.

How much more tax could the IRS collect with better enforcement?

Claiming to be able to raise more revenue without increas-ing tax rates and sparing honest (hard-working) Americans is nearly irresistible for most, especially Democratic, politicians. The nearly $400 billion tax gap becomes an inviting target. But, realistically, more and smarter enforcement could bring in no more than one-fifth of that total. This would come from expanding information reporting, targeting the cash econ-omy, and from special initiatives such as the IRS crackdown on offshore bank accounts. However, while only a small por-tion of the tax gap could be collected with more enforcement, it remains the case that spending on enforcement, at least at current levels, brings in much more revenue than it costs.

Why not audit everyone?

A more interesting question is how much more tax the IRS *should* collect. The IRS does not audit everyone for good

Figure 9.2 Cagle Cartoons, Inc.

reason, for the same reason we don't station a police officer at every street corner, or a parking enforcement officer at every meter: it would be too costly, relative to the social benefits of reduced—or even eradicated—crime. The same is true for beefing up income tax enforcement so much that no one attempts to evade.

Jacking up the penalties for tax evasion might also deter tax evasion. Right now a "substantial understatement" penalty applies to individuals whose tax is understated by the greater of 10 percent of the correct tax or $5,000 and a "negligence or disregard of the rules of regulations" penalty is assessed on individuals who "carelessly, recklessly or intentionally disregard IRS rules and regulations." Both penalties are equal to 20 percent of the net understatement of tax. The penalty for underpayment resulting from fraud—intentionally falsifying information on a tax return—is equal to 75 percent of the underpayment of tax. In fiscal year 2010, the IRS assessed 37 million civil penalties amounting to $28 billion, $10 billion of which was eventually abated.[14] In 2010, they initiated nearly 5,000 investigations into fraudulent returns, which led to 2,184 convictions with over 80 percent of those convicted sentenced to prison.[15]

We resist substantially increasing the penalty for tax evasion for a couple of reasons. There is a vague but widespread belief that the punishment should fit the crime, and we are also reluctant to inflict very high penalties when we occasionally misidentify perpetrators.

Are refundable tax credits especially prone to tax evasion?

Soon after the Earned Income Tax Credit was introduced, an IRS audit program found that 34 percent of claimants filed for too large a credit, and 29 percent of claimants were completely ineligible.[16] Although this could be due to honest mistakes, as well as negligence or fraud, it provoked a lot of indignation. Congress required more audits of returns with EITC claims, and several statutory and administrative changes were made. Amazingly, in 2002 over 80 percent of all IRS compliance examination resources were devoted to the EITC.[17] This is even though, as of 2001, overstated credits, including the EITC, accounted for just under 5 percent of the estimated tax gap.[18]

Whether the EITC is especially prone to fraud is hard to tell. No other group of individual taxpayers is audited at such a high rate. When the Treasury Inspector General for Tax Administration examined tax compliance among EITC recipients, he concluded that they were most likely to cheat in the same circumstances as higher-income taxpayers. For example, self-employed people were much more likely to misstate their incomes or other eligibility criteria than wage and salary workers.

Do most people get tax refunds? Should I?

In fiscal year 2010, 85 percent of individual income tax returns filed provided a refund that averaged $3,000.[19] Why this is so is somewhat of a mystery. From the IRS point of view, it is not hard to see why they set up the standard employer withholding tables so that withholding exceeds tax liability and generates a refund. This provides a financial incentive for people to file a tax return in order to receive a refund, and the filing provides the IRS with information about the taxpaying population that is helpful in monitoring the tax collection process. Also, taxpayers are more likely to underreport if they owe money at tax time than if they expect a refund.

But why do taxpayers go along? By filing a Form W-4, taxpayers can adjust their withholding to minimize or even eliminate their refund. This way their refund would be lower, but their tax payments early in the tax year would be lower, too. By so doing, they could stop providing the government the equivalent of an interest-free loan. These days, when interest rates are very low, the cost of having the government take a larger bite of one's paycheck only to have it refunded back at the end of the year with no interest paid is not large, but most people were getting refunds even when interest rates were sky-high in the early 1980s.

Several factors might come into play. Some people may be afraid of incurring the penalty for under-withholding. Others may simply not be aware that they can adjust how much is withheld from their paychecks. Finally, for some people overpaying their tax during the year so as to qualify for a large refund is the best, or maybe only, way to accumulate a substantial sum of money, so that the refund is a form of self-induced forced saving.[20]

How many people use tax preparers? Do they help or hinder compliance?

The IRS has estimated that there are between 900,000 and 1.2 million paid tax return preparers.[21] In 2008, 58 percent of individual income tax returns were filed with the help of a paid tax preparer.[22] Only 5 percent of individuals filing Form

1040EZ used a paid preparer and 6 percent of those filing a 1040A used a paid preparer.[23] Somewhat surprisingly, of those returns that qualify for the EITC, generally low-income individuals and families, 67 percent used a paid preparer.[24] The 58 percent overall rate is certainly one of the highest in the world, but is not the highest—in 2006, 76 percent of Australian income tax returns were filed with professional preparer assistance.[25] The high U.S. preparer usage rate is in part a symptom of the complexity of the income tax system, as taxpayers want to be sure they comply with the law but also want to make sure that they take advantage of all the tax breaks they legally qualify for. It certainly makes sense that not everyone need be an expert on the tax system, and that professional expertise is available for hire. In this capacity tax preparers improve the quality of the income tax system.

Tax preparers are a heterogeneous bunch, to be sure. Most view their job as helping taxpayers comply with the law, and alerting them to credits, deductions, and other tax-saving provisions they qualify for. But a few are in cahoots with unscrupulous taxpayers, and a few others actively pursue tax cheating. Return preparer fraud generally involves the preparation and filing of false income tax returns by preparers who claim inflated personal or business expenses, false deductions, unallowable credits or excessive exemptions on returns prepared for their clients. Preparers may also manipulate income figures to fraudulently obtain tax credits, such as the Earned Income Tax Credit. In some situations, the taxpayer may not even know about the false expenses, deductions, exemptions, and/or credits shown on their tax returns.

The IRS is taking the role of tax preparers very seriously and has recently taken several measures to improve the quality and oversight of the tax preparation industry.[26] As of January 1, 2011, tax preparers must register with the IRS and obtain identification numbers, which must be used on all returns they help prepare. Beginning in the fall of 2011, certain paid preparers had to pass a competency test, and the IRS will conduct background checks on certain preparers. Starting in 2012, the IRS will require preparers to complete fifteen hours of annual continuing professional education consisting of three hours of federal tax updates, two hours of ethics, and ten hours of general federal taxation.

How should tax complexity be measured?

The federal income tax code had 172,000 words in 1955, but 3.8 million in 2010, and the number of words in federal tax regulations increased from 547,000 to more than 7 million during the same period.[27] Ten million plus words to lay out the tax law seems complex, indeed. The problem with the number of words or pages as a measure of complexity is that although more pages and more words in the tax code and tax regulations are symptomatic of more complexity, it is also true that

Figure 9.3 http://www.stus.com

more words may clarify otherwise uncertain areas of the tax law, and thus reduce complexity in some cases.

A more useful summary measure of the cost of tax complexity is the total resource cost of collecting the revenue—also called the cost of collection or operating costs. The cost of collection is the sum of the tax authority's budget (*administrative costs*) and the compliance costs incurred both by taxpayers themselves and by third parties such as employers, who withhold and remit tax on behalf of their employees and provide information reports. This includes both the involuntary costs that must be incurred to comply with the tax law and discretionary costs that are incurred voluntarily to facilitate avoidance or even evasion of tax liability.

Although the resource cost of collection is a useful measure of complexity, it does not capture all of its implications for policy. To see this, consider the following "simplification" proposal: relax the recordkeeping and calculation requirements of a particular tax credit, so that the average taxpayer would need to spend only one-half the time as before in order to qualify for the credit. Suppose that, in response to this change, the number of people who apply for and receive the credit quadruples. If judged solely on the resource cost measure, the tax system has become more complicated—total costs have doubled, after all. The policy question, though, is whether the process simplification is worthwhile, and to assess that one must also consider the social value of the credit being made available to more households who "deserve" it (and maybe also to some who do not).

Do fewer tax brackets promote simplicity?

Not really. Although many tax reform plans tout that they will cut the number of brackets (sometimes to just one, under a flat tax), the number of brackets does not matter much for tax simplicity. The complicated part of income tax is figuring out one's taxable income. Once that's done, figuring out tax liability is easy. In the old days, you could use a tax table printed in the 1040 instruction booklet; these days tax software does the calculation in a nanosecond.

Why is there a trade-off between simplicity and other goals such as fairness?

For one thing, fine justice, rather than rough justice, is costly. If we think it is fair that taxable income should be measured net of medical expenses, then people have to report—and the IRS has to monitor—people's medical expenses. If we think it is fair that people should get to deduct their charitable contributions, then we have to measure and monitor these deductions. Otherwise we could dispense with having to track these things and have a simpler income tax, but one in which tax liability would be the same between two families, each with $70,000 of income, but where one family incurred $20,000 of medical expenses and the other incurred none.

Should states be able to tax Internet and mail-order sales from other states?

The Internet and e-commerce have a direct and important impact on states' retail sales taxes. Imagine if a Michigan resident buys a bookcase over the Internet from Ikea. Like all 45 states with a retail sales tax, Michigan residents owe tax at the retail sales tax rate on purchases from out of state that are used at home. Technically, this is called a use tax, but the base and rate are the same as the sales tax. But who must remit this tax liability? The remote seller? Not necessarily, because the Supreme Court has ruled that out-of-state retailers need not remit the sales tax liability to the purchaser's state of residence unless that company happens to have a physical presence, such as a store, business office, or warehouse in that state. The Court ruled in 1992 that requiring the remote seller to remit the tax would violate the Commerce Clause of the Constitution. When an Internet retailer doesn't remit the tax, consumers

Figure 9.4 © 2012 Ted Rall. All Rights Reserved. www.rall.com

are required to remit the tax to their state when they file their annual state tax returns, but the rate of compliance of the "use tax" is very low; the Michigan Treasury estimated that in 2010, it collected about 1.3 percent of the use tax due on remote sales to Michigan residents.[28] In recent years, several states, led by New York, have enacted laws that require any remote retailer partnering with an in-state retailer to remit sales taxes due on purchases made by residents. Amazon, in particular, has fought these laws, and even shut down some local affiliates to escape the tax. But many prominent "brick-and-mortar" retailers, including Wal-Mart, have argued (reasonably, in our opinion) that there's no reason to provide remote retailers with a tax-connected advantage.

How fast are we moving toward e-filing?

More than 116 million returns, including almost 70 percent of individual tax returns but less than one-third of corporation income returns, were filed electronically in FY 2010.[29] Of the 98 million plus individual returns filed electronically, 34 million were filed online by the taxpayers, and 64 million were practitioner filed. Almost 3 million taxpayers, all with adjusted gross income below $58,000, used the IRS Free File program. This is a free federal income tax preparation and filing service developed through a partnership between the IRS and a group of private-sector tax software companies that can be accessed through www.irs.gov. For those with income below $58,000, it provides brand-name software for free; for those with higher income it offers online versions of the IRS paper forms and performs only basic calculations. Many believe the government should expand access to this free software, but this has been fiercely resisted by the software companies who see it as an incursion into their business.

Processing and managing a tax return filed electronically is less resource-intensive for the IRS than processing one filed manually, which is why they prefer e-filing. The rapid increase in electronically prepared returns suggests that most taxpayers prefer it, too, in part because refunds are received significantly faster.

If almost everyone uses tax software or paid preparers, should we stop worrying about complexity? Should we start worrying about democracy?

Once most everyone, or their tax preparer, uses software, the consequences of complexity change. If the data inputted must be subject to complex calculations, they are done automatically and correctly. So, calculation complexity becomes a nonissue. (If more and more data must be inputted, that remains a concern.) Thus, the outcry of citizens might be less of a bulwark against an even more labyrinthine tax system in the future.

This would be a problem for two reasons. First, an opaque tax system, where taxpayers have little sense how their inputted data affects their tax liability, limits how engaged they can be in the tax policy-making process. Taxpayers have no way to evaluate the fairness—or any other criterion—of the tax system, as applied either to themselves or to others. As Charles McLure of Stanford University has said, "Taxation without comprehension is as inimical to democracy as taxation without representation."[30]

An incomprehensible tax system may also render ineffective the incentives it is meant to provide such as encouraging charitable contributions. This may on balance be a good or a bad thing depending on how one judges the appropriateness of these incentives.

Could most taxpayers be spared any filing requirement (as in the United Kingdom)?

In several countries with an income tax most people need not file tax returns at all. We could do it here, but it would require major tax law changes. Return-free filing relies heavily on a process called "exact withholding," in which employers, financial institutions, and others remit tax liability on taxpayers' behalf in exactly the right amount so that no end-of-year reconciliation is necessary.

The main requirement for a return-free system is a relatively flat-rate tax schedule and few deductions and credits. In the simplest case, if we had a flat 25 percent income tax with no credits or deductions, then employers could withhold and remit 25 percent of wages and banks could withhold and remit 25 percent of interest and that would equal final tax liability for a taxpayer with only those two forms of income. However, under our current income tax, the personal exemption varies with family size and the standard deduction varies with filing status and there are multiple income tax brackets. Even if your employer knew your family size and filing status, your actual tax liability depends not only on your earnings from that job, but earnings from other jobs, spouse's earnings, and income from other sources. Deductions complicate tax liability even more, as do tax credits, eligibility for which may also depend on income and filing status. For that reason, return-free filing is infeasible without significant simplification and substantial reform.

The Bipartisan Policy Center's debt reduction task force (which Burman served on) proposed a tax reform plan that the Tax Policy Center estimated would not require income tax filing for about one-half of households. The proposal would have replaced personal exemptions, child-related tax credits (including the EITC), and the standard deduction with two refundable tax credits—one based on the number of children in the household and another based only on earnings of each spouse. The deductions for mortgage interest and charitable contributions would have been replaced with flat 15 percent refundable tax credits, paid directly to the mortgage holder or charity. There would be only two tax brackets—15 and 27 percent—and wages, interest, and dividends would be subject to withholding at a 15 percent rate. For most households in the 15 percent bracket, withholding would exactly match income tax liability. Households with income from self-employment, in the 27 percent tax bracket, or with complex tax situations would still have to file.

Could the IRS fill out our tax returns for us?

It is feasible, at least for relatively simple returns, but it's not easy to implement. The basic idea is that data from information returns (e.g., wages from W-2s, interest and dividends from 1099s) would automatically be entered onto a form for taxpayers and all they would have to do is check to make sure that the information is accurate and complete, and sign (electronically). If information was missing or inaccurate, the taxpayer would have to do some work, but this process could still give most taxpayers a head start on filing. This is how it works in Australia, Belgium, Denmark, Norway, and Spain.

But it's not something the IRS could implement tomorrow. For one thing, the IRS does not get some information returns until after the filing season is over. Employers and financial institutions would have to file sooner and the IRS would have to overhaul their information systems to match the data with taxpayer IDs early in the tax season. They would also have to invest in people to track down anomalies and answer questions from taxpayers. Economists Joe Cordes and Arlene Holen concluded that it would likely cost the IRS, employers, and financial institutions more than it would save taxpayers. California, however, which offers something called ReadyReturn for singles and heads of households with straightforward returns, says it saves a lot of money on every return filed through the automated system.

Only a fraction of eligible Californians take advantage of the automated return filing system. Critics say this is because the prefilled returns are rife with errors and taxpayers fear that the government has no incentive to let filers know about money-saving deductions and credits. On the other hand, lack of participation may primarily be due to ignorance—California has a tiny budget for publicizing the program—and the fact that federal tax returns must still be filed the old-fashioned way. A well-publicized federal program might attract much more widespread participation. There is also a concern that taxpayers might assume that the information on the government-filled return is accurate, which could increase the incidence of errors and penalties if, in fact, the government's information is flawed.

The Obama Administration has proposed a similar program to California's, which it calls Simple Return, and estimated that 40 percent of filers could use it, but the federal program has yet to be implemented.

Would simplifying tax compliance be unfair to H&R Block and Intuit?

One of the most peculiar arguments against process simplification is that it infringes on the inherent right of tax software makers' to profit from the current complex tax system.

That's not exactly the way the software companies put it, but that's the gist. They fought tooth and nail against California's ReadyReturn—actually killing it for one year (2006)—and have also been implicated in the demise of Virginia's free online system for preparing and filing state tax returns. The tax software firms complain that the government has a conflict of interest because it benefits financially if it overstates taxpayers' liability. On the other hand, unlike businesses, the government works for the voters so has an incentive to represent their best interest. And, as Joe Thorndike points out, if free file returns have errors, taxpayers can vote with their feet and choose to continue using software and paid preparers.[31]

Joseph Cordes and Arlene Holen argue that "Government involvement in personal income tax preparation...would reduce competition in existing markets.... It could also have the unintended effect of reducing innovation in rapidly evolving software markets."[32] But the market only exists because the tax-filing requirement created it. By mitigating the burden of filing, the government is lessening a burden that it imposed itself. And we find the idea that the government should maximize taxpayers' burdens as a way to boost innovation in the software industry bizarre.

What is a data retrieval platform?

One other process innovation, much less radical than a return-free system, is worth considering. Under a data retrieval system, taxpayers and paid preparers could view, access, and download tax information from a secure database maintained by the federal government, thus relieving them of having to obtain this information from employers, financial institutions, and other third parties as they have to do now. Supporters argue that having such a platform would facilitate communication between the IRS, on the one hand, and between taxpayers and return preparers, on the other.[33]

PART III

A TOUR OF THE
SAUSAGE FACTORY

10

MISPERCEPTIONS AND REALITY IN THE POLICY PROCESS

What does the public know about taxes?

Not all that much. For example, according to a comprehensive survey done by the National Public Radio, Kaiser Family Foundation, and the Kennedy School of Government, only 40 percent of respondents knew that the federal income tax system is progressive.[1] Only 5 percent of respondents knew that most Americans pay less than 10 percent of their household income on federal income taxes (table 10.1). A poll by CBS News/*New York Times* found that only 10 percent of respondents were aware that the Obama administration lowered taxes.[2]

Self-interest is not enough to get some people to stay informed on taxes. According to the IRS, one in five people eligible for the Earned Income Tax Credit do not receive it because they failed to claim it or they did not file a tax return.[3]

People were unaware that the estate tax only applies to the extremely wealthy people, less than 1 percent of decedents in 2010. One in five people inaccurately believed that the estate tax applies to 40 percent or more of Americans.[4]

The public's ignorance is not limited to federal taxes. Only one in three Californian voters knew the personal income tax was the main source of revenue for California,[5] and only a third

Table 10.1 Americans' Perception of Federal Income Tax Burdens on Most Americans

Average Tax Rate	All Americans	Tea Party Supporters	Actual Distribution
Less than 10 percent	5 percent	11 percent	86.5 percent
10–20 percent	26 percent	25 percent	12.9 percent
20–30 percent	25 percent	26 percent	
30–40 percent	10 percent	14 percent	0.6 percent
40–50 percent	2 percent	3 percent	
More than 50 percent	1 percent	1 percent	
Don't know	31 percent	20 percent	

Note: The survey question was: "On average, about what percentage of their household incomes would you guess most Americans pay in federal income taxes each year—less than 10 percent, between 10 and 20 percent, between 20 and 30 percent, between 30 and 40 percent, between 40 and 50 percent, or more than 50 percent, or don't you know enough to say?"

Source: Bruce Bartlett (2010) based on the *New York Times*/CBS News Poll and estimates on the distribution of tax burdens by the Joint Committee on Taxation.

of respondents knew that Proposition 13, the tax cap on proper-ties, applied to both residential and commercial property.[6]

What does the public think about taxes?

The public is unhappy with the tax system, although there's dis-agreement about what the most pressing problem is. In a poll conducted in December 2011 by the Pew Research Center, 55 percent of respondents said they thought the tax system was not too fair or not at all fair. Only 43 percent said the tax system was very or moderately fair.[7] A similar poll from March 2003 found that a slim majority (51 percent) thought the tax system was moderately or very fair, with 48 percent disagreeing (table 10.2).

Perhaps reflecting a decade of tax cuts, only 38 percent thought they paid more than their fair share in 2011, compared with 55 percent in 2003. When asked what bothers them most, 57 percent said it was that the wealthy did not pay their fair share (51 percent in 2003), 28 percent thought complexity was the top problem, and 11 percent thought their own tax burden was most troubling.

More people in 2011 than in 2003 thought that a complete overhaul was necessary to repair the tax system—59 percent in 2011 compared with 52 percent in 2003. Only about one-

Table 10.2 The Public's View of Federal Taxes

Shares in Percent	March 2003	December 2011
Federal tax system is...		
Very/Moderately fair	51	43
Not too/at all fair	48	55
You pay...		
More than fair share	55	38
Less than fair share	1	5
About right amount	41	52
What bothers you most...		
Amount you pay	14	11
Complexity of system	32	28
Feel wealthy people don't pay fair share	51	57
Tax system...		
So much is wrong, Congress should completely change	52	59
Works pretty well, Congress should make minor changes	44	34

Source: Pew Research Center, "Tax System Seen as Unfair, in Need of Overhaul," December 20, 2011, http://www.people-press.org/2011/12/20/tax-system-seen-as-unfair-in-need-of-overhaul/

third of respondents thought minor revisions would suffice (compared with 44 percent in 2003).

The survey also attempted to gauge the partisan divide between Democrats and Republicans. Republicans were much more likely than Democrats or independents to say that the tax system was fair (51 percent versus 40 percent and 42 percent, respectively). Unsurprisingly, none of the groups was prone to complaining about their own personal tax burden, and Republicans were most likely to report that they are paying the right amount of tax. All three groups believe major overhaul is needed; 63 percent of independents, 60 percent of Republicans, and 55 percent of Democrats.

The big difference by political party allegiance concerns what bothers people most. Forty-two percent of Republicans said it was complexity, compared with only 38 percent who thought the wealthy don't pay their fair share. But only 17

Table 10.3 Prime Complaint about Our Tax System, by Party, December 2011 (in percent)

	Total	Republicans	Democrats	Independent
Amount you pay	11	15	9	9
Complexity of system	28	42	17	29
Feel wealthy people don't pay fair share	57	38	73	57

Source: Pew Research Center, "Tax System Seen as Unfair, in Need of Overhaul," December 20, 2011, http://www.people-press.org/2011/12/20/tax-system-seen-as-unfair-in-need-of-overhaul/

percent of Democrats complained about complexity, while 73 percent said the wealthy should pay more. Most independents (57 percent) also thought the wealthy don't pay their fair share, while 29 percent were most troubled by complexity (table 10.3). This division may explain in part why bipartisan cooperation is so challenging on tax policy.

Perhaps not surprisingly, there is also a divide by income. Most low- and middle-income people believe that the wealthy are undertaxed, compared with only 44 percent of those with higher incomes.

How are new taxes enacted?

According to the U.S. Constitution, all tax bills must originate in the House of Representatives: "All bills for raising Revenue shall originate in the House of Representatives; but the Senate may propose or concur with Amendments as on other Bills" (Article 1, section 7). This would seem to constrain the legislative process, but it does so less than you might imagine. In every session of Congress, dozens of bills containing tax provisions pass the House. At that point, the provision allowing the Senate to propose amendments gives them carte blanche to substitute their own tax bill as a replacement for the House legislation.

Some tax proposals originate in the White House. The President must submit a budget to the Congress on or about the first Monday in February. The budget always includes many tax proposals. The Treasury Department produces an accompanying document called "A General Explanation of the Administration's Fiscal Year 2013 [or whatever year applies] Revenue Proposals," which contains a description of current law, reasons for change, and a discussion of each specific revenue proposal, as well as a detailed table of the Treasury Department's Office of Tax Analysis revenue estimates for each proposal and the package as a whole.

Both the House and Senate hold hearings on tax legislation where they hear from Administration witnesses, experts, and stakeholders. Generally, when the House and Senate pass different versions of tax bills, the leaders of each body appoint members of a conference committee with the mandate to vote out a conference report—a version that resolves differences in the two bills. If the House and Senate agree on the conference bill, it is sent to the president for his approval. If the president vetoes the bill, it can still become law if two-thirds of the members of the House and Senate vote to override the veto.

What are regulations and why are they important?

Often legislative language is only an outline of Congress's intentions that leaves many details unspecified. The executive branch implements the law via regulations. Sometimes legislation specifically instructs the Secretary of the Treasury (or of some other agency in the case of legislation that crosses jurisdictions) to promulgate regulations to implement the law. Other times Treasury writes regulations to provide guidance to taxpayers where the law is unclear. The regulations may be quite lengthy.[8] (See page 188, "How should tax complexity be measured?")

The Office of the Chief Counsel at the Internal Revenue Service takes the lead on the regulatory process in consultations with lawyers from the Treasury's Office of Tax Policy. Although critics sometimes complain that the IRS oversteps its authority by redefining the scope of legislation via regulations, the IRS and Treasury are required to implement the intent of the law and nothing more. However, the complexity of tax law often leaves much ground for interpretation. When the statute is unclear, regulators may consult the legislative history as embodied in the General Explanation document published by Congress's Joint Committee on Taxation. The IRS seeks advice from stakeholders and publishes draft versions for feedback before finalizing regulations.

Without regulations, taxpayers would have tremendous uncertainty about the law. Some might avoid taking advantage of murky tax incentives while others might use the fog to hide sketchy activities. That is, both avoidance and evasion would be more likely without adequate guidance. However, regulators also have to be very careful in interpreting the law. By clearly laying out the tax parameters, regulations may also create inadvertent avenues for legal tax avoidance. As in many other areas of government, regulators may profit handsomely passing through the revolving door to work for those who would like to find and exploit loopholes.

How does the tax sausage get made? (House and Senate rules)

Several rules may limit tax (and spending) legislation in Congress. A budget process sets limits for spending and targets for tax revenues. Legislation that would cut taxes below the level specified in the budget resolution may be blocked by any member who raises a "point of order" against it. In the House, this does not much constrain activity, because the leadership-appointed Rules Committee may waive the point of order and the rule is enacted by a simple majority vote. In the Senate, points of order carry more weight because waiving them requires 60 (out of 100) votes. Thus, a minority of 41 senators can block tax cuts that exceed the budget resolution targets.

Figure 10.1 © T- McCracken

In addition, Pay-As-You-Go (PAYGO) rules require that all tax cuts and spending increases be offset by other tax increases and spending cuts, respectively. The House let the PAYGO rule lapse in 2011, but it is still in force in the Senate. Tax cuts that are not offset are subject to a point of order and, again, may be blocked by a minority.

Sometimes Congress uses a special procedure called "reconciliation." Originally intended to facilitate difficult deficit reduction proposals, it has sometimes been used to increase deficits. If Congress opts for reconciliation, the House and the Senate agree to a set of spending and tax targets and the enacting legislation is "fast-tracked" for approval; it is not subject to points of order or a filibuster (the procedure by which one member may halt all activity in the Senate). The so-called Byrd Rule, named after the late Senator Robert Byrd (D-WV), does place some constraints on reconciliation. Members may raise a point of order in objection to the introduction of any provisions that are extraneous to taxes and entitlements in the reconciliation bill. Changes in discretionary programs or new regulations would fall afoul of this rule. That effectively would bar the provision unless 60 Senators agreed to override the point of order. The Byrd Rule also bars legislation that would increase the deficit outside the ten-year budget window. This is one reason why the Bush tax cuts were originally designed to expire after ten years.[9]

Who estimates the revenue impact of tax changes?

The nonpartisan Joint Committee on Taxation (JCT) is the official scorekeeper for changes in tax law. JCT has a staff of fifteen to twenty economists, most with Ph.D. degrees, who are charged with providing expert guidance regarding the effects of tax changes on federal revenues.

There are also revenue estimators at the Office of Tax Analysis (OTA) at the Department of the Treasury. They estimate the revenue effects of proposed tax changes used in preparation of the Administration's budget. Treasury revenue estimators also advise on revenue costs of bills as they are being developed. OTA and JCT are also responsible for producing estimates of tax expenditures. (See page 151, "What exactly is a tax expenditure?")

Although the JCT was created to provide an independent source of information for Congress, relations between the professional staffs of the two groups are generally cordial and respectful. Estimators at Treasury and the JCT consult informally about data sources and methods, and it is unusual for estimates to vary by a large amount between the two organizations.

How do they do it? Do they ignore behavioral responses to taxation?

Revenue estimates reflect the estimators' best judgment about the effect of a tax change, subject to some ground rules, which we'll return to. Estimators have large databases of individual, corporate, and estate tax returns and detailed calculators that allow them to estimate tax liability under current law and under alternative policies. Where necessary, they also use data from other sources or draw on evidence from published research.

The estimates account for likely changes in behavior in response to taxation; thus they are not "static," as is sometimes alleged by tax-cut supporters who complain that the JCT methods overstate the likely revenue loss because they understate the positive response of economic activity to the tax cuts. For example, if JCT were asked to estimate—"score" in Washington-speak—the effect of an increase in taxes on capital gains, they would account for the fact that, based on historical patterns, taxpayers are likely to report fewer capital gains when tax rates increase. Similarly, they account for more tax avoidance and evasion when ordinary income tax rates increase. So, for example, if tax rates were to increase by 10 percent across the board, they would estimate a change in tax revenues of less than 10 percent.

The revenue consequences of some provisions are easier to estimate than others. Provisions where eligibility is based entirely on information already reported on tax returns are comparatively simple to measure because those data are in the estimators' database. Forecasting the revenue consequences of new provisions based on information not currently reported to the IRS is more problematic. The estimators must estimate the eligible population, the amounts subject to taxation, deduction, or credit, and the take-up rate for the new provision. All of these elements may be highly uncertain. Also, sometimes estimates are very sensitive to projections of the overall level of economic activity. The Congressional

Budget Office makes those forecasts for the JCT, and the JCT revenue estimates must be consistent with this aggregate economic forecast, which often constrains what kinds of behavioral responses can be built into the revenue estimates. For example, consider a proposal to reinstate an investment tax credit. In this case the estimated response of investment could not be so large that it would imply GDP growth that exceeded the CBO estimate.

Finally, about those ground rules. Estimators must usually estimate the cost under a "current law baseline." This means that the basic assumption is that all provisions in current law will play out exactly as legislated unless they are modified in the bill under consideration. This technical-sounding rule can make a big difference to revenue estimates. For example, all of the Bush tax cuts are currently scheduled to expire at the end of the 2012. Starting in 2013, the revenue cost of all deduction and exemptions will increase because tax rates will be higher. Also, nonrefundable tax credits will cost more revenue because taxpayers will have more tax liability before credits. If estimators reasonably assumed that most of the tax cuts would be extended because the president and Congress seem to agree on that, these revenue estimates would change markedly. But JCT is barred from making that judgment.

Most controversially, the official estimators must assume that macroeconomic aggregates are fixed. That means that even if the economists at the JCT believed that a particular tax change would boost the economy, they would have to ignore the additional revenues that would come as a result. This seems like an extreme assumption, but it probably protects estimators from even more controversy. (See below.)

There are some other potentially important scoring conventions. For one thing, estimators typically must provide their best guess of the most likely outcome, rather than estimate the average expected revenue effect. This can be significant in the case of provisions that only take effect in rare circumstances. For example, there is a tax credit for oil production from relatively unproductive oil wells (so-called marginal wells) when oil prices fall below a certain level. Because oil prices are not expected to fall that much, the credit is scored as having zero revenue cost, even though it is clearly valuable to the industry when oil prices fall, which lobbied heavily for it. The problem with this scoring convention is that it treats quasi-insurance programs run through the tax code as if they cost little or no revenue because, except when the insurance is actually needed, they do cost little. The drawback of changing the rule, however, is that JCT revenue estimates would more often turn out to be off the mark.

Another important feature of the revenue estimation process is that estimators do not score the long-run effect of tax policies, even if they are markedly different from the effects within the official ten-year budget window. This can be important for provisions that shift the timing of economic activity. For example, Congress is currently debating whether to allow multinational firms a tax break if they repatriate dividends from foreign subsidiaries during a "repatriation holiday" period. Most observers expect that if the law were enacted, it would produce a surge in tax revenues during the repatriation period, but lose even more revenue over ensuing years. JCT can only show the lost revenue to the extent that it occurs over the budget period. Another example is a provision that allowed taxpayers to convert traditional IRAs into Roth IRAs, which increased revenue during the conversion period at the expense of much larger revenue losses over ensuing decades. (See page 114, "Stupid Tax Tricks: Roth IRA conversions.") A concern is that this rule makes such policies that bring revenue from the future into the ten-year window look more attractive than they really are, exacerbating the large long-term fiscal imbalance the country already faces.[10]

What is dynamic scoring?

Dynamic scoring involves incorporating macroeconomic feedback effects into estimates of tax changes. Most economists would agree that a major tax reform in which loopholes were eliminated and tax rates lowered, holding overall revenues constant, would increase economic growth, although there would be a wide range of estimates of how much. And indeed, official scorers were instructed to modify the baseline to account for the salutary effects of the Tax Reform Act of 1986 while it was being debated.

Unfortunately, the vast majority of tax proposals considered by Congress would not fit into this category of likely growth enhancers. While everyone likes lower tax rates, base broadening is a lot more popular with economists than it is with the people who pay higher taxes as a result. Tax cuts enacted since 2001, for example, have lowered marginal tax rates, but they also narrowed the tax base by creating a slew of new targeted tax breaks—including the one for unproductive oil wells mentioned earlier—that are likely to hurt the overall economy rather than help it. This makes assessing the net effect problematic.

The biggest problem, though, is that recent tax bills have produced significant revenue losses with no indication of how those losses will be offset. Without knowing that, it is impossible to assess the economic effects, or even to measure whether the economy will be stronger or weaker in the long run.

Depending on how the increased deficits are closed, there could be dramatically different economic results. The best-case scenario for economic growth is for deficits to be financed by cuts in transfer programs or increases in relatively efficient taxes. That deficits might force spending constraint appears to be the logic behind the "starve the beast" rationale for deficit-financed tax cuts, but there is no evidence that this tactic actually works. It is not clear why spending cuts would be easier in the future than they are now. Will it be easier to cut Social Security and Medicare twenty years from now when all the baby boomers are retired (and AARP's membership has exploded)?

The worst-case scenario for economic growth is this: years from now, our profligate budgetary policies lead to dramatically higher interest rates as the federal government's solvency comes into doubt, triggering a massive recession. Taxpayers blame this on the tax cuts for the rich and decide to deal with budget problems by raising tax rates on high-income folks. (And they leave in place all the middle-class tax cuts like the child credit, higher standard deduction, and 10 percent bracket.) We think it is safe to say that in JCT's, CBO's, and Treasury's models, such a tax increase would prove most damaging to growth. The net effect would be a much weaker economy than would exist had the tax cuts never been enacted.

To be clear, this long-term risk also means that deficit-financed spending could also be more costly than would appear in either a balanced-budget scenario or one assuming less damaging deficit offsets in the future.

Because it is impossible for official revenue scorers to predict how the deficits will be closed, it is impossible to reliably predict the long-term effect of deficit-financed tax cuts. For related reasons, it is a challenge to predict the short-term effects as well. In the standard Keynesian macroeconomic model, short-term fiscal stimulus (a spending increase or tax cut) boosts the economy during downturns by spurring households to spend and businesses to invest, creating more demand and thus more jobs. When the economy is at full employment, deficit-financed tax cuts can damage the economy by creating inflationary pressure.

The wild card is the Federal Reserve, which tries to stimulate the economy when it is underperforming and slow it down when inflationary pressures arise. Fed policymakers might respond to tax cuts by tightening up monetary policy to prevent inflation. Because monetary policy affects the economy more slowly than fiscal policy, short-term deficits that are larger than the Fed had expected can still have an immediate effect, but the effect beyond that is complicated by the Fed's response. While this is probably more predictable than how future Congresses will deal with the national debt, it significantly complicates forecasting the effects of fiscal policy beyond a year or so.

Must taxes be raised?

No. While tax revenues are at the lowest level as a share of GDP in more than fifty years, they are expected to increase as the economy rebounds and the stimulus measures expire. However, population aging and rising health care costs will put unprecedented pressures on the federal budget. Unless Congress figures out a radical cure for health cost inflation, services would have to be cut drastically from current levels to balance the budget with the tax system of current law.

Figure 10.2 shows CBO projections for spending for Social Security, Medicare, Medicaid, and health reform assuming recent health care trends continue indefinitely and assuming that excess health care cost growth can be stopped after ten years. Even if we are remarkably successful at controlling

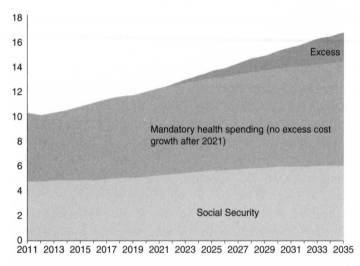

Figure 10.2 Federal mandatory spending on health care and Social Security, with and without excess health cost growth after 2021, as percentage of GDP. *Source*: CBO Long-Term Budget Outlook, 2011.

health care costs, federal government spending on these programs will exceed 14 percent of GDP by the year 2035. That is roughly the current level of total tax revenues.

Either there will have to be unprecedented cuts in public programs or revenues will have to rise significantly. Over the long term, the best solution is probably a mix of higher revenues and spending cuts.

Can we solve the problem by raising tax rates only on those with high incomes?

Not unless spending is cut drastically. Rosanne Altshuler and colleagues at the Tax Policy Center estimated what top tax rates would need to be to get the deficit down to 2 percent of GDP by 2019 assuming no change in spending patterns. If only the top two tax brackets (applying to married couples with income above $250,000) are adjusted, the top rate would have to increase to almost 91 percent, if we ignore the likely behavioral responses to such rates. Considering that there would be an enormous amount of avoidance at such high rates, it's clearly not feasible to tame the deficit by simply raising top tax rates. It's probably not even feasible if the top three rates are adjusted. (See table 10.4.)

Table 10.4 Income Tax Rates Required to Cut Deficit to 2 percent of GDP in 2019, Administration Baseline

Current Tax Rates	Raise All Rates	Raise Top Three Rates	Raise Top Two Rates
10.0	14.9	10.0	10.0
15.0	22.3	15.0	15.0
25.0	37.2	25.0	25.0
28.0	41.7	60.8	28.0
33.0	49.1	71.7	85.7
35.0	52.1	76.1	90.9

Source: Rosanne Altshuler, Katherine Lim, and Roberton Williams, 2010, Desperately Seeking Revenue, Tax Policy Center, presented at "Train Wreck: A Conference on America's Looming Fiscal Crisis," January 15, 2010, available at: http://www. taxpolicycenter.org/publications/url.cfm?ID=412018

Another option would be to raise the tax burdens on those with high incomes by paring or eliminating preferences that disproportionately benefit the wealthy, such as the low tax rates on capital gains and dividends. Unlike increases in tax rates, broadening the tax base actually reduces the scope for tax avoidance. Nonetheless, given the size of our long-term fiscal imbalance, it is likely that spending will need to be cut and taxes raised on more than the highest earners.

11

SNAKE OIL

The FairTax sounds, well, fair. Is it?

Well, it depends on your definition of fair, but it would be a large tax increase on the middle class, would invite tax evasion, and at the rates advertised would not come close to raising enough revenue to fund the government without massive borrowing. And, one more quibble: the advertised rates are misleading.

The FairTax is the name given by supporters to a national retail sales tax. In principle, it's similar to the sales taxes levied by most states, but the FairTax would apply to all goods and services while most state sales taxes exempt some crucial expenditure items, such as food, medical expenses, and housing, from the tax base. Advocates recognize that a sales tax is regressive and propose to offset the impact on the poor by providing an annual "prebate"—a payment equal to the sales tax liability of a family at the poverty level if they spend all of their income. FairTax advocates claim that a 23 percent tax would bring in enough revenue to replace all federal taxes plus cover the cost of the prebate.

This sounds really good, but it's very misleading. For one thing, state sales taxes are added onto the price of goods, so a 30 percent sales tax would raise the after-tax price of a $1.00 item to $1.30. In the FairTax publicity, the tax rate is expressed as a percentage of the tax-inclusive price. So what we would naturally consider to be a 30 percent sales tax is reported by advocates as a 23 percent tax (0.30/1.30). FairTax proponents say this makes the FairTax comparable to income taxes (recall that a 100 percent sales tax rate is akin to a 50 percent income tax rate), which are reported as a share of before-tax income, but it does also make the FairTax rate seem like a smaller sales tax than it is.

A more fundamental problem is that the 23 (or 30) percent tax rate would not come close to replacing the revenue lost from repealing other federal taxes. William Gale of the Brookings Institution shows that the FairTax calculations are based on a set of logically inconsistent assumptions. In particular, when the FairTax designers estimated government revenues under the sales tax, they (implicitly) assumed that consumer prices would rise by the full amount of the sales tax; when they estimated government spending needs, they (implicitly) assumed consumer prices would stay constant. Both of those assumptions cannot be valid at the same time. As a result, the calculation either overstates revenues, understates spending needs, or both.

The FairTax people also assume that there would be no evasion under their plan, which is Pollyannaish at best. A 30+ percent sales tax would provide a huge incentive to move sales underground, especially in sectors like grocery stores where gross margins are often 1 or 2 percent. The income tax is estimated to have a 15 percent "tax gap." It's likely that evasion would be even more of a problem with the FairTax. All told, the actual tax rate would likely have to be more like 50 percent or more to replace all other federal taxes.[1]

But the fatal flaw is probably the effect of such a tax on the middle class. The prebate would protect those with low incomes and, given the clear tax break it provides to high-income families, middle-class people have to make up the lost revenue. President Bush's tax reform panel estimated that replacing just the federal income tax with a national sales tax would on average boost middle-income tax bills by $5,000—and that's after the prebate!

For that reason alone, notwithstanding its appeal to occasional presidential contenders like Mike Huckabee and Ron Paul, the FairTax is not going to ever become law, nor should it.

Wouldn't a flat tax be super-simple and efficient?

As discussed in chapter 4 the flat tax is basically a VAT, but with a wrinkle: businesses are allowed a deduction for wages paid, but the employees are subject to a "flat tax" on their wages above an exemption level, typically set at around the poverty level. (See page 105, "What is the flat tax?") Overall, a flat tax would be substantially simpler than a similarly comprehensive income tax. But the same pressures that make the current tax system riddled with deductions and credits would apply to the flat tax. It is not clear that it could stay pristine. Indeed, Texas governor Rick Perry proposed to allow deductions for charitable contributions and mortgage interest under his "flat tax" proposal in the recent Republican presidential primary campaign. So the comprehensive tax base of the flat tax may not be very durable.

While applauding the simplicity of a flat tax, many economists are even more drawn to the fact that it is a consumption tax and therefore, for reasons explained in chapter 4, does not distort savings and investment decisions.

How about offering a new tax system on an elective basis?

Rick Perry attempted to allay concerns about the regressivity of his flat tax proposal by saying that taxpayers could elect to stay in the current tax system if they like. Republican presidential candidate John McCain made a similar proposal in the 2008 campaign, and that elective alternative tax system was adopted by House Budget Committee Chairman Paul Ryan (R-WI) in his tax reform proposal.

The main problem with these take-your-pick tax systems is that they would lose an enormous amount of tax revenue. As a general rule, taxpayers will only elect an alternative if they expect to save money. Yes, they might make an election to save hassle, but they're unlikely to pay much for simplification. The chances are excellent that if Rick Perry's optional alternative flat tax became law, TurboTax® would include a calculator to determine which alternative would result in lower taxes.

The Tax Policy Center estimated that the Perry plan would reduce revenues by between $600 billion and $1 trillion per year (depending on unspecified assumptions). John McCain's optional alternative tax plan would have reduced revenues by around $7 trillion over a decade.

Besides being fiscally irresponsible, these optional alternative systems would also add new complexity. They would effectively create an alternative maximum tax—mimicking (and compounding) the complexity of the existing alternative minimum tax. Taxpayers would have the incentive to game the system by switching from one system to the other to minimize tax liability; limiting the ability to switch back and forth would penalize those people whose circumstances change unexpectedly, and provoke serious tax envy among those who are stuck with the less attractive of the two options.

The bottom line is that offering a radical reform plan as an optional system might be good politics, but it's not good tax policy.

What is the "starve-the-beast" theory?

The "starve-the-beast" theory argues that more tax revenues don't reduce the deficit; they just enable more (wasteful) government spending. The only way to restrain spending is to cut taxes—that is, starve-the-beast (i.e., the government).

On its face, this argument appears plausible, but the evidence, especially the recent evidence, is not kind to it. Indeed, it is hard to imagine that spending could have been higher as tax revenues were slashed by the Bush tax cuts. Government grew much faster from 2001 to 2009 than during the Clinton administration. While some of that was war-related, nondefense discretionary spending also grew and there was a major expansion in Medicare—the largest expansion of entitlement spending since Medicare was first enacted. It appears that instead of constraining spending, deficit financing was contagious. If deficits don't matter when considering tax cuts, why should they be considered when evaluating a new drug benefit or a "bridge to nowhere?"

The late William Niskanen, former president of the libertarian Cato Institute, posited an intriguing critique of "starve-the-beast."[2] If deficits finance 20 percent of government spending, he argued, then citizens perceive government services as being available at a discount. Services that are popular at 20 percent off the listed price would garner more support than if offered at full price.

He found statistical support for his theory by comparing the time patterns of revenues and changes in spending. He hypothesized that higher—not lower, as suggested by the starve-the-beast theory—revenues could constrain spending and found strong support for that conjecture based on data from 1981 to 2005. Another Cato researcher, Michael New, tested Niskanen's model in different time periods using a more restrictive definition of spending (nondefense discretionary spending) and found the same result as Niskanen did.[3]

Niskanen and New might even have understated the effect of deficits on spending. The message during the last decade seems to have been not that spending and tax cuts were available at a discount, but that they were free. Spending for wars, Medicare expansion, and "No Child left Behind" happened at the same time that taxes were falling. Citizens could be forgiven for forgetting that there is *any* connection between spending and taxes.

We surmise that if President Bush had announced a new war surtax to pay for Iraq, or an increase in the Medicare payroll tax rate to pay for the prescription drug benefit, these initiatives would have been less popular. Given that the prescription drug benefit only passed the House of Representatives by one vote after an extraordinary amount of arm-twisting, it seems unlikely that it would have passed at all if accompanied by a tax increase.

Starve-the-beast doesn't work. Indeed, columnist Bruce Bartlett called it "the most pernicious fiscal doctrine in history."[4] The cost of what government does is not measured by the taxes in place to fund it, but rather by what it spends.

Does the taxpayer protection pledge protect taxpayers?

Obviously, protecting taxpayers sounds great, but the pledge will do anything but (in our opinion). The pledge is the brain-child of Grover Norquist, president of a group called Americans for Tax Reform that favors a much smaller federal government. The pledge—a promise to never, under any circumstances, raise taxes—has been signed by 235 Congressmen and 41 Senators.

The pledge works to achieve a smaller government if starve-the-beast works, but it doesn't. And every time legislators vote for a deficit (which is to say, almost every year), they implicitly vote for higher future taxes. Over the long run, taxes must equal spending. Spending that is not paid for now must be paid, with interest, in the future. As the oil filter commercial used to warn, "You can pay me now, or pay me later." Large-scale cutbacks in entitlement programs could help to complete the square, but the American public has not yet shown any appetite for this.

Moreover, the taxpayer protection pledge applies not just to tax rate increases, but also to scaling back tax expenditures, which are more appropriately considered to be spending cuts. Any plan that cuts spending reduces the present value of current and future taxes. The major bipartisan debt reduction plans protect future taxpayers much more than the status quo, but they are off limits to the tax-pledge signatories because of the cuts in tax expenditures.

What is the "two Santa Claus" theory?

Conservative writer Jude Wanniski came up with the idea of the two Santas as a way to revive the Republican Party in the 1970s.[5] He argued that the Democratic Party won elections

Figure 11.1 Cagle Cartoons, Inc.

because it always played Santa—promising more and more new government programs without worrying about who would pay for them.

Republicans back then were the party of fiscal responsibility, playing Scrooge to the Democrats' Santa. Mr. Wanniski might have forgotten that Republican President Richard M. Nixon expanded both the social safety net and the military, and that Republican President Dwight D. Eisenhower created the national highway system. But this simple explanation for why the Democrats had controlled Congress for so long resonated with Mr. Wanniski's audience.

He told the Republicans that if the Democrats were going to play Santa, the Republicans had to be Santa, too. When the Democrats promised more spending, the Republicans should promise lower taxes—two Santas. And, for heaven's sake, don't worry about the deficit.

But Mr. Wanniski also thought that if the Republicans cut taxes, tax revenue would rise—that we were on the wrong side of the Laffer curve. (See page 135, "What is the Laffer Curve?")

Tax cuts would pay for themselves, the budget would be balanced, no deficits would ensue, and Republicans would win.

Republicans never really tried Mr. Wanniski's prescription until George W. Bush entered the White House in 2001. True, in 1980 Ronald Reagan ran on a platform of tax cuts, but soon after his election backed off and raised taxes when the deficit exploded and interest rates spiked. In 1990, the first George Bush famously raised taxes in an attempt to tame the deficit—and paid the ultimate political price in the 1992 election.

President Clinton might have wanted to spend more; and the congressional Republicans, led by Newt Gingrich, desperately wanted to cut taxes. Instead of compromising on a giant underfunded government, those two Santas fought to a stalemate and created the first budget surpluses in a generation.

But both parties embraced the "two Santa theory" in the 2000 presidential election. Al Gore promised lots of new spending and big tax cuts. Mr. Bush promised an expanded role for government in education and much bigger tax cuts than Mr. Gore.

The era of surpluses died because the younger Mr. Bush was not about to repeat his dad's mistake. His vice president, Dick Cheney, growled that "deficits don't matter." Mr. Bush cut taxes by trillions of dollars while creating a huge prescription drug entitlement program, waging two wars, and increasing nondefense discretionary spending even faster than Mr. Clinton. Mr. Bush left office with a burgeoning deficit and record-low approval ratings, but both sides continued to embrace the two Santa theory. Candidate Barack Obama criticized Mr. Bush's fiscal profligacy, but proposed new spending programs and tax cuts that would have increased the deficit almost as much as Mr. Bush's policies. Candidate John McCain was more restrained on spending, but his huge promised income tax cuts would have led to even larger deficits.

12

TAX REFORM

Tax reformers talk about a broad base and low rates. What does that mean?

The base refers to the definition of income subject to tax. The broader the base—meaning the fewer the deductions, exclusions, and credits—the lower tax rates can be to raise a given amount of revenue. So a broader base is consistent with lower tax rates. Lower tax rates are more efficient and fewer deductions, exclusions, and credits make the tax code simpler. Also, a broad base is generally easier for the tax authorities to administer and less prone to tax avoidance and evasion.

Is the broadest base always the best base?

No. There are good reasons to allow certain deductions and exclusions. Some deductions, like for legal expenses in a lawsuit, are necessary to measure income properly. Taxing businesses' gross receipts rather than net income—as some states have recently started doing—would be quite simple, but would distort economic activity on a number of dimensions. Deductions for business costs are necessary to properly measure income. As we have already argued, a deduction for extraordinary medical expenses, which reduce a family's well-being below what their pre-deduction income suggests, narrows the personal income tax base but arguably makes the distribution of tax burdens more equitable.

It also makes sense to run some subsidies through the tax code. The challenge for reformers is to balance out the gains from the subsidy against the costs of complicating the tax base.

Does the framing of taxes matter?

Sometimes it does, both politically and substantively.[1] For example, the move to scale back or eliminate the estate tax really gained steam when repeal advocates started calling it the "death tax." Polls showed that opposition to the "death tax" was much higher than opposition to the "estate tax," even though the difference is purely semantic.

Another example is the almost ubiquitous state sales tax. Typically the tax is not visible on the store shelves, but is added to the price of goods purchased at the checkout counter. Harvard economist Raj Chetty and coauthors wondered whether people would react differently if the tax was displayed along with the pre-tax price on grocery aisles. Chetty found that people were significantly less likely to buy items when the sales tax was included with the price shown on the shelf. (See page 24, "Are there cases in practice where it does matter who writes the check?")

What is a revenue-neutral tax change?

Revenue-neutral means that the tax change is not expected to add or subtract from the deficit over the budget period, which is typically ten years. The Tax Reform Act of 1986 was designed to be revenue-neutral over the five-year budget period then used by official scorekeepers. It was designed to be revenue-neutral to remove deficit politics from the political debate. (It actually turned out to lose revenue because official scorekeepers overestimated the revenue gain from the corporate tax changes.)[2]

Should tax reform and deficit reduction be separated?

One critical point in the current (circa 2012) debate about tax reform is whether it should be revenue-neutral. Some argue that it should be so as to follow the successful blueprint laid out in 1986. Also, many advocates of revenue-neutrality object to tax increases on principle. But some counter that our long-run budget problems are so severe that more revenues will be needed and potentially tying tax reform to lessening future debt burdens could be an effective strategy.

We side with those who think more revenue will be needed and that tax reform should be part of a revenue-raising, deficit-reducing plan. The two go together in that raising revenue is less damaging if done with a more efficient tax system. As discussed below, the Bowles-Simpson deficit reduction plan and the proposal by the Bipartisan Policy Center's Debt Reduction Task Force both followed this approach. They would eliminate many tax expenditures to finance income tax rate cuts, as in 1986, but reserve some of the revenue gains for deficit reduction. The BPC plan cut fewer tax expenditures, but would introduce a new VAT to augment federal revenues.

Are there some sensible tax reform ideas?

Sure. President George W. Bush put together a blue ribbon panel to propose fundamental tax reform, and they came up with two alternative packages that would have each been simpler and more efficient than the existing tax code. One option would have radically simplified the tax code by eliminating many tax expenditures and converting many of the remaining tax deductions to flat credits. One insight of the Bush tax reform panel was that while tax experts view the standard deduction as a simplification—because people who do not itemize don't need to keep records on charitable contributions, mortgage payments, taxes, and so on—most real people think it's unfair that high income people can deduct those items while lower income people can't. The proposal would have dispensed with itemization.

The "simplified income tax" under the Bush panel's scheme would have reduced the number of tax brackets and cut top rates, eliminated the individual and corporate alternative minimum tax, consolidated savings and education tax breaks to reduce "choice complexity" and confusion, simplified the Earned Income and Child Tax Credits, simplified taxation of Social Security benefits, and simplified business accounting. The alternative "growth and investment" tax plan would have lowered the taxation of capital income compared with current law—somewhat similar to Scandinavian dual income tax systems.

As mentioned earlier, the Bipartisan Policy Center Debt Reduction Task Force contained a tax reform plan aimed at simplifying the tax code enough so that half of households would no longer have to file income taxes. That plan would create a new value-added tax and use the revenue to cut top individual and corporate income tax rates to 27 percent.[3]

President Obama empaneled another commission, commonly called the Bowles-Simpson Commission (after its two heads) with the mandate to reform the tax code and reduce the deficit. (The Bush panel had been instructed to produce a revenue-neutral plan.) The commission failed to achieve the super-majority required to force legislative consideration, but a majority supported the chairmen's blueprint. Bowles-Simpson would have eliminated even more tax expenditures than the BPC Task Force, allowing substantial tax rate cuts without the need for a new VAT or other revenue source.[4]

Senators Ron Wyden (D-OR) and Dan Coats (R-IN) produced a more incremental tax reform plan, designed to be revenue-neutral and preserve the most popular tax breaks.[5] It would eliminate the AMT and cut the corporate tax rate to 24 percent while capping individual income tax rates at 35 percent. The cost of these provisions would be offset by closing or scaling back various tax expenditures. The proposal would raise tax rates on high income taxpayers' long-term capital gains and dividends from 15 to 22.75 percent. It would revise the formula the federal government uses to adjust tax parameters for inflation, generally cutting the revenue cost of annual inflation adjustments. (See page 50, "How does inflation affect the income tax?") The plan would also reduce businesses' interest deductions. It would consolidate and simplify individual tax breaks for saving and education. The most radical process change is that the plan would require the IRS to prepare pre-filled tax returns for lower-income filers. (See page 194, "Could the IRS fill out our tax returns for us?")

Columbia law professor Michael Graetz has an even more sweeping proposal.[6] He proposes to raise the income tax exemption level so high that 100 million households would no longer owe income tax. To make up the lost revenue a new 10 to 15 percent VAT would be enacted. Only families with incomes above $100,000 would have to file an income tax return. The plan would also substantially simplify the income tax for those few who continued to file, but the main simplification would be to take most households off the income tax rolls entirely. (However, households would still have to supply information to claim new refundable tax credits aimed at offsetting the regressivity of the VAT.)

What have we learned?

Tax policy is, and will continue to be, a tremendously contentious issue in the United States. In part this is because taxes come out of our pocketbooks, whether we like it or not. The issue inflamed American revolutionaries at the birth of the nation and still resonates to this day.

Alas, the stirring call to arms of "no taxation without representation" has devolved considerably so that today the American public debate about taxation—even during, or especially, in a presidential election year—rarely goes beyond platitudes and accusations. The rhetoric and misinformation is abetted by the extreme complexity of the tax system, which makes it incomprehensible to all but a handful of experts. On crucial questions that should inform tax policy choices, such as how features of the tax system affect economic growth, the supposed economics experts disagree and there is little hope that this will change any time soon. Beyond economics, the right tax policy also depends on societal values about equity, privacy, and freedom—equally contentious issues.

Our hope is that this book has helped to penetrate the fog of tax policy in America by explaining what economists do and do not know so you can evaluate what the sensible alternatives are. Rather than try to summarize all that's come before, we'll close by offering a few lessons.

- There's no such thing as a free lunch. Except in very special circumstances, cutting tax rates does not stimulate the economy enough to increase revenues.
- Taxes collected do not measure the social cost of government; spending is a much better metric. If the government cuts tax collections without restraining spending, all it's done is put off the reckoning of who will bear the cost.
- Tax policy changes create winners and losers, both within and across generations. Talking about this is not class warfare.
- Taxes entail economic cost. They reduce the incentive to work, save, and invest, and encourage taxpayers to engage in unproductive tax shelters. Centuries of experience proves that taxpayers do respond to those incentives, but there is considerable disagreement about how much they respond. Nonetheless, it is apparent that the all-in economic cost of a dollar of government services is significantly more than a dollar.

- If we value services the government provides more than their cost, we should grow up and tax ourselves to pay for them. If not, they should be eliminated.
- A large and growing number of spending programs are now run through the tax system. Policymakers should apply the same scrutiny to those "tax expenditures" as to traditional spending. If they are not worth the cost, they should be eliminated. And if they would work better as a traditional spending program, they should be removed from the tax code.
- The tax code could be made simpler and more efficient by eliminating preferences and loopholes, consolidating tax subsidies with similar aims (such as the vast array of education credits and deductions), and eliminating the ultra-complex AMT. This is easy for tax policy experts to say and hard for politicians to do (because those preferences and loopholes all have powerful constituencies).

NOTES

Chapter 1

1. For popularity of federal agencies, see: http://www.theacsi.org/
   index.php?option=com_content&view=article&id=238&Itemi
   d=298.

2. The quote from Will Rogers on the income tax making liars of
   people is available at: http://www.quotegarden.com/taxes.html.

3. The reference to the ethanol tax subsidy repeal supported by
   Senator Tom Coburn of Oklahoma and the subsequent criti-
   cism by Grover Norquist is available at: http://www.rollcall.
   com/issues/56_139/grover-norquist-ethanol-tax-206489-1.
   html?zkMobileView=true.

4. The number of nations that have military conscription is from:
   http://www.nationmaster.com/graph/mil_con-military-
   conscription.

5. The inflation figures for the Weimar Republic are from a presentation on "Globalization and the Washington Consensus,"
   available at: http://www.uvm.edu/~gflomenh/St_Lucia/ppts/
   Globalization.ppt.

6. The inflation figures for Zimbabwe are from: http://www.nytimes.
   com/2006/05/02/world/africa/02zimbabwe.html?pagewanted=all.

7. The numbers regarding states with the highest and least burden are drawn from page 3 of Mark Robyn and Gerald Prante,

"State-Local Tax Burdens Fall in 2009 as Tax Revenues Shrink Faster than Income," *Tax Foundation Special Report* 189 (February 2011), available at: http://taxfoundation.org/files/sr189.pdf.

8. The figure on the composition of federal taxes for FY 2009 is drawn from: http://www.fms.treas.gov/annualreport/cs2009/receipt.pdf.

9. The figures on composition of state and local taxes are taken from: http://www.taxpolicycenter.org/taxfacts/displayafact.cfm?Docid=507 and http://www2.census.gov/govs/estimate/09_summary_report.pdf.

10. The data for tax as a share of GDP are drawn from: http://stats.oecd.org/Index.aspx?DataSetCode=REV. The 26.1 percent figure from the text is lower than the 30 percent number used earlier because the former applies to 2008, when the severe recession sharply reduced tax collections.

11. The official version of the long-term fiscal imbalance is on page 62 of http://www.ssa.gov/OACT/TR/2009/tr09.pdf. For some perspective on the problem, read Alan J. Auerbach and William G. Gale, "The Economic Crisis and the Fiscal Crisis: 2009 and Beyond," *Tax Notes* 123, 1 (2009): 101–130.

12. On what people think about whether taxes should be reduced or spending cut, see: http://www.gallup.com/poll/1714/Taxes.aspx and http://www.gallup.com/poll/145790/Americans-Oppose-Cuts-Education-Social-Security-Defense.aspx.

Chapter 2

1. The principles of tax incidence are explained in Harvey S. Rosen and Ted Gayer, *Public Finance*, 9th ed. (New York: McGraw-Hill, 2009), ch. 14.

2. See Joel Slemrod, "Does It Matter Who Writes the Check to the Government? The Economics of Tax Remittance," *National Tax Journal* 61, 2 (June 2008): 251–275.

3. The Tax Protester FAQ, available at http://evans-legal.com/dan/tpfaq.html, dispels the myths about the validity of the income tax in forceful terms. The FAQ first clarifies that it is "not a collection of frequently asked questions, but a collection of frequently made assertions, together with an explanation of why each assertion is false."

4. Tons of income tax statistics are available at http://www.taxpolicycenter.org/taxfacts. The percentage of tax filers who claim the standard deduction can be found at: http://www.taxpolicycenter.org/taxfacts/displayafact.cfm?Docid=392.

5. Income tax parameters, including the personal exemption, can be found at: http://www.taxpolicycenter.org/taxfacts/displayafact.cfm? Docid=474.

6. See Roberton Williams, "Why So Few People Pay Income Tax," *TaxVox* blog, February 25, 2010, http://taxvox.taxpolicycenter.org/2010/02/25/why-so-few-people-pay-income-tax/.

7. Net capital loss (losses in excess of gains) deductions are limited to $3,000 per year. Losses that cannot be deducted in the current year may be carried over to later tax years. This prevents wealthy taxpayers from selectively realizing losses to shelter other income, but they can often shelter their realized gains from tax by selling assets with offsetting losses. High-income, high-wealth taxpayers are most likely to do this. Evidence from the 1980s (the most recent available) suggests that taxpayers with net losses in excess of the $3,000 annual deduction limit were usually able to deduct them within a year or two. See Alan J. Auerbach, Leonard E. Burman, and Jonathan Siegel, "Capital Gains Taxation and Tax Avoidance: New Evidence from Panel Data," in *Does Atlas Shrug? The Economic Consequences of Taxing the Rich*, ed. Joel Slemrod (New York, Cambridge, Mass.: Russell Sage Foundation and Harvard University Press, 2000), 355–388.

8. See Leonard E. Burman, "The Alternative Minimum Tax: Assault on the Middle Class," *The Milken Institute Review* (October 2007): 12–23. For more recent stats and analysis, see: http://www.taxpolicycenter.org/taxtopics/quick_amt.cfm.

9. For an amusing discussion of Warren Buffett's "secretary" and her supposed tax status, see Annie Lowrey, "Who Is Warren Buffett's Secretary?" *Slate* (September 20, 2011), available at: http://www.slate.com/articles/business/moneybox/2011/09/who_is_warren_buffetts_secretary.html. As of this writing, she has not released her tax return.

10. For a critique of the Buffett Rule, see Leonard E. Burman, "The Buffett Rule: Right Goal, Wrong Tool," *New York Times* (April 16, 2012), available at: http://www.nytimes.com/2012/04/16/opinion/the-buffett-rule-right-goal-wrong-tool.html.

11. The Congressional Budget Office (CBO) study, "For Better or for Worse: Marriage and the Federal Income Tax," June 1997, although dated, is still the best overview of what generates marriage penalties and options to eliminate them, see: http://www.cbo.gov/ftpdocs/0xx/doc7/marriage.pdf.

12. The GAO count of federal law provisions in which marital status is a factor was first done in United States General Accounting Office, "Defense of Marriage Act" (GAO/OGC-97-16), January 31, 1997, available at: http://www.gao.gov/archive/1997/og97016.pdf. That report was updated in 2004, "Defense of Marriage Act: Update to Previous Report" (GAO-04-353R), January 23, 2004, available at: http://www.gao.gov/new.items/d04353r.pdf.

13. For the share of taxpayers who pay more payroll tax, see: http://www.taxpolicycenter.org/T11-0192. For the distribution of average tax burdens by income, see: http://www.taxpolicycenter.org/T11–0099.

Chapter 3

1. The data about corporate tax liability for corporations of different sizes is found in: Table 22—Number of Returns and Selected

Tax Items, by Size of Total Income Tax After Credits, available at: http://www.irs.gov/pub/irs-soi/08coccr.pdf.

2. The data, which pertains to the 2008 tax year, come from the following sources:

   • Partnership returns: Statistics of Income—Partnership Returns. http://www.irs.gov/pub/irs-soi/08pareturnsnap .pdf, p. 1.

   • S corp. returns: Table 1—S Corporations: Total Receipts and Deductions, Portfolio Income, Rental Income, and Total Net Income, by Major Industry: http://www.irs.gov/pub/irs-soi/ 08coo1s.xls.

   • Sole proprietorship returns: Business Receipts, Selected Deductions, Payroll, and Net Income: http://www.irs.gov/uac/ Tax-Stats-2.

3. The number of shareholders in S corps is drawn from: Table 6—S Corporation Returns: Balance Sheet and Income Statement Items, by Major Industry (2008): http://www.irs.gov/uac/ Tax-Stats-2.

4. Richard M. Bird provides a well-balanced survey of the arguments for and against a separate tax on corporations in "Why Tax Corporations?" available at: http://publications.gc.ca/collections/ Collection/F21-4-96-2E.pdf. The majority of Americans support taxing businesses when given a choice between raising taxes on corporations and raising taxes on households making more than $250,000 a year, available at: http://www.nytimes.com/2011/05/03/ business/economy/03poll.html?_r=2.

5. Value-added by corporations can be found in: BEA Table 1.14 for FY 2010, p. D-19: http://www.bea.gov/national/pdf/dpga .pdf.

6. Value-added by businesses and entire economy can be found in: BEA Table 1.3.6 for FY 2010, p. D-9: http://www.bea.gov/national/ pdf/dpga.pdf.

7. Wal-Mart's revenue and profits for 2011 are available at: http://walmartstores.com/sites/annualreport/2011/financials/2011_Financials.pdf.

8. Exxon's profits for 2011 are available at: http://money.cnn.com/magazines/fortune/fortune500/2011/full_list/.

9. The distribution of corporate ownership based on income and wealth are authors' calculations from SCF tables, available at: http://www.federalreserve.gov/econresdata/scf/files/2007_SCF_Chartbook.pdf. Tables used are: Mean value of directly held stocks for families with holdings, Mean value of stock holdings for families with holdings, Mean value of directly held stocks for families with holdings, and Mean value of stock holdings for families with holdings.

10. The discussion on the incidence of the corporate tax draws from: http://economix.blogs.nytimes.com/2010/07/23/who-ultimately-pays-the-corporate-income-tax/.

11. This controversial assumption is not terribly important to distributional analysis. The corporate income tax is mostly borne by taxpayers with high incomes whether the burden is assumed to be borne by capital or labor. That is because wage and capital income are highly correlated across households. See Benjamin J. Harris, "Corporate Tax Incidence and Its Implications for Progressivity," Tax Policy Center, 2009, available at: http://www.taxpolicycenter.org/UploadedPDF/1001349_corporate_tax_incidence.pdf.

12. For the story of General Electric, see David Kocieniewski, "G.E.'s Strategies Let It Avoid Taxes Altogether," *New York Times* (March 24, 2011), available at: http://www.nytimes.com/2011/03/25/business/economy/25tax.html. GE apparently did actually remit a little tax in 2010. See Alan Sloan and Jeff Gerth, "The Truth about GE's Tax Bill," *Fortune* (April 4, 2011), available at: http://features.blogs.fortune.cnn.com/2011/04/04/the-truth-about-ges-tax-bill/. Nonetheless, its prowess at avoiding income tax is legendary.

13. In "Book-Tax Conformity for Corporate Income: An Introduction to the Issues," Michelle Hanlon explains the differences between the tax and financial accounting definition of corporate profits and assesses proposals to conform the two definitions. Her article is in *Tax Policy and the Economy*, Vol. 19, ed. James Poterba (Chicago: University of Chicago Press, 2005), 101–134.

14. The difference between income as reported in the financial statements and as reported for tax purposes is drawn from Figure 3, available at: http://www.nber.org/chapters/c11538.pdf and http://www.nber.org/chapters/c0166.pdf.

15. The survey that reports the proportion of tax executives who rate minimizing the effective tax rate as extremely or very important is discussed in: http://www.kpmginstitutes.com/taxwatch/insights/2010/pdf/tax-dept-svy-2009.pdf.

16. Tom Neubig's argument that many corporations prefer tax rate cuts to accelerated depreciation is explained in "Where's the Applause? Why Most Corporations Prefer a Lower Tax Rate" *Tax Notes* (April 24, 2006): 483–486.

17. The anecdotes about preferential tax treatment for some corporations are taken from: http://www.usnews.com/opinion/blogs/robert-schlesinger/2009/03/20/targeted-tax-provisions-have-a-history-before-aig-bonus-tax. The Sonat story is from: http://www.gpo.gov/fdsys/pkg/USCODE-2009-title26/pdf/USCODE-2009-title26-subtitleA-chap1-subchapB-partVI-sec168.pdf.

18. The number of countries in which Nike and McDonald's operate is found in: http://faculty.chicagobooth.edu/ralph.ossa/course%20materials/Lec%208a%208b%20-%20Multinational%20firms%20and%20foreign%20direct%20investment.pdf.

19. For states within the United States, details on whether they use sales or property or payroll for determining state income tax liability is drawn from: http://www.taxadmin.org/fta/rate/apport.pdf.

20. The figures on the ratio of the profits of U.S.-controlled foreign corporations relative to GDP are taken from Table 4, U.S. Foreign Company Profits Relative to GDP, Small Countries on Tax Haven Lists, on p. 736 of Jane G. Gravelle, "Tax Havens: International Tax Avoidance and Evasion," *National Tax Journal* 62, 4 (December 2009): 727–753. An overview of the issues raised by tax havens is in Dhammika Dharmapala, "What Problems and Opportunities Are Created by Tax Havens?" *Oxford Review of Economic Policy* 24, 4 (Winter 2008): 661–679.

21. The figure is taken from: http://economix.blogs.nytimes.com/2011/04/08/the-logic-of-cutting-corporate-taxes/.

22. The discussion about corporate tax rates from around the world is drawn from Joel Slemrod, "Are Corporate Tax Rates, or Countries, Converging?" *Journal of Public Economics* 88, 6 (June 2004): 1169–1186.

23. Joel Slemrod presents an overview of these issues in "Competitive Tax Policy," available at: http://webuser.bus.umich.edu/jslemrod/. Our discussion draws on the arguments presented there.

Chapter 4

1. The Hobbes quote is from *Leviathan* (London: Andrew Crooke, 1651).

2. Tax rates by state (2011) can be found at: http://taxpolicycenter.org/taxfacts/displayafact.cfm?Docid=411.

3. State and local tax rates (2010) can be found at: http://taxpolicycenter.org/taxfacts/displayafact.cfm?Docid=492.

4. For the tax rate in Tuba City, AZ, see William P. Barrett, "Average U.S. Sales Tax Rate Hits Record High," *Forbes* (February 17, 2011), available at: http://www.forbes.com/2011/02/17/average-sales-tax-rate-record-high-shopping-arizona-25-highest-sales-taxes.html.

5. California's compliance statistics are available at: http://www.lao.ca.gov/handouts/Econ/2011/CA_Use_Tax_2_28_11.pdf (pg. 2).

6. The national estimate of uncollected sales tax is available at: http://www.streamlinedsalestax.org/index.php?page=faqs.

7. A nice discussion of the telephone excise tax and its history is available at: http://www.irs.gov/pub/irs-soi/99extele.pdf. The website (http://nwtrcc.org/phonetax.php) urges continued resistance to the telephone excise tax to protest war.

8. Eric Toder and Joseph Rosenberg have the best analysis of the revenue and distributional effects of a VAT in the United States. See "Effects of Imposing a Value-Added Tax to Replace Payroll Taxes or Corporate Taxes," Tax Policy Center, March 18, 2010, available at: http://www.taxpolicycenter.org/UploadedPDF/412062_VAT.pdf.

9. The CBO did a comprehensive study of the issues involved in implementing a VAT. See *Effects of Adopting a Value-Added Tax*, February 1992, available at: http://www.cbo.gov/ftpdocs/102xx/doc10288/1992_02_effectsofadloptingavat.pdf.

10. The estimate for the sales tax revenue loss from Internet and mail order sales comes from: http://cber.utk.edu/ecomm/ecom0409.pdf.

11. Alan Viard of the American Enterprise Institute has an excellent explanation of this somewhat complex issue. See "Border Tax Adjustments Won't Stimulate Exports," March 2, 2009, available at: http://www.aei.org/article/economics/fiscal-policy/border-tax-adjustments-wont-stimulate-exports/.

12. Robert E. Hall and Alvin Rabushka are the intellectual fathers of the flat tax. They updated their book, *The Flat Tax* (Stanford, Calif.: Hoover Institution Press) and have made it available free online: http://www.hoover.org/publications/books/8329.

13. David Bradford explained how to make the flat tax more progressive in *Untangling the Income Tax* (Cambridge, Mass.: Harvard University Press, 1986), 329–334. At that time he hadn't yet dubbed the tax scheme the "X Tax."

14. The Treasury analysis of the progressive consumption tax is discussed in President's Advisory Panel on Federal Tax Reform, *Simple, Fair, and Pro-Growth: Proposals to Fix America's Tax System*

(2005), chapter 7, available at: http://www.treasury.gov/resource-center/tax-policy/Documents/Simple-Fair-and-Pro-Growth-Proposals-to-Fix-Americas-Tax-System.pdf.

15. Robert Carroll and Alan Viard have an excellent new book on the subject of progressive versions of consumption taxes such as the X Tax and the consumed income tax, see *Progressive Consumption Taxation: The X Tax Revisited* (Washington, D.C.: AEI Press, 2012).

16. This section is adapted from Leonard E. Burman, "We Are All Keynesians Now (Heaven Help Us!)," *TaxVox* blog, December 31, 2007, available at: http://taxvox.taxpolicycenter.org/2007/12/31/we-are-all-keynesians-now-heaven-help-us/.

17. For a discussion of how the VAT (and other consumption taxes) would affect the elderly and other groups, see Eric Toder, Jim Nunns, and Joseph Rosenberg, "Methodology for Distributing a VAT," Tax Policy Center, April 2011, available at: http://www.taxpolicycenter.org/UploadedPDF/1001533-Methodology-Distributing-VAT.pdf.

Chapter 5

1. An accessible treatment of the pros and cons of the U.S. estate tax is found in William G. Gale and Joel Slemrod, "Overview," in *Rethinking Estate and Gift Taxation*, ed. William G. Gale, James R. Hines Jr., and Joel Slemrod (Washington, D.C.: Brookings Institution Press, 2001), 1–64.

2. Wojciech Kopczuk and Joel Slemrod won an Ig Nobel Prize in Economics for reporting evidence that the timing of death is tax-sensitive in the United States (see "Dying to Save Taxes"). Others have found similar responses in Australia and Sweden. ("The Ig Nobel Prizes honor achievements that first make people laugh, and then make them think." See: http://improbable.com/ig/.)

3. The estimate of the value of minority discounts comes from: http://www.appraisaleconomics.com/family.html. For the value

of farm and business estate tax provisions, see: http://www.journalofaccountancy.com/Issues/2009/Jul/20091463.

4. A discussion of credit shelter trusts is available at: http://www.prudential.com.

5. For estimates of the distribution of the estate tax burden, see: http://www.taxpolicycenter.org/T09-0201.

6. The CBO study is available at: http://www.cbo.gov/ftpdocs/108xx/doc10841/Estate_GiftTax_Brief.shtm. The TPC data are from: http://www.taxpolicycenter.org/briefing-book/key-elements/estate/who.cfm.

7. For a capsule history of Margaret Thatcher's rise and fall, see: http://www.spartacus.schoolnet.co.uk/COLDthatcher.htm.

8. Greg Mankiw argues that the rejection of this idea suggests that the rationale behind a progressive tax system is fundamentally flawed. See: http://gregmankiw.blogspot.com/2007/04/optimal-taxation-of-height.html. We think the problem is that height is a very imperfect predictor of income. So while it might improve fairness on average, it would create large and inexplicable inequities. (Disclosure: Both of us are over six feet tall.)

9. For the science fiction buffs out there, Kyle Logue and Joel Slemrod speculate on the tax implications of easily available information about one's genomes and its probabilistic consequences for one's standard of living. This article is "Genes as Tags: The Tax Implications of Widely Available Genetic Information," published in the *National Tax Journal* special issue on taxes and technology (December 2008): 843–863.

Chapter 6

1. Claudia Sahm, Matthew Shapiro, and Joel Slemrod present evidence from consumer surveys that suggest that for only 20 percent of people did the rebates lead people to mostly spend more. See "Household Response to the 2008 Tax Rebate: Survey Evidence and Aggregate

Implications," in *Tax Policy and the Economy*, Vol. 24, ed. Jeffrey R. Brown (Chicago: University of Chicago Press, 2010), 69–110.

The research of Jonathan Parker and his co-authors suggest higher spending out of the tax cuts. See, e.g., David S. Johnson, Jonathan Parker, and Nicholas Souleles, "Household Expenditure and the Income Tax Rebates of 2001," *American Economic Review* 96, 5 (December 2006): 1589–1610.

2. Victor Fuchs, Alan Krueger, and James Poterba, "Economists' Views about Parameters, Values, and Politics: Survey Results in Labor and Public Economics," *Journal of Economic Literature* 36, 3 (September 1998): 1387–1425.

3. The evidence is discussed at more length in chapter 4 of Joel Slemrod and Jon Bakija, *Taxing Ourselves: A Citizen's Guide to the Debate over Taxes*, 4th ed. (Cambridge, Mass.: MIT Press, 2008), 99–158.

4. For an opinionated but sophisticated survey of the state-of-the-art research about how taxes affect labor supply, see Michael Keane, "Labor Supply and Taxes: A Survey," *Journal of Economic Literature* 49, 4 (2011): 961–1075.

5. Economists Julie Berry Cullen and Roger Gordon argue that there are many other implicit subsidies to entrepreneurship, including the ability to deduct many expenses that are nondeductible for wage earners and the option to incorporate and pay a 15 percent corporate tax rate if the business prospers (while deducting losses at higher individual rates if the business fails). See Julie Berry Cullen and Roger H. Gordon, "Taxes and Entrepreneurial Risk-Taking: Theory and Evidence for the U.S.," *Journal of Public Economics* 91, 7–8 (2007): 1479–1505.

6. The study cited is Nick Bloom, Rachel Griffith, and John Van Reenen, "Do R&D Tax Credits Work? Evidence from a Panel of Countries 1979–1997," *Journal of Public Economics* 85, 1 (July 2002): 1–31.

7. The analysis of trickle-down economics is taken from Thomas Piketty, Emmanuel Saez, and Stefanie Stantcheva, "Optimal

Taxation of Top Labor Incomes: A Tale of Three Elasticities," National Bureau of Economic Research Working Paper No. 17616, November 2011.

8. For a very comprehensive and clear analysis of the economics of deficits, see Doug Elmendorf and Greg Mankiw, "Government Debt," in *Handbook of Macroeconomics*, Vol. 1, ed. John B. Taylor and Michael Woodford (Amsterdam: Elsevier, 1999), 1615–1669.

9. The revival of the Ricardian view of deficits is due to the article by Robert Barro, "Are Government Bonds Net Wealth?" *Journal of Political Economy* 82, 6 (November–December 1974): 1095–1117. Doug Bernheim extended the idea to its logical extreme in "Is Everything Neutral?" *Journal of Political Economy* 96, 2 (April 1988): 308–338.

Chapter 7

1. The title for this chapter is borrowed from the excellent book by political scientist Christopher Howard, *The Hidden Welfare State: Tax Expenditures and Social Policy in the United States* (Princeton: Princeton University Press, 1997).

2. See Stanley S. Surrey and Paul R. McDaniel, *Tax Expenditures* (Cambridge, Mass.: Harvard University Press, 1985), 3.

3. See Donald Marron and Eric Toder, "Measuring Leviathan: How Big is the Federal Government?" Tax Policy Center, Presentation at "Starving the Hidden Beast: New Approaches to Tax Expenditure Reform," Loyola Law School, Los Angeles, January 14, 2011, available at: http://events.lls.edu/taxpolicy/documents/PANEL2Marr onToderSizeofGovernment-presentationFinal01-06-11.pdf.

4. See also John L. Buckley, "Tax Expenditure Reform: Some Common Misconceptions," *Tax Notes* 132 (July 18, 2011): 255–259.

5. Leonard E. Burman, Christopher Geissler, and Eric J. Toder estimated the distribution of tax expenditures in "How Big Are Total Individual Income Tax Expenditures, and Who Benefits from Them?" *American Economic Review Papers and Proceedings* 98, 2 (May 2008): 79–83.

6. Leonard E. Burman and Marvin Phaup explore this question in "Tax Expenditures, the Size and Efficiency of Government, and Implications for Budget Reform," NBER Working Paper No. 17268, August 2011.

7. For the income and payroll tax expenditures attributable to the tax exclusion for health insurance, see Joint Committee on Taxation, Tax Expenditures for Health Care (JCX-66–08), July 30, 2008.

8. See Bruce F. Davie, "Tax Expenditures in the Federal Excise Tax System," *National Tax Journal* 47, 1 (March 1994): 39–62.

9. The quotes are from Neil Brooks, "Review of Surrey and McDaniel (1985)," *Canadian Tax Journal* 34, 3 (May–June 1986): 681–694.

10. Dan Shaviro argues compellingly that a big problem is that our "fiscal language" is very imprecise and sometimes misleading. See Daniel Shaviro, "Rethinking Tax Expenditures and Fiscal Language," *Tax Law Review* 57, 2 (2004): 187–231.

Chapter 9

1. The IRS budget for Fiscal Year 2010 is drawn from the 2010 IRS Data Book, available at: http://www.irs.gov/pub/irs-soi/10databk.pdf.

2. The assertion that the IRS is one of the most efficient tax administrators can be found at: http://www.irs.gov/app/understanding-Taxes/student/whys_thm03_les01.jsp#taxTrivia.

3. The compliance cost estimate is detailed in Testimony Submitted to the Committee on Ways and Means, Subcommittee on Oversight, Hearing on Tax Simplification, Washington, D.C., June 15, 2004.

4. The data about the percentage of returns that are audited in broad classes of taxpayers are taken from Table 9a of the 2010 IRS Data Book, available at: http://www.irs.gov/pub/irs-soi/10databk.pdf.

5. The data about the number of information returns, number of contacts generated, and amount collected in additional assessments can be found in Table 14, Information Reporting Program, Fiscal Year 2010, available at: http://www.irs.gov/pub/irs-soi/10databk.pdf.

6. The states offering vendor discounts are listed in: http://www. taxadmin.org/fta/rate/vendors.pdf.

7. For an overview of the facts and policy issues regarding tax evasion, see Joel Slemrod, "Cheating Ourselves: The Economics of Tax Evasion," *Journal of Economic Perspectives* 21, 1 (Winter 2007): 25–48. Our text draws on this article.

8. The numbers regarding the rate of noncompliance and estimated noncompliance rate for self-employment income are from: http:// www.irs.gov/pub/irs-news/tax_gap_figures.pdf.

9. The story of the day-care experiment in Israel is related in Uri Gneezy and Aldo Rustichini, "A Fine is a Price," *Journal of Legal Studies* 29, 1 (January 2000): 1–17.

10. The discussion on effect of war on compliance draws on the work of Naomi Feldman and Joel Slemrod, "War and Taxation: When Does Patriotism Overcome the Free-Rider Impulse?" in *The New Fiscal Sociology*, ed. Isaac William Martin, Ajay K. Mehrotra, and Monica Prasad (Cambridge: Cambridge University Press, 2009), 138–154.

11. How tax cheating varies by demographic and other characteristics is based on information in pages 30 and 31 of Joel Slemrod, "Cheating Ourselves: The Economics of Tax Evasion," *Journal of Economic Perspectives* 21, 1 (Winter 2007): 25–48. The original sources vary and are mentioned in the paper.

12. The variation in the percentage of true income not reported and tax liability with income can be found in Andrew Johns and Joel Slemrod, "The Distribution of Income Tax Noncompliance," *National Tax Journal* 63, 3 (September 2010): 397–418.

13. The amount of underreporting based on type of income is taken from: http://www.irs.gov/pub/newsroom/overview_tax_ gap_2006.pdf .

14. The number and amount of civil penalties assessed and number of criminal investigations initiated are from p. 39 of the IRS 2010 Data Book.

15. The proportion of criminal investigations that led to convictions and sentences are from Table 18 "Criminal Investigation Program, by Status or Disposition, Fiscal Year 2010" of the IRS 2010 Data Book.

16. The extent of fraud in the EITC program can be found in Steve Holt, "The Earned Income Tax Credit at Age 30: What We Know," Brookings Institution Research Brief, February 2006. The original source is George K. Yin, John Karl Scholz, Jonathan Barry Forman, and Mark J. Mazur, "Improving the Delivery of Benefits to the Working Poor: Proposals to Reform the Earned Income Tax Credit Program," *American Journal of Tax Policy* 11, 2 (Fall 1994): 225–298.

17. The share of compliance resources devoted to auditing EITC compliance is from "Final Audit Report—More Information Is Needed to Determine the Effect of the Discretionary Examination Program on Improving Service to All Taxpayers," Reference Number: 2003-40-185, dated August 2003, available at: http://www.treasury.gov/tigta/auditreports/2003reports/200340185fr.html.

18. The amount of overstatement on credits using the 2001 tax gap numbers for the gross tax gap and that due to credits are taken from the table on p. 2 of the report, available at: http://www.irs.gov/pub/irs-news/tax_gap_figures.pdf.

19. Figures regarding number of tax refunds, number of tax returns, and amount of tax refunds are from Tables 7, 4, and 8, respectively, of the 2010 IRS Data Book.

20. On the reasons why most individuals settle for getting a tax return, see Damon Jones, "Inertia and Overwithholding: Explaining the Prevalence of Income Tax Refunds," *American Economic Journal: Economic Policy* 4, 1 (February 2012): 158–185.

21. The number of tax preparers is from: http://www.irs.gov/uac/Return-Preparer-Review-Leads-to-Recommendations-For-New-Requirements-of-Paid-Tax-Return-Preparers.

22. The number of returns that are prepared with the help of a tax preparer can be found in Table 22 "Taxpayers Using Paid Preparers,

Tax Years 2000–2008," available at: http://www.irs.gov/pub/
irs-soi/09resconeitcpart.pdf.

23. The number of returns filed in individual categories is from Figure
A, Individual Income Tax Returns, Preliminary Data: Selected
Income and Tax Items, Tax Years 2007 and 2008 in Individual
Income Tax Returns, Preliminary Data, 2008, available at: http://
www.irs.gov/pub/irs-soi/10winbulindincretpre.pdf.

24. The number of EITC returns that use tax preparers can be
found in "Earned Income Tax Credit Effectiveness and Program
Management FY 1998—FY 2002. Department of the Treasury,
Internal Revenue Service, February 28, 2002," available at: http://
www.irs.gov/pub/irs-utl/eitc_effectiveness.pdf.

25. Data about the fraction of Australians who used a tax preparer's assistance to prepare a return in 2006 are from: http://
www.ato.gov.au/corporate/content.aspx?menuid=0&doc=/con-
tent/00177078.htm&page=37&H37, and for 2008 are from:http://
www.ato.gov.au/corporate/content.aspx?menuid=0&doc=/con-
tent/00268761.htm&page=36&H36.

26. Information about the regulation of tax preparers is from:
http://www.irs.gov/uac/Return-Preparer-Review-Leads-to-
Recommendations-For-New-Requirements-of-Paid-Tax-Return-
Preparers.

27. The number of words in the IRS code and federal tax regulations
is taken from "Number of Words in Internal Revenue Code and
Federal Tax Regulations, 1955–2005," available at: http://www.
taxfoundation.org/taxdata/show/1961.html.

28. The fraction of Michigan's use tax liability that is remitted by
taxpayers is available at: http://www.michigan.gov/documents/
treasury/Sales__Use_Tax_Report_2010_August_2011_360206_7.pdf.

29. The number of returns that are filed electronically including
numbers on how many of them used a tax preparer is from Table
4 "Number of Returns Filed Electronically, by Type of Return and
State, Fiscal Year 2010" of the IRS 2010 Data Book.

30. The quote by Charles McLure of Stanford University is from Lawrence Zelenak, "Complex Tax Legislation in the TurboTax Era," *Columbia Journal of Tax Law* 1, 1 (2010): 91–119.

31. See Roberton Williams, "Shutting Down Virginia's iFile," *TaxVox* blog, April 26, 2010; and Joseph J. Thorndike, "Why Everyone Should Like ReadyReturn—Even the Tax Foundation," October 8, 2009, available at: http://www.tax.com/taxcom/taxblog.nsf/ Permalink/JTHE-7WMJ94?OpenDocument.

32. See Joseph Cordes and Arlene Holen,"Should the Government Prepare Individual Income Tax Returns?" Technology Policy Institute, September 2010, available at: http://www.techpolicy-institute.org/files/should%20the%20government%20prepare%20 individual%20income%20tax%20returns.pdf.

33. The argument for a data retrieval platform is made in Dennis Ventry, "Americans Don't Hate Taxes, They Hate Paying Taxes," *University of British Columbia Law Review* 44, 3 (2011): 835–889.

Chapter 10

1. The NPR poll is available at: http://www.npr.org/news/specials/ polls/taxes2003/20030415_taxes_survey.pdf.

2. The *New York Times*/CBS News poll is available at: http:// s3.amazonaws.com/nytdocs/docs/312/312.pdf.

3. The IRS estimates of EITC take-up are available at: http://www. irs.gov/uac/SOI-Tax-Stats—Historical-Table-1 and http://www. irs.gov/uac/SOI-Tax-Stats—Historical-Table-22.

4. Perceptions of the estate tax from the 2007 and 2008 Cooperative Congressional Election Surveys are reported in John Sides, "Stories, Science, and Public Opinion about the Estate Tax," George Washington University, July 2011, available at: http://home.gwu. edu/~jsides/estatetax.pdf.

5. The California data are reported in: http://www.economist.com/ node/18563612.

6. See also Bruce Bartlett, "What People Don't Know About Federal Income Taxes," *Capital Gains and Games* Blog, April 15, 2010, available

at: http://capitalgainsandgames.com/blog/bruce-bartlett/1653/ what-people-dont-know-about-federal-income-taxes.

7. This data is from: http://www.people-press.org/2011/12/20/tax-system-seen-as-unfair-in-need-of-overhaul/.

8. For more information on the regulatory process, see Internal Revenue Service, "Overview of the Regulations Process," available at: http://www.irs.gov/irm/part32/irm_32-001-001.html.

9. This section draws heavily from the Center on Budget and Policy Priorities, "Policy Basics: Introduction to the Federal Budget Process," December 6, 2010, available at: http://www.cbpp.org/files/3-7-03bud.pdf.

10. For more on the JCT's role in the revenue-estimating process, see: http://www.jct.gov/about-us/revenue-estimating.html.

Chapter 11

1. See William G. Gale, "The National Retail Sales Tax: What Would the Rate Have to Be?" *Tax Notes* (2006): 889–911.

2. See William A. Niskanen, "Limiting Government: The Failure of 'Starve the Beast'," *Cato Journal* 26, 3 (Fall 2006): 553–558.

3. See Michael J. New, "Starve the Beast: A Further Examination," *Cato Journal* 29, 3 (Fall 2009): 487–495.

4. See Bruce Bartlett, "Tax Cuts and 'Starving the Beast'," *Forbes.com* (May 7, 2010), available at: http://www.forbes.com/2010/05/06/tax-cuts-republicans-starve-the-beast-columnists-bruce-bartlett.html.

5. This is adapted from Leonard E. Burman, "We Need to Ban the Evil Santas," *Washington Times* (December 22, 2009), available at: http://www.washingtontimes.com/news/2009/dec/22/we-need-to-ban-the-evil-santas/.

Chapter 12

1. See Raj Chetty, Adam Looney, and Kory Kroft, "Salience and Taxation: Theory and Evidence," *American Economic Review* 99, 4 (September 2009): 1145–1177.

2. For the corporate tax shortfall after Tax Reform Act of 1986, see James M. Poterba, "Why Didn't the Tax Reform Act of 1986 Raise Corporate Taxes?" in *Tax Policy and the Economy*, Vol. 6, ed. James M. Poterba (Cambridge, Mass.: MIT Press, 1992), 43–58.

3. See Bipartisan Policy Center, *Restoring America's Future*, available at: http://bipartisanpolicy.org/sites/default/files/BPC%20FINAL %20REPORT%20FOR%20PRINTER%2002%2028%2011.pdf.

4. See the National Commission on Fiscal Responsibility and Reform, *The Moment of Truth*, available at: http://www.fiscal-commission.gov/sites/fiscalcommission.gov/files/documents/TheMomentofTruth12_1_2010.pdf.

5. An overview of the Bipartisan Tax Fairness and Simplification Act of 2011, sponsored by Ron Wyden (D-OR) and Dan Coats (R-IN), is available at: http://www.wyden.senate.gov/imo/media/doc/Wyden-Coats%20Two%20Pager%20FINAL1.pdf. Legislative language with all the gory details is available at: http://www.wyden.senate.gov/download/bipartisan-tax-fairness-and-simplification-act-of-2011-legislative-text&ei=FOenT72ZBcfnggeiwPymAQ&usg=AFQjCNHCF2i21VNywXNwbd7QjM8mp63u_g&sig2=28bK5YCtJv27qA2gKkwqDw.

6. See Michael Graetz, *100 Million Unnecessary Returns* (New Haven: Yale University Press, 2008).

GLOSSARY

This glossary is an edited and abridged version of the one that appears in the Tax Policy Center's excellent *Briefing Book*, available at http://www.taxpolicycenter.org/briefing-book. Used with permission.

A

Accelerated depreciation. See **depreciation**.

Adjusted Gross Income (AGI). A measure of income used to determine a tax filing unit's tax liability (before subtracting **Personal exemptions** and the **Standard deduction** or **Itemized deductions**). AGI excludes certain types of income received (e.g., municipal bond interest, most Social Security income) or payments made (e.g., alimony paid, **IRA** deductions, moving expenses). (See also **Taxable income**.)

Alternative minimum tax (AMT). The individual alternative minimum tax is a supplemental income tax originally intended to ensure that high-income filers not take undue advantage of tax preferences to reduce or eliminate their tax liability. The most common "preference" items, however, are for state and local tax deductions, personal exemptions, and miscellaneous itemized deductions—not items normally thought of as preferences or shelters. Increasingly, this complicated tax applies to middle-class families, in part because its exemption and tax bracket thresholds are not indexed for inflation and in part because Congress has not adjusted the

AMT to coordinate with recent tax cuts. There is also a corporate alternative minimum tax, but few companies are subject to it.

AMT patch. Since 2001, lawmakers have periodically raised the **AMT**'s rate bracket thresholds to offset the effects of inflation. This ad hoc adjustment of the AMT is sometimes referred to as the "patch," because it is a stopgap remedy for a basic design flaw—the fact that the AMT is not indexed for inflation, unlike most other income tax provisions. Patch legislation also typically extends a temporary provision allowing AMT taxpayers the full benefit of personal tax credits, such as the child and dependent care tax credit. (See also **Indexation of the tax system.**)

Average effective tax rate (ETR). A widely used measure of tax burdens, equal to tax paid divided by some measure of income. ETRs may be calculated with respect to a single tax, such as the individual income tax, or with respect to all taxes together (i.e., including payroll taxes, corporate income taxes, and estate taxes). However, the ETR may differ substantially from the economic incidence of tax. (See also **Tax incidence.**)

B

Base broadening. A term applied to efforts to expand the tax base, usually by eliminating deductions, exclusions, and other preferences from the tax base. A broader base allows more revenue to be raised without increasing tax rates or for rates to be cut without sacrificing revenues.

Bracket creep. The movement of taxpayers into higher tax brackets caused by inflation. Under a progressive tax system, rising nominal income can move taxpayers into higher tax brackets, even if their real income (after adjusting for inflation) remains constant. Congress indexed tax rate schedules for inflation in the early 1980s to prevent general increases in the price level from causing bracket creep. (See **Price indexing.**)

Budget baseline. The baseline is the level of revenue (or spending) expected under a given set of assumptions. Traditionally, Congress and the administration have used a "current law baseline" that assumes that discretionary spending grows at the rate of inflation and mandatory spending and tax revenues are determined by current law. In particular, temporary tax provisions expire as scheduled. However, the Obama administration has advocated using a "current policy baseline," which assumes that **Bush tax cuts** enacted in recent years would be extended indefinitely (and that a politically unpopular Medicare provision would never be allowed to take effect).

Budget scoring. The process of estimating the budgetary effects of proposed changes in tax and expenditure policies and enacted legislation. The budget score represents the difference from baseline revenues or spending.

Bush tax cuts. A set of tax provisions that were originally enacted in the administration of President George W. Bush—mostly in 2001 and 2003. The first installment, the **Economic Growth and Tax Relief Reconciliation Act of 2001** (EGTRRA), cut individual income tax rates, phased out the estate and gift tax, doubled the child tax credit, provided marriage penalty relief, expanded retirement tax incentives, and temporarily raised the threshold for taxation under the individual **Alternative minimum tax** (AMT). The provisions of EGTRRA phased in slowly and were all set to expire at the end of 2010. Subsequent legislation in 2003, the **Jobs and Growth Tax Relief Reconciliation Act of 2003**, sped up many of the 2001 tax cuts, added cuts in the tax rates on long-term capital gains and dividends, and again temporarily patched the AMT, but preserved the 2010 expiration date. The Pension Protection Act of 2006 made the retirement savings provisions of EGTRRA permanent and the AMT has been continually patched since 2001. In 2010, President Obama signed legislation extending the Bush tax cuts, as well as several new tax cuts he had initiated through 2012. It is likely that at least some of the tax cuts will again be extended past 2012. (See also **AMT patch.**)

C

Capital cost recovery. Income tax features intended to allow businesses to deduct over time the costs of tangible capital assets that are used to produce income. It is similar to a depreciation allowance, except that "depreciation" in principle relates the timing of the deductions to changes in asset value over time. (See **Depreciation.**)

Capital gains. The difference between the sale price and purchase price of capital assets net of brokers' fees and other costs. Capital gains are generally taxable upon sale (or "realization"). Long-term gains, those realized after holding the asset for a year or longer, face lower tax rates (no more than 15 percent) than short-term gains, which are taxed the same as earned income. Taxpayers can deduct up to $3,000 of net losses (losses in excess of gains) each year against other income; taxpayers can carry over losses above that amount and subtract them from future gains.

Charitable deductions. Deductions allowed for gifts to charity. Subject to certain limits, individual taxpayers who itemize deductions and corporations are allowed to deduct gifts to charitable and certain other nonprofit organizations. In part, the deduction is intended to subsidize the activities of private organizations that provide viable alternatives to direct government programs. (See **Itemized deductions.**)

Child and dependent care tax credit (CDCTC). A tax credit based on eligible child care expenses incurred by taxpayers who are employed or in school. The credit varies with the expenses incurred, the number of eligible children, and the taxpayer's **AGI**. A separate exclusion is available for some employer-provided child care.

Child Tax Credit (CTC). A tax credit of $1,000 per qualifying child (as of 2011). The credit is partially refundable for filers with earnings over a threshold ($3,000 in 2011). The refundable portion is limited to 15 percent of earnings above the threshold. (See **Refundable tax credit.**)

Consumer Price Index (CPI). A measure of the average level of prices, inclusive of sales and excise taxes, faced by urban households for a given "market basket" of consumer goods and services.

Consumption tax. Tax on goods or services. In the United States, most consumption taxes are levied by states and local governments (as retail sales taxes), although the federal government does levy some selective consumption taxes, called "**Excise taxes.**" The **Value-added tax (VAT)** is a consumption tax that is common in the rest of the world.

Corporate income tax. A tax levied on corporate profits. A corporation's taxable income is its total receipts minus allowable expenses, including capital depreciation.

D

Deduction. A reduction in **Taxable income** for certain expenses. Some deductions, such as that for contributions to an **Individual Retirement Account (IRA)**, reduce **AGI**. Most deductions, such as those for home mortgage interest and state and local taxes, are only available to those who **Itemize deductions**. Most taxpayers choose not to itemize and instead claim the **Standard deduction** because it provides a greater tax benefit. Because tax rates increase with taxable income, a dollar of deductions generally benefits a high-income taxpayer more than a low-income taxpayer. Deductions cannot reduce taxable income below zero.

Dependent. An individual supported by a tax filer for more than half of a calendar year. Federal tax law stipulates five tests to determine whether a filer may claim someone as a dependent and thus qualify for an exemption: a relationship test, a joint return test, a citizen-or-resident test, an income test, and a support test. In 2011, a tax filer could reduce taxable income by $3,700 for each dependent exemption.

Depreciation. A measurement of the declining value of assets over time because of physical deterioration or obsolescence. The actual rate at which an asset's value falls is called economic depreciation, which depends on wear and tear and the rate of technological obsolescence. In practice, tax depreciation is calculated by a schedule of deductions, usually over the asset's "useful life" specified in the tax code through which the full cost of an asset can be written off. Accelerated depreciation refers to a depreciation schedule that allows larger deductions in early years than would be expected due to economic depreciation.

Distortion. The economic cost of changes in behavior due to taxes, government benefits, monopolies, and other forces that interfere with the otherwise-efficient operation of a market economy. For example, employees might choose to work fewer hours because taxes reduce their after-tax wage.

Distribution table. A table that details how a proposal or policy is estimated to affect the distribution of tax burdens across income categories, demographic groups, or sets of taxpayers defined by other characteristics.

Dividends. Profits distributed by a corporation to its shareholders. Under 2003 tax law, most dividends are taxed at the same lower tax rates that apply to **Capital gains**.

Double taxation of dividends. Most tax systems that have both corporate and individual income taxes levy tax on corporate profits twice, once at the corporate level and again at the individual level when shareholders receive profits in the form of dividends or capital gains. The reduced tax rates on capital gains and dividends are intended in part as an offset to double taxation.

Dynamic modeling. Computer-based simulation of how tax policy or tax reform affects the economy taking into account how individuals, households, or firms alter their work, saving, investment, or consumption behavior, and how those effects feed back to affect tax revenues.

E

Earned Income Tax Credit (EITC). A refundable tax credit that supplements the earnings of low-income workers. The credit is a fixed percentage of earnings up to a base level, remains constant over a range above the base level (the "plateau"), and then phases out as income rises further. Those income ranges depend on both the taxpayer's filing status and number of children in the taxpayer's family. In contrast, the credit rate depends only on the number of children. Married couples with three or more children receive the largest credit, a maximum of $5,751 in 2011. Childless workers get the smallest credit, no more than $464 in 2011. Originally enacted in 1975, the EITC is now the largest federal means-tested cash transfer program.

Economic Growth and Tax Relief Reconciliation Act of 2001 (EGTRRA). A tax bill passed under the presidency of George W. Bush (and therefore often referred to as the "**Bush tax cut**") that reduced most tax rates, increased the **Child Tax Credit** and made it partially refundable, expanded tax-free retirement savings, reduced **Marriage penalties,** increased the **Child and dependent care tax credit,** and phased out the **Estate tax**. Most provisions were scheduled to phase in slowly between 2001 and 2010, and then expire at the start of 2011. **JGTRRA** accelerated some of the EGTRRA tax cuts and added others.

Economic income. A very broad income concept that includes cash income from all sources, fringe benefits, net realized capital gains, both cash and in-kind transfers, the employer's share of payroll taxes, and corporate income tax liability. The Treasury Department's Office of Tax Analysis developed a similar measure in the 1980s and used it for **Distribution tables** until 2000.

Economic Recovery Tax Act (ERTA). Tax legislation enacted in 1981 (and often referred to as the "Reagan tax cut") that significantly reduced income taxes on individuals and businesses. The Tax Equity and Fiscal Responsibility Act (TEFRA) scaled back the cuts in 1982.

EGTRRA. See **Economic Growth and Tax Relief Reconciliation Act of 2001.**

Employer-sponsored health insurance. Health insurance offered by an employer to some or all employees. Employer contributions to health insurance plans are exempt from both income and payroll taxes. Economists believe that workers receive lower wages in exchange for the valuable tax-free fringe benefit. The exclusion from tax of employer-sponsored health insurance is the single biggest **Tax expenditure.**

Entitlements. Payments to individuals, governments, or businesses which, under law, must be made to all those eligible and for which funds do not have to be appropriated in advance. Major entitlement programs include Social Security, Medicare, Medicaid, and Temporary Assistance to Needy Families (TANF).

ERTA. See **Economic Recovery Tax Act.**

Estate tax. A tax levied on a person's estate at the time of his or her death. The federal estate tax applies only to large estates, those worth over $5 million for people dying in 2012. No tax is owed on transfers to spouses or to charities, and special provisions apply to farms and small businesses. (See also **Gift tax.**)

Excise tax. A tax on specific goods and services, levied at federal, state, and local levels. The most common excise taxes are on gasoline, alcohol, and tobacco products.

Expensing. Allows businesses to immediately deduct the entire cost of a capital asset, rather than claiming depreciation deductions over the useful life of the asset. (See also **Depreciation.**)

F

Federal poverty levels. See **Poverty levels.**

Federal fiscal year (FY). The period commencing October 1 and ending September 30 of the following year. For example, fiscal year 2012 runs from October 1, 2011 to September 30, 2012.

Filing status. Tax filers fall into one of five categories, depending on their marital status and family structure. A single person without children files as a single; a single parent with dependent children files as a head of household; a married couple, with or without children, files either as married filing joint or married filing separate; and a recent widow(er) may file as a qualifying widow(er), which is the same, in effect, as married filing joint. The standard deductions, bracket widths, and qualification criteria for certain credits and deductions vary by filing status.

Flat tax. A proposal for tax reform that would replace the income tax system with a single-rate (or flat-rate) tax on businesses and on individuals after an exempt amount. Many flat tax proposals are designed to be consumption rather than income taxes (see **VAT**), many would retain politically sensitive deductions such as for mortgage interest payments, and most are really not "flat" because they grant an exemption for a certain amount of earnings.

Foreign tax credit. A credit that allows U.S. residents to subtract foreign income taxes paid from the U.S. income tax due on income earned abroad.

G

Gift tax. A tax levied on gifts in excess of a specified threshold. In 2012, no tax is levied on annual gifts of up to $13,000 per donor, per recipient; gifts in excess of the limit are taxable but no tax is due until lifetime taxable gifts total more than $5 million. Any tax still due must be remitted when the donor dies and is incorporated into the decedent's estate tax. (See also **Estate tax**.)

H

Health savings account (HSA). A special tax-favored account for deposits made to cover current and future health care expenses paid by the individual. Like defined contribution retirement plans, contributions to HSAs and any earnings are generally deductible (or excluded from income if made by an employer). Unlike defined contribution retirement plans, withdrawals from the account are also tax-free as long as they are used to pay for medical expenses. Enacted in 2003 as part of legislation providing prescription drug benefits under Medicare, the tax preference is only available if the individual purchases a high-deductible health insurance policy.

Horizontal equity. (See also **Vertical equity.**) The concept that people of equal well-being should have the same tax burden.

Human capital. Knowledge and skills that people acquire through education, training, and experience.

I

Indexation of the tax system. Annual adjustments to various parameters in the tax code to account for inflation and prevent **Bracket creep.** Since 1981, many features of the federal individual income tax, including personal exemptions and tax brackets, have been automatically indexed for inflation based on changes in the **Consumer Price Index.** For instance, after a year with 5 percent inflation, a personal exemption of $1,000 would be raised to $1,050. More broadly, the term applies to all efforts to adjust measures of income to account for the effects of price inflation.

IRA (Individual Retirement Account). Retirement accounts funded by individuals through their own contributions or by rolling over benefits earned under an employee-sponsored plan. An IRA is a kind of defined contribution retirement account. In traditional IRAs, contributions and earnings are tax-free, but withdrawals are taxable. In Roth IRAs, contributions are not deductible, but withdrawals are exempt from income tax.

Itemized deductions. Particular kinds of expenses that taxpayers may use to reduce their taxable income. The most common itemized deductions are for state and local taxes, mortgage interest payments, charitable contributions, medical expenses larger than 7.5 percent of AGI, and certain miscellaneous expenses. Individuals may opt to deduct these expenses or claim a **Standard deduction.**

J

JGTRRA. See the **Jobs and Growth Tax Relief Reconciliation Act of 2003**.

Jobs and Growth Tax Relief Reconciliation Act of 2003 (JGTRRA). The 2003 tax act that accelerated the phase-in of tax rate reductions scheduled under **EGTRRA**, reduced the taxation of **Capital gains** and **Dividends**, accelerated increases in the **Child Tax Credit** amount, and temporarily raised the exemption for the **Alternative minimum tax (AMT)**. Most provisions were set to expire at the end of 2010, but have since been extended through 2012. (See also **Bush tax cuts**.)

L

Low-income housing tax credit. A tax credit given to investors for the costs of constructing and rehabilitating low-income housing. The credit is intended to encourage the acquisition, construction, and/ or rehabilitation of housing for low-income families. Credits are allocated to state housing agencies based on state population. The agencies select qualifying projects and authorize credits subject to statutory limits.

M

Marginal tax rate. The additional tax liability due on an additional dollar of income. It is a measure of the effect of the tax system on incentives to work, save, and shelter income from tax. Provisions such as the phase out of tax credits can cause marginal tax rates to differ from statutory tax rates.

Marriage bonus. The reduction in the tax liability of some married couples that arises from filing as married rather than as single filers. Marriage bonuses result from the combination of treating a family as a single tax unit and progressive tax rates. In general, couples in which spouses have quite different incomes receive marriage bonuses. (See also **Marriage penalty**.)

Marriage penalty. The additional tax that some married couples pay because they must file as married rather than as single filers.

Marriage penalties result from the combination of treating a family as a single tax unit and progressive tax rates. In general, couples in which spouses have similar incomes incur marriage penalties. (See also **Marriage bonus**.)

Medicaid. A federal entitlement program that reimburses states for a portion of the costs associated with providing acute and long-term care services to certain low-income individuals. States determine which services and categories of people, beyond the minimum required by federal law, to cover. States also establish payment rates for providers and administer the program.

Medicare Part A. (See also **Medicare Part B**.) The part of Medicare that covers hospital services, skilled nursing facility services, and some home health care. Anyone over age 65 who is eligible for Social Security and persons under age 65 who have received Social Security disability payments for two years are eligible. Participants pay no premiums for Part A coverage.

Medicare Part B. (See also **Medicare Part A**.) Supplementary medical insurance for Medicare beneficiaries that provides physician services and other ambulatory care (such as outpatient hospital services and tests). Beneficiaries must pay a premium to join; premiums cover about one-fourth program costs. All persons over the age of 65 and other Medicare beneficiaries can enroll.

Moral hazard. The incentive created by insurance (explicit or implicit) to engage in behaviors that raise the expected cost of insurance. The moral aspect refers to the observation that unscrupulous people covered by fire insurance were sometimes tempted to engage in arson. However, less insidious behavior, such as using more health services when they are covered by insurance, is also covered by the term.

N

Nominal income. A measure of income that is not adjusted for inflation. That is, nominal income is expressed in current dollars. (See also **Real income**.)

Non-filer. A person or household who does not file an individual income tax return. Most non-filers are not employed; many are elderly.

O

OASDI (Old Age, Survivors, and Disability Insurance). The Social Security programs that pay monthly benefits to retired workers and their spouses and children, to survivors of deceased workers, and to disabled workers and their spouses and children.

Omnibus Budget Reconciliation Act of 1987. Legislation that attempted to decrease the budget deficit through tax increases and expenditure decreases.

Omnibus Budget Reconciliation Act of 1990 (OBRA90). This Act increased excise and payroll taxes, added a 31 percent income tax bracket, and introduced temporary high-income phase-outs for personal exemptions and itemized deductions. OBRA93 made these changes permanent.

Omnibus Budget Reconciliation Act of 1993 (OBRA93). This Act introduced 36 percent and 39.6 percent income tax brackets, repealed the wage cap on Medicare payroll taxes, increased the portion of Social Security benefits subject to income taxation for those with higher incomes, made more workers with children eligible for the **Earned Income Tax Credit** and increased their benefits, and made permanent the temporary high-income phase-outs of the personal exemption and itemized deductions. Overall, the bill was focused on deficit reduction.

P

Pay-as-you-go system (PAYGO). A retirement system in which benefits for current retirees are funded by taxes on today's workers in return for the implicit promise that those workers will receive retirement benefits funded by future workers. Social Security operates largely on this system.

Payroll taxes. Taxes imposed on employers, employees, or both that are levied on some or all of workers' earnings. Employers and employees each remit Social Security taxes equal to 6.2 percent (4.2 percent in 2011 and 2012) of all employee earnings up to a cap ($106,800 for 2011 and $110,100 in 20012) and Medicare taxes of 1.45 percent on all earnings with no cap. Those taxes are referred to by the names of their authorizing acts: FICA (Federal Insurance Contributions Act) or SECA (Self-Employment Contributions Act), depending on the worker's employment status. Employers also remit State and Federal Unemployment Taxes (SUTA and FUTA) that cover the costs of unemployment insurance.

Personal exemption. A per-person amount of income that is shielded from income tax. In calculating taxable income, tax filers may subtract the value of the personal exemption times the number of people in the tax unit. The personal exemption—$3,800 in 2012—is indexed for inflation to maintain its real value over time.

Poverty levels. (Also called "poverty thresholds.") The level of pre-tax cash income below which a family is considered to be officially "poor." Thresholds vary by family size, age of head, and number of children. When established in 1965, the thresholds were set at three times the cost of a minimally adequate diet and indexed annually for changes in the price of food. The basis for indexing changed to the Consumer Price Index for all goods and services in 1969.

Price indexing. (See also **Wage indexing**.) Adjusting monetary values by the change over time in prices. For example, many parameters in the federal individual income tax system are price-indexed annually.

Progressive tax. A tax that levies a larger percentage of the income of higher-income households than from lower-income households. (See also **Regressive tax**.)

Progressivity. A measure of how tax burdens increase with income. A progressive tax claims a proportionately larger share of income from higher-income than from lower-income taxpayers. Conversely, a **Regressive tax** levies a larger share of income from lower-income households than from higher-income ones. Taxes that claim the same percentage of income from all taxpayers are termed "proportional."

Property tax. A tax based on the value of property owned by an individual or household. In the United States, most property taxes are levied by local governments.

R

Real income. The value of income after accounting for inflation. Real income is typically converted in terms of a particular year's prices— for example, a table may show income in 2010 dollars, meaning that the incomes are shown in terms of purchasing power in 2010. (See also **nominal income**.)

Refundable tax credit. A tax credit that is payable even when it exceeds an individual's tax liability. Tax credits generally may be used only to reduce positive tax liability and are therefore limited to the amount of tax the individual otherwise would owe. Unlike other tax credits, the refundable portion of a tax credit is scored as an outlay in government budget accounts—that is, it is treated the same as direct spending. (See, e.g., **Earned Income Tax Credit**.)

Regressive tax. A tax that claims a larger percentage of the income of lower-income households than of higher-income households. (See also **Progressive tax**.)

Revenue-neutral. A term applied to tax proposals in which provisions that raise revenues offset provisions that lose revenues so the proposal in total has no net revenue cost or increase.

S

SSDI (Social Security Disability Insurance). Social insurance that provides benefits to the disabled who qualify on the basis of years of work covered by Social Security. (See also **OASDI**.)

Stagflation. The combination of stagnant growth and high inflation, a situation that occurred in the United States during the 1970s.

Standard deduction. A deduction that taxpayers may claim on their tax returns in lieu of itemizing deductions such as charitable contributions, mortgage interest, or state and local taxes. Typically, taxpayers with modest deductible amounts that could be itemized choose to take the standard deduction. Single filers, heads of household, and married couples filing jointly have different standard deductions. Roughly two-thirds of tax filers claim a standard deduction. (See also **Itemized deductions**.)

Sunset. Provision of a tax act that terminates or repeals parts of the act on a certain date unless legislation is passed to extend them.

T

Taxable income. The final income amount used to calculate tax liability. Taxable income equals adjusted gross income (**AGI**) less **Personal exemptions** and the **Standard deduction** or **Itemized deductions**.

Tax after credits. A filer's calculated, final tax liability after all credits (e.g., the **Earned Income Tax Credit**, the **Child Tax Credit**, the **Child and dependent care tax credit**, and the **Foreign tax credit**) have been applied. If this amount is less than taxes paid via withholding or estimated tax payments, the taxpayer receives the difference as a refund. If the amount exceeds taxes paid, the taxpayer must remit the difference as a final payment.

Tax burden. The total cost of taxation borne by a household or individual. The burden accounts not only for taxes remitted directly but also for burden incurred indirectly through lower wages or a reduced return on an investment and for **Distortions** due to tax-induced changes in behavior. For example, in addition to the employee portion of payroll taxes, a worker may also bear the employer's share in the form of lower compensation.

Tax credit. A reduction in tax liability for specific expenses such as for child care or retirement savings. Unlike deductions, which reduce taxable income, a tax credit reduces tax liability dollar for dollar. Nonrefundable credits may only offset positive tax liability; in contrast, if a refundable credit exceeds the taxpayer's tax liability, the taxpayer receives the excess as a refund. (See also **Refundable tax credit**.)

Tax expenditure. A revenue loss attributable to a provision of federal tax laws that allows a special exclusion, exemption, or deduction from gross income or provides a special credit, preferential tax rate, or deferral of tax liability. Tax expenditures often result from tax provisions used to promote particular activities in place of direct subsidies.

Tax filing threshold. The level of income at which filing units of specific size and filing status first owe a tax before considering tax credits. The amount varies with filing status, allowable adjustments, deductions, and exemptions. Tax credits can further increase the amount of untaxed income.

Tax incidence. A measure of the actual burden of a tax. Tax incidence may deviate from statutory tax liability because the imposition of a tax may change pre-tax prices. For example, retailers remit sales taxes, but those taxes raise the prices faced by consumers, who ultimately bear much of the burden of the tax.

Tax liability. The amount of total taxes owed after application of all tax credits.

TRA86 (Tax Reform Act of 1986). Revenue-neutral legislation passed in 1986 that simplified the tax code, lowered marginal tax rates, and closed corporate loopholes.

TRA97 (Taxpayer Relief Act of 1997). Tax legislation passed in 1997 that reduced capital gains tax rates, introduced the child credit, created education credits, raised the estate tax exemption level, created Roth IRAs, and increased the contribution limit for traditional IRAs.

U

Unemployment insurance (or **Unemployment compensation**). A government program that provides cash benefits to some jobless workers for limited periods. Supervised by the federal government, the state-run programs are funded by payroll taxes states impose on employers.

V

Value-added tax (VAT). A form of consumption tax collected from businesses based on the value each firm adds to a product (rather than, say, gross sales). VATs are almost universal outside the United States.

Vertical equity. A value judgment about whether the net tax burden on people at different levels of well-being is appropriate. (See also **Horizontal equity.**)

INDEX